Law, Literature and the [illegible] Reading

At the intersection of law, literature and history, this book interrogates how a dominant contemporary idea of law emerged out of specific ideas of reading in the nineteenth century. Reading shapes our identities. How we read shapes who we are. Reading also shapes our conceptions of what the law is, because the law is also a practice of reading. Focusing on the works of key Victorian writers closely associated with legal practice, this book addresses the way in which the identity of the reader of law has been modelled on the identity of the political elite. At the same time, it shows how other readers of law have been marginalised. The book thus shows how a construction of the law has emerged from the ordering of a power that discriminates between different readers and readings. More specifically, and in response to the emerging media of photography – and, with it, potentially subversive ideas of exposure and visibility – the book shows that there have been dominant, hidden and unrecognised guides to legal reading and to legal thought. And in making these visible, the book also aims to make them contestable. This secret history of law will appeal to legal historians, legal theorists, those working at the intersection of law and literature and others with interests in law and the visual.

Suneel Mehmi is an independent, early career researcher.

Part of the
DISCOURSES OF LAW
series

series editors
Peter Goodrich, *Benjamin N. Cardozo School of Law, USA*
Michel Rosenfeld, *Benjamin N. Cardozo School of Law, USA*
Arthur Jacobsen, *Benjamin N. Cardozo School of Law, USA*

for information about the series and details of previous and forthcoming titles, see
https://www.routledge.com/Discourses-of-Law/book-series/SE1036

The publisher gratefully acknowledges the support of the Jacob Burns Institute for Advanced Legal Studies of the Benjamin N. Cardozo School of Law to the series *Discourses of Law*.

Law, Literature and the Power of Reading

Literalism and Photography in the Nineteenth Century

Suneel Mehmi

Routledge
Taylor & Francis Group
LONDON AND NEW YORK

First published 2022
by Routledge
2 Park Square, Milton Park, Abingdon, Oxon OX14 4RN

and by Routledge
605 Third Avenue, New York, NY 10158

Routledge is an imprint of the Taylor & Francis Group, an informa business

British Library Cataloguing-in-Publication Data
A catalogue record for this book is available from the British Library

Library of Congress Cataloging-in-Publication Data
A catalog record has been requested for this book

ISBN: 978-0-367-76032-8 (hbk)
ISBN: 978-1-032-00372-6 (pbk)
ISBN: 978-1-003-17385-4 (ebk)

DOI: 10.4324/9781003173854

Typeset in Bembo
by SPi Technologies India Pvt Ltd (Straive)

Contents

Acknowledgements

This book would not have been possible if it were not for my parents, Gurmit Kaur and Manjit Kumar. All my PhD supervisors also deserve many thanks and recognition: Leigh Wilson, Alexa Wright, Julia Chryssostalis and Sas Mays. Last but not least, Peter Goodrich assisted me in various ways to get this book to publication despite the fact that I was a complete stranger to him. I am very grateful for all the help, assistance and encouragement I have received from those mentioned and also from the University of Westminster and its staff and students.

Introduction

How does fiction respond to the invention of photography? If we investigate fiction's response to photography, does an identifiable, historic visual regime emerge in writing around ideas and representations of photography? What relationship, if any, would this historic visual regime have with ideas and representations of the law and reading? And with the workings and transmission of power? There has been scholarship which would suggest that fiction would support a particular, identifiable visual regime, although it does not include the analysis of representations of photography, the law or reading. Works such as Jonathan Crary's *Techniques of the Observer: On Vision and Modernity in the Nineteenth Century* (1992) have focused on the prime influence of scientific understandings of vision and changing ideas about the role of the observer. They have suggested that such scientific conceptions have influenced cultural production after the invention of photography. Thus, one crucial, exemplary artwork for Crary is J. M. W. Turner's painting *Light and Colour (Goethe's Theory) – The Morning After the Deluge* (1843), which was influenced by Goethe's writings on physiological optics. Crary sees this painting as symptomatic of the broader nineteenth century visual regime because he sees it as showing a complete collapse of 'the older model of representation' based on the optics of the *camera obscura*.[1] As he writes, the work, in which he sees the sun as representative of the eye, accords a 'central' emphasis on 'the retinal processes of vision; and it was the carnal embodiment of sight that the camera obscura denied or repressed'.[2] Does Crary's model of vision allow us to understand the central concerns of this painting and perhaps fiction and its construction of reading and readers after the invention of photography?

Along with Crary, I share the idea that this painting shows what is central to understandings of vision in the nineteenth century, and that it makes evident the underpinnings of the visual regime at the time. However, what I see as central are not changes in scientific understandings of sight which influenced the construction of art. Rather, the themes shown in the painting that are absolutely central to the visual regime after the invention of photography are the figure of the author and the implicit invocation of the law and its reading. In the centre of the painting, is Moses who, according to the Bible, received the tablets of the Law from God that were

1 Jonathan Crary, *Techniques of the Observer: On Vision and Modernity in the Nineteenth Century* (Cambridge, Massachusetts: MIT Press, 1992), 139.
2 Ibid.

DOI: 10.4324/9781003173854-1

inscribed with God's own writing; Moses as the first reader of God's law. In addition, Moses is writing – he is not just reader of the law, but also the author that is divinely inspired. Yet Crary's understanding of the painting, reflected in his shortening of its title, does not address such related themes of authorship, the law and of its reading which I understand as absolutely crucial to understanding how nineteenth-century commentators represented themselves as seeing. The emphasis of commentators such as Crary in understanding the visual regime of the nineteenth century has been on science, not the law, or ideas of reading. In this book, I will show that an emphasis on ideas of authorship, law and reading allows us to see the visual regime more accurately and to understand it in the terms that nineteenth-century individuals understood it in. I argue that constructions of the reader and the law in fiction, and fiction's intended control of an intended audience, were heavily influenced by ideas of an ideal law and legal interpretation, or the reading of the law. The larger visual regime is one in which constructions of the law and legal interpretation simultaneously inform and control ideas of the reader and the viewer.

In the painting, the law is invoked repetitively. Besides including the figure of Moses, who received the tablets of the law, Turner represents and celebrates the rainbow of the Covenant between the Father and man after the deluge, the light of the law. The celebration of law's light, its truth, is conflated with the image of the male writer, himself the first reader of the law, writing scripture. Moses himself appears in the absolute centre of a circle of light, which Crary tells us represents both the sun and a huge eyeball, a circle which touches a heaven outside of the frame of the picture at its top and participates in the mystery of the Father, the mystery of divine vision. The reader of the law as author is the central figure. Not only this, but he therefore represents the pupil of the eye, which accepts 'light-writing' (truth) from the Father, or the divine revelation of scripture. That is, the 'light-writing' of the Christian God rather than the 'light-writing' of photography which had just been invented and which seems to be implicitly opposed to the truth of divine revelation and divine vision. Thus, in this eye, through implicit suggestion, the law is divinely inspired and outside the photographic manufacture of man, an object of worship since it comes from the Father. What adds to this subtle definition of God's law against photography is the viewer's awareness of the story that Moses the reader obeyed God's law which prohibited the worship of the graven image, an alternative source of power and divine authority. The painting's form may recall this patriarchal legal fight against the image that Moses as the reader of God's law was recruited in: representation is blurred rather than clear, like art photography in the period which imposed a concealing 'veil' upon what is portrayed. Like the authors examined in this book, Moses, reader and author, is involved in a legal war against an image with a rival power. It is this which appears central to nineteenth-century vision, including the emphasis on a patriarchal law: the figure of both the reader of the law and receiver of inspired vision presented as author of patriarchal 'truth' (scripture), a figure who is implicitly opposed to photography and its way of seeing. Lastly, one notes that Moses the reader against photography and the graven image is at one with the immense power of God and his law. This is a game of power and the positions in which nineteenth century readers could take in a hierarchy which placed reading and the law over vision and the image.

As in the above discussion of Turner's painting, this book aims to investigate the ways in which reading is related to photography and the law through the idea of writing and authorship in mainly English but also some American fiction from the mid-nineteenth century to the end of the 1920s. I show how and why intended readers were recruited by authors to oppose photography and to fashion a law and an interpretation and reading of the law against the image. I argue that law required of its readers an appreciation of an idealism that lay beneath the surface of the text and what it thought of as 'appearances'. This form of reading was attached to a class of political and mostly legally trained elites. Photography, on the other hand, was contrasted with the supposedly 'deeper' reading as a more superficial ('literalist') form of interpretation. I focus on how power was sustained through the construction of these visual codes around ideas of the law, reading and the reader. The majority of authors studied moved in professional legal circles, so their fiction represents to me the production and thought of a unified legal culture and is about real legal interpretation in the period, rather than the laboured fancies of novelists. Although, along with other scholars investigating the area, I share the idea that photography was hugely significant for fiction, law and reading during the period, this study complicates the understanding of the nature of that significance within fiction. I argue that the role of photography in fiction and in relation to representations of law and reading in that fiction is to act not as a model, but as a foil. I contend that late nineteenth- to early twentieth-century fiction creates an opposition between photography and the law in order to discipline its readers in certain kinds of reading practice. In the fiction I've studied, representations of photography engage with and invite discussions of the larger nature of order, art, representation, truth, law and fiction as prominent commentators such as Nancy Armstrong have argued.[3] These authors also provoke and foreground questions as to the nature of seeing and reading and the subjectivity of the seers and readers in the period, especially as they relate to the construction and transmission of identities, power relations and asymmetries of power. But, as this work aims to show, photography is also used in the fiction as a subversive, contrary form of seeing and reading associated with perceived outsiders to the political elite such as women, natives and the lower class. As such, a 'photographic' reading is denounced while an 'anti-photographic' reading is valorised.

I will argue that, by concentrating on investigating photography as a positive model for the representational modes of nineteenth-century fiction, previous scholars have neglected a nuanced study of representations of photography and photographers in relation to representations of reading and the law in fiction. In the writings of canonical authors such as Charles Dickens, Wilkie Collins and Henry James and in key works of fiction in the period such as Wilkie Collins' *The Woman in White* (1860), photography is consistently associated with villains who threaten 'correct' reading practices, the existing order and the law. Through its associations with criminality and its threats to truth in these fictions photography

3 Nancy Armstrong, *Fiction in the Age of Photography: The Legacy of British Realism* (Cambridge, Massachusetts and London, England: Harvard University Press, 2002). I discuss this work in greater detail below.

functions to delineate ideas of legitimacy and authorised and acceptable reading practices. This function was assigned to photography in spite of, and perhaps because of, the multiplicity of uses to which it was put in the wider culture. I aim to show how representations of photography in fiction supply an immensely fertile site in which to explore ideas of fiction, order and legal truth.

The primary methodology employed in this monograph is close reading of a limited selection of primary source material. This monograph is about ideas presented in fiction and how they can be historically placed within the context of legal knowledge and political strategies. I have made a conscious decision not to employ any particular theoretical approach because I aim to understand the fiction on its own terms, so far as it is possible. I had noticed the number of times photography and photographers were seen negatively in the fiction of the nineteenth century. Accounting for this occurrence has informed my method and I have used various critical positions (such as Michel Foucault's) to the extent that they help me explicate what I find in the fiction: many instances of photography being seen as problematic, and used in plots to bring about deceit, disorder and illegality. I have selected fiction for discussion where I have seen it as representative of the central case in fiction from the mid-nineteenth century to the 1920s, particularly but not exclusively the fiction of writers involved in various ways in the professions of the law. This is to show that I am talking about a 'real' legal culture rather than the representation of the law in fiction which could be conjectured to be apart from the rarefied legal universe. However, the authors were not selected in the first place because of their legal connections. It was after tracing the resistance of the law to photography in fiction that I discovered a shared and consistent legal culture amongst the authors. The recognition and assessment of such a coherent and unified, albeit clandestine, legal culture fuelled by involuntary and unconscious, compulsive membership is one of the key contributions of this work. I realised that this was an artistic-legal culture (see below for a discussion of the formative relationships between idealist art and the law), and therefore I have included a concentrated analysis of Henry James and Wilkie Collins in two chapters, since they were trained as both artists and lawyers. What unified such a culture can be conjectured to be a will to power, since it is power above all else with which the hierarchies of reading and readers are concerned. I have aimed to include key authors and key works rather than emphasising the legal professions of authors, demonstrating that the boundaries between the law and culture were porous and that the shared and surreptitious legal culture had a wider net and a wider, if unrecognised, membership. The most popular and significant names, such as Charles Dickens and Wilkie Collins, all figure. The most popular and influential and important works of the period, such as *The Woman in White* have all been shown to form part of the anti-photographic regime. At the same time, I have made an attempt at inclusivity and have shown that lesser known writers share in the modelling of reading and the reader and their differentiation from photography and photographs. I have done so to indicate how widely shared such constructions were. My focus has been on texts in which the anti-photographic regime is most evident rather than focusing on fiction which might be read as supporting photography as the truth. This is because I see fiction which denounces photography to predominate. The authors here are all male, but this is so because of the evident nature of the complex I am studying in their work and how much it can reveal about the law and legal interpretation. Certainly, writers like Mrs Margaret Oliphant also portrayed the separation between the law, reading and photography in works like *Mrs Marjoribanks* (1866). There, the heroine refuses an offer of marriage with a lawyer in a library (where reading takes place) in full view of a glass-house where women do their photography. However, ideas of reading the law are not very explicit in such portrayals. In their readings of fiction, prominent women authors such as Charlotte Brontë also denounced writers such as Jane Austen for allowing their writing to become like a photograph and, more implicitly, for imposing photographs on the reader.[4] However, here, explicit ideas of the law are not invoked and neither is there any substantial mention of photography in Brontë's fiction which allow her ideas on the subject to be developed (*Shirley* (1849), the only novel explicitly to refer to photography, mentions daguerreotypes in just two instances). The women authors I came across largely seem to have adopted the complex studied in a much more implicit and concealed manner than male authors, perhaps as a result of their greater distance from the professional legal sphere. In my treatment of the authors studied, I have emphasised the sharing of ideas and the resemblance between authors rather than their individuality. My focus has been on a unitary logic in their work. This limitation that was imposed on the texts has been enabling in a number of ways. It provided focus and highlighted the connections between the chosen texts. It allowed me to move away from the ahistorical idea that authors were discrete individuals with an ahistorical genius. It emphasised connections rather than separations. The relatively small size of the sample of fiction as representative of a larger body of writings allowed a more detailed reading in which the main coordinates of the model of anti-photographic and anti-literalist invisibility could be explored. In my analysis, I have not considered the fiction as multi-voiced or involved in a dialogic encounter with the political and legal context. This is because I wanted to concentrate my full attention on a single voice within fiction which, as I show, strongly determines its nature and purpose. I also wonder if an emphasis on the supposedly many voices within fiction can adequately describe this repressive legal voice I have heard, a voice which is based on systematic exclusion and the silencing and marginalisation of voices which represent difference, such as the voices of women, natives and the lower class.

My reading of the fiction is analytical because it aims to construct relationships and identify recurring and previously unidentified patterns between terms such as art, the law and reading and ideas of power. The interest is in an area outside of the conscious control and intentions of authors: the implicit, given conditions of representation in a situated period which influence and shape thought without being explicitly or consciously recognised. My analysis of the fiction focused on its content rather than its form. As I will show below, literary investigations of the relationship between photography and literature have been preoccupied with questions of form and the construction of fiction. My analysis therefore redresses what appears

4 Brontë to George Lewes, 12 January 1848, in *The Letters of Charlotte Brontë, vol. 2*: 1848–1851 (Margaret Smith (ed), Oxford: Clarendon Press, 2000), 10.

to me to be a critical neglect. For similar reasons, I have concentrated on how the fiction supported the structures of power through its representations. Questions of literary form and the influence of photography upon it in previous scholarship did not appear to directly address questions of power, although they made implicit assumptions about it. Since my study involved an analysis of the law, it seemed to not only raise the question of power, but also to bring it to the foreground in an analysis. As I read the fiction, the law represented within it seemed to be the expression of power: an exclusionary and discriminating power that was patriarchal, based on economic dominance, a power that was misogynistic and xenophobic, determined to eliminate difference, opposition and possible reform or rebellion. If there is a theoretical perspective in my reading, it is conditioned by this larger understanding of power, a version of power that has been presented in Marxist, Feminist and Postcolonial studies, and in the work of Friedrich Nietzsche and Michel Foucault, with varying nuances. My analysis is an analysis of the operation of power throughout society because it appeared to me through reading it, rather than through seeing it through a theoretical framework, that the prime function of the fiction I have analysed was the propping up of power structures. Indeed, contemporary commentators like John Ruskin explicitly said that this was the function of literature, as I will discuss at length in the first chapter of this monograph.

As for the representations of photography, and of the law and reading, I have analysed them by considering them to be entangled or enmeshed in each other and in fiction as a dense web of meaning. I have not considered them to be discrete entities, but as interwoven products that relate to each other and wider ideas, such as understandings of art and idealism. I have understood this web as a collection of subtle suggestions, hints and insinuations to be extracted through working out heavily nuanced implications, associations, contextualisation, comparisons and contrasts. In my readings, I have constantly been reminded and my reading has been shaped by the awareness that ideas about the subjects I have addressed have not been directly expressed, they have been indirectly expressed. The tools of my literary analysis have therefore aimed to expose and reveal the presentation and representation of the terms I have studied in the original fictions in their naked rather than their veiled significance.

Scholarship on the relationship between Victorian photography and the law

As I will demonstrate, the characterisation of photography as crucially related to ideas of truth is repeatedly contested by writers of fiction from the invention of photography to the 1920s. Scholarship over the last three decades which has, in contrast to this, seen photography as wedded to ideas of truth in the nineteenth century has often been based on the reading of archives, not fiction. In historical accounts of the late nineteenth century, truth and order are often understood to depend upon photographic evidence. Alan Sekula's essay on the subject, 'The Body and the Archive' (1986) appears to be the earliest example of such an argument.[5]

5 Allan Sekula, 'The Body and the Archive', *October*, 39 (1986), 3.

Sekula believes that photography was used to tell 'the truth' about personhood and identity through supposedly truth-telling disciplines such as law and criminology. In Sekula's account, it is photography that seemingly orders society through mechanisms of 'truth' since it is fully integrated into the state and legal apparatus. Sekula presents the argument that there is a close connection between the historical use of photography and the operations of power that regulate 'the deviant body' and also 'the social body' and 'the normal body'. As he writes, 'photography came to establish and delimit the terrain of the *other*, to define both the *generalized look* – the typology – and the *contingent instance* of deviance and social pathology'.[6] He associates the emergence of photography with the development of police acts and technologies of surveillance. Thus, he states that the 'socially instrumental realism' of photography 'was central to the process of defining and regulating the criminal'.[7]

John Tagg, who writes after Sekula, but does not cite his work, also links photography to truth and order in the Victorian period by focusing on the situation in America. In *The Burden of Representation: Essays on Photographies and Histories* (1988), for example, Tagg argues that because photography was widely seen as a truthful representation, it became the medium through with power circulated, supporting certain forms of law, discipline and control. Tagg investigates photography as it functioned throughout a series of nineteenth- and early twentieth-century practices such as photographic portraiture, the establishment of the photograph as a legal document, the use of photography in medical and police practices, and the documentary work of the Farm Security Administration in America. He argues that the 'coupling of evidence and photography in the second half of the nineteenth century was bound up with the emergence of new institutions and new practices of observation and record-keeping'.[8] The extent to which the photographic process and the legal realm which is associated with the truth are synonymous in this argument is evidenced in Tagg's linkage of the police service and photography. He writes:

> The early years of the development of the photographic process coincided approximately with the period of the introduction of the police service into this country, and for more than a hundred years the two have progressed together. As photographic processes and equipment have been evolved and refined, so have police forces expanded and become more efficient.[9]

Tagg's account, based on archival research, would indicate that truth, the law and the photographic image were inseparable in the period. As I aim to show, however, photography is carefully separated from the truth in the fiction that I analyse, particularly from the discipline of law and ideas of legal truth. The manufacture of the sharp, clean figure portrait is described in both Sekula and Tagg's accounts as an

6 Ibid., 7.

7 Ibid.

8 John Tagg, *The Burden of Representation: Essays on Photographies and Histories* (London: The Macmillan Press Ltd, 1988), 5.

9 Ibid., 74.

unquestionable (if unattainable and unrealistic) corollary of the will to power and the repressive mechanisms of the state. However, in the fiction I'm looking at, the photographic portrait is a site of deception and confusion.

Tagg and Sekula's accounts have been influential and have been echoed more recently in Jonathan Matthew Finn's book, *Capturing the Criminal Image: From Mug Shot to Surveillance Society* (2009). The linking of photography and disciplinary knowledge or truth is also clear in this book. The title is indicative of how photography is seen as synonymous with the rise of surveillance of the body. Finn also sees photography as part of the disciplinary classifying and ordering of bodies in the carceral network of modern governmentality in the nineteenth century. He writes, for example,

> [b]y the close of the nineteenth century, the photographic representation of the criminal body was enmeshed in a socially defined binary of normal versus deviant and in questions of power, surveillance and privacy.[10]

Photography is here seen to feed the surveillance society. Thus:

> [a] central effect of photography's use in law enforcement and criminal identification practices of the nineteenth century was to bring more bodies under police and state surveillance through their representation and inclusion in the police file or, in Sekula's term, the archive. To be photographed was to be recorded as a subject of the state.[11]

Like Tagg, Finn also writes of the photographic vision creating new subjects of knowledge to be disciplined according to the needs of the new society:

> [a]s a representational device, the camera effectively extended the disciplinary mechanism manifest in Bentham's Panopticon: it isolated and made visible bodies as they moved through the social and institutional spaces of the carceral network. As an inscription device, the camera facilitated the production of new forms of disciplinary knowledge, which, in turn, helped describe the types of subjects that were to be made visible.[12]

Photography is seen by these writers as creating new forms of disciplinary knowledge because of its status as evidence and therefore as new truth. In this account, photography enables the construction not only of truth, but also of order. All of the above scholars have shown that in certain circumstances, photography was widely held to tell the truth and thus formed the foundation of 'legal truth'. These readings are based on an investigation of the archive, not of fiction. However, in the

10 Jonathan Mathew Finn, *Capturing the Criminal Image: From Mug Shot to Surveillance Society* (Minnesota: University of Minnesota Press, 2009), ix.

11 Ibid., 29.

12 Ibid., 29–30.

fiction I will discuss, photographic portraits, the photographic archive and photographic evidence are all seen as deceptive.

Within these different areas of science and the arts, photography took on seemingly contradictory and opposing meanings. From the mid-nineteenth century to the end of the 1920s, photography played a very different role in science than in the law, art and fiction I have studied here. The association of photography with scientific vision and observation is considered problematic in this fiction. The accounts of Tagg and others seem more apposite for the study of the scientific use of photography and do not appear to apply to the way photography is used in the fiction I am studying. To understand the larger picture, I argue, scholarship has to pay attention to the relationship between truth, legal truth, seeing and reading. This is why the fiction is crucial to analysis: it relates reading to the law and truth.

The influence and reinterpretation of Michel Foucault's panopticism

How can the larger historical construction of vision be understood to be characterised by its relationship to power and its modality? This is a crucial issue which I will address in this monograph. Scholars such as Tagg and Finn have clearly used Michel Foucault's concept of panopticism which he outlined in *Discipline and Punish* (1975) to describe the expansion of nineteenth-century photography and the state. However, their interpretations of panopticism emphasise surveillance rather than any linkages with the law and concealment, or invisibility, which have influenced my own readings. Concealment of the central figure of authority and the law was the crucial condition for how Jeremy Bentham's Panopticon (the prison house, a legal apparatus) was constructed and how it operated. As Bentham emphasised, the architecture of the inspection house was to allow '*seeing without being seen*'.[13] Thus, in the proposed plans, to the windows of the central Inspector's Lodge 'there are blinds, as high up as the eyes of the prisoners in their Cells can, by any means they employ, be made to reach'.[14] There was also strategic partitioning in place so that there was no way 'the prisoners would see from the Cells whether or not any person was in the Lodge'.[15] As Foucault summarised the situation, 'in the peripheric ring, one is totally seen, without ever seeing; in the central tower, one sees everything without ever being seen'.[16] For Foucault, the Panopticon is Jeremy Bentham's construction of light, visibility and invisibility, a diagram of power and a type of legal soft technology which structures diverse institutions such as factories, schools, hospitals and asylums. As he wrote, the 'panoptic schema, without disappearing as such or losing any of its properties, was destined to spread throughout the social body; its vocation was to become a generalized function'.[17]

13 Jeremy Bentham, *Panopticon; or, The Inspection-House* (London: T. Payne, 1791), 23 (original emphasis).

14 Ibid., 7.

15 Ibid.

16 Michel Foucault, *Discipline and Punish: The Birth of the Prison* (Alan Sheridan (tr), Vintage Books New York 1995), 202.

17 Ibid., 207.

Invisibility and loss of vision as well as concealment of power was therefore the crucial condition for the totalising vision of power throughout the historical formation of society. It is these conditions that I have emphasised in my research on photography and its relationship to understandings of reading and the law in fiction. A deference to a bodiless (and anti-photographic) 'invisibility' understood as powerful and legitimate structures the way in which reading and the reader are controlled through visual codes.

Foucault's ideas on panopticism and the concealment of the figure of the law, power and authority at its centre were developed over a number of years. Significantly enough, where Foucault considered modern law in fiction in *Maurice Blanchot: The Thought from Outside* (1966), he emphasised its 'hidden' character, stating that the law is not self-evident but that the sovereignty and the 'presence of the law is its concealment'.[18] To describe the status of modern law in fiction, this 'concealment' and indeed law's 'invisibility' had to be taken into account seriously. Therefore, in his analysis of Maurice Blanchot's novel *Le Très-Haut* (*The Most High*) (1948), Foucault wrote that:

> when Sorge leaves state service, where he was responsible for ordering other people's existence, he does not go outside the law. Quite the opposite, he forces it to manifest itself at the empty place he just abandoned. The movement by which he effaces his singular existence and removes it from the universality of the law in fact exalts the law; through that movement he serves the law, shows its perfection, 'obliges' it, while at the same time linking it to its own disappearance (which is, in a sense, the opposite of transgressive existence exemplified by Bouxx and Dorte); he has become one with the law.[19]

The law is thus associated in Foucault's thinking not only with concealment, but also with 'disappearance' or invisibility. The hidden nature of modern law is emphasised. Why does Foucault link law with concealment and invisibility? The ideas are developed at length in *Discipline and Punish* (1975) in the discussion of panopticism.

In *Discipline and Punish*, Foucault argues that modern legal punishment reflects a general historical shift from the production of the law and legal truth as a spectacle of the body. As he writes:

> Punishment had gradually ceased to be a spectacle. And whatever theatrical elements it still retained were now downgraded, as if the functions of the penal ceremony were gradually ceasing to be understood, as if this rite that 'concluded the crime' was suspected of being in some undesirable way linked with it.[20]

18 Michel Foucault, "Where Is the Law, And What Does It Do?" in Michel Foucault (ed), *Maurice Blanchot: The Thought from Outside* (Brian Massumi (tr), New York: Zone Books, 1987), 33.
19 Ibid., 38.
20 Foucault, *Discipline and Punish: The Birth of the Prison* (n 16) 9.

This is a spectacle of the body since Foucault argues that in the older form of punishment, the force of the King's own body is triumphant.[21] The new form of punishment stands in contrast to the spectacle of the body. The new form of punishment instead models the law as a hidden or invisible, bodiless entity. This historical shift is seen to reflect a seizure of power and law by the middle class from the sovereign. This idea is developed by pairing the law's constructed 'invisibility' with the middle class' need to 'hide' its lack of legitimacy in its control of the legal apparatus. As a result, the modern period is productive of the form of legal institutions such as the prison, which is hidden away from the public's sight, which reflects the new modality of truth and power. Foucault therefore writes:

> It is ugly to be punishable, but there is no glory in punishing. Hence that double system of protection that justice has set up between itself and the punishment it imposes. Those who carry out the penalty tend to become an autonomous sector; justice is relieved of responsibility for it by a bureaucratic concealment of the penalty itself.[22]

Importantly, Foucault again couples the law with 'concealment'.

Invisibility is paramount in such constructions of the law and of legal punishment. This is evident in the construction of the Panopticon, for instance. The Panopticon must have an invisible watcher or knower, whether real or, indeed, imaginary (since the Inspector is not compelled to be always present), as the position of legal power and authority must be invisible, a reaction against the body as image. It is this very invisibility that is constructed and accepted as the face of power that forces deference and submission. The body of law and power has to be structured away from the idea of spectacle and image in the new modality of power. Not only this, but the shift from torture to the prison is understood as a shift from corporal punishment which has to bear scars to a rigorous timetabling and disciplining. As Foucault comments:

> The disappearance of public executions marks therefore the decline of the spectacle; but it also marks a slackening of the hold on the body.[23]

What becomes important to law and the social formation in regulating the individual and the community is not the materiality of the body and its status as image which broadcasts information about the law, but rather the potentiality of the body and its possibility of being 'docile' and productive in line with the larger requirements of society. What becomes important is 'soul' or 'spirit' rather than the image

21 The culmination of a ritual of truth that reflects 'the principle that in criminal matters the establishment of truth was the absolute right and the exclusive power of the sovereign and his judges'. Ibid., 35. Furthermore, 'The search for truth through judicial torture was certainly a way of obtaining evidence, the most serious of all-the confession of the guilty person; but it was also the battle, and this victory of one adversary over the other, that "produced" truth according to a ritual'. Ibid., 41.

22 Ibid., 10.

23 Ibid.

of the body, of any body. The condition for this is itself the invisibility or concealment of the (king's) body which was once a spectacle of power.

Discipline and Punish has influenced my research because of its focus on the law's strategies of concealment. It shows how heavily invested the law is in the invisibility/visibility or 'hidden' dynamic in the modern period. It shows how law is related to the body and 'the non-corporal nature of the penal system'.[24] *Discipline and Punish* also suggests that law's concealment is the modality of power. The book shows how this form of power produces and regulates truth and power relations in order to build knowers, subjects and communities around the central core of the concealed body, like Bentham's non-visible body in the Panopticon. I have extended Foucault's ideas about the law's concealment in several ways in exploring how and why fiction has exploited the figure of the law's imaginary, bodiless 'invisibility', including how this idea is related to the power and the reading of the law, the identity of the reader of the law and the law's influence on art and its marginalisation of photography. In particular, I have shown how the idea of panopticism has been taken up by individuals in detail and how they have attempted to reconstruct and reinstitute this idea throughout society through their readership set against a photography of bodies. Thus, through my reinterpretation of Foucault's work, I see the law's relationship to power and vision to characterise it in a different way to understandings of Panopticism, photography and surveillance in works like those of Tagg and Finn.

Scholarship on the relationship between Victorian photography and fiction

The idea that Victorian fiction, like the law, is modelled upon photography has determined several recent investigations into the connections between Victorian photography and fiction. This work, which I will now consider, seems to follow the earlier claims made by scholars such as Tagg and Sekula about the power of photography to shape extra-photographic practices and discourses and sees fictional writing as considerably influenced and shaped by photographic processes and photographic discourses.

Nancy Armstrong, one of the most influential commentators on the novel, in *Fiction in the Age of Photography: The Legacy of British Realism* (1999), reflects this approach. She argues that there is a 'mutually authorizing relationship between fiction and Photography':[25]

> Victorian fiction was the first English fiction, I am suggesting, to convert a particular kind of visual information—infinitely reproducible and capable of rapid and wide dissemination—into what was both a way of seeing and a picture of the world that a mass readership could share.[26]

24 Ibid., 15.
25 Armstrong (n 3) 5.
26 Ibid., 7.

For Armstrong, fiction attempted to represent the photographic representation of reality. She summarises the relationship between photography and fiction in terms of interdependency, aiming '[t]o show how photography authorized fiction as a truth-telling medium'. She attempts to demonstrate 'that in order to convince readers fiction was indeed offering them mastery of the world of objects, fiction had to authorize the transparent, reproducible image'.[27] Armstrong sees the identity of Victorian readers as depending upon photographic images which she sees as the crucial resource which was drawn upon to construct ideas of personhood and individuality. She writes that '[t]he iconography of the period clearly shows that individuals were 'hailed' into various social categories, more by recognizing themselves in an image than, as Althusser assumes, by recognizing themselves as the target of 'a verbal call or whistle''.[28] According to Armstrong, the photograph is so foundational to the construction of identity that there is no visual influence outside of photography upon identity since even strategies which counter photographic representations of persons are ultimately reliant upon mass-produced photographic stereotypes which frame and thus effectively dictate how difference is conceived and articulated. This can be seen where Armstrong writes:

> I have tried to combat the assumption that we can get rid of harmful stereotypes simply by refusing to think in terms of mass-produced images. If it is by differentiating ourselves from one or more of these stereotypes that one acquires individuality, then without them we would have no identity, or at least no modern identity.[29]

In Armstrong's account, photography is the most powerful influence on ideas of reading, fiction and identity. However, as I will go on to show, in much fiction after the invention of photography until the 1920s, the representation of photography does not play out the relationship set out by Armstrong. Rather, accepted conventions of art-viewing and legal positions and the roles that they call for appear to determine the nature of reading and identity within fiction. Where Armstrong sees photography as an accepted form of truth and fiction to attempt to share in its method of truth-telling, I have seen photography as it is represented in fiction to be associated with deception and lying. Fiction has therefore attempted to dissociate itself from photography to suggest its greater ability to represent the truth. However, paradoxically, as I argue in Chapter Four, where I show that illegitimate and 'photographic' plots of deception only trouble fiction because they may supplant 'legitimate' plots of deception, if fiction has done this, fiction has at the same time emphasised itself as having a monopoly on untruth and deception. As I see it, fiction and photography therefore seem to collide because they clash over the perceived ability to represent untruth, because both photography and fiction are seen as untrue, even while this is framed as a contest of truth against deception.

27 Ibid., 27.
28 Ibid., 22.
29 Ibid., 3.

In *Realism, Photography and Nineteenth-Century Fiction* (2008), Daniel Novak also sees the form of the Victorian novel as modelled on a photographic process in 'the age of photography'.[30] Indeed, for him, fiction and photography are somewhat interchangeable. Thus, arguing that his approach to fiction and photography represents the interdisciplinary nature of Victorian thinking on their intersections, he writes that, 'Victorians *already* read photography as a form of literary fiction and literary fiction as a form of photographic representation'.[31] For him, fictional works and photographs are in some ways equivalent because they are the outcome of a 'technology of realism [which] produced what appears to be its opposite: the non-existent, the fictional, and the abstract'.[32] Novak sees 'composition photography' as the dominant practice in Victorian 'art photography' in the 1850s. This was a process which put together a collection of parts to fit together into a new whole, such as Henry Peach Robinson's photograph *Fading Away* (1858), which merged together several individual photographs so as to create a new scene. He argues that the Victorian novel mimics this process which offered 'new techniques of totalization … to turn these fragments into the picture perfect scenes of convincing and compelling fictions'.[33] As he elaborates, the process resulted in a composition:

> in which figures were transposed from one scene to another, bodies from different images juxtaposed in new (and often compromising) contexts, and single bodies even sutured together from different models.[34]

Here, composition photography is presented as the dominant model for Victorian fiction and as such is seen to define its nature and limits because fiction is said to mimic its processes.

Novak argues in particular that identity in Victorian novels is modelled on Francis Galton's 'composite-photography' which aims to portray ideal 'types'. Identity in fiction is said by him to depend upon photographic representations where photographs are layered upon each other and present the refined result as the isolated resemblances across groups. In a discussion of the identity of Daniel Deronda in George Eliot's novel, *Daniel Deronda* (1876), Novak writes:

> this amorphous yet seemingly individual figure, this spectral and typological body, is both the product of a technological novelistic vision and a reproduction of visual technology in the age of photography. This immaterial and fictional figure finds its material embodiment in Galton's 'composite-photography', which he used to isolate the pure type of family inheritance, pathology, and race.[35]

30 Daniel A. Novak, *Realism, Photography and Nineteenth-Century Fiction* (Cambridge: Cambridge University Press 2008), 92.

31 Ibid., 6.

32 Ibid., 1.

33 Ibid., 68.

34 Ibid., 1–2.

35 Ibid., 92.

For Novak, identities in fiction are presented as photographic 'types' based on the idea of resemblance. They derive from photographic practices. The ultimate aim of Novak's work is to redefine 'photographic realism'. He accepts and does not question the idea that the Victorian novel is based on 'photographic realism',[36] but goes beyond existing understandings of this by arguing that photographic realism is constructed as a fiction, rather than concluding that the fiction is claiming to be in some way 'real'. His redefinition of Victorian photography and 'photographic realism' is founded upon the claim that they are both a type of fiction with similar methods of construction. Novak goes on to 'show how photography set the standard for what was not real. Photographic fictions … defined and produced the impossible and the abstract'.[37] He writes that 'far from capturing particularity and individuality, technologies of realism rendered its subjects at once dismembered and disembodied'.[38] Novak does mention the negative characterisation of individual photographs in the novels of George Eliot and the practices of art photographers. He states that there is 'a wide-spread conviction that the photograph could not represent individuality, particularity, and even the temporal moment'.[39] However, like the other critics I have mentioned above, he does not investigate the widespread negative depictions of photography and photographers in fiction.

Owen Clayton's work in *Literature and Photography in Transition, 1850-1915* (2015) builds upon Novak's. Clayton models Victorian fiction on photographic processes in more detail by studying the relationship between shifts in photographic processes and Victorian writing. He writes, for example, that:

> Mayhew's journalism, for instance, was undertaken during the period in which the daguerreotype was displaced by the wet plate collodion process. Stevenson engaged with a variety of photographic innovations in his work, including the zoopraxiscope photographic projector and the Galtonian composite.[40]

Clayton argues that specific photographic processes informed the way that Victorian authors 'engaged with photography as both metaphor and mode of literary organisation'.[41] For Clayton, like Novak, photographic processes are integrally tied to formal constructions of fiction. Specific photographic processes are also tied to constructions of identity. Thus, Clayton argues that 'Robert Louis Stevenson's model of the divided self was influenced by specific photographic and projection methods'.[42] By concentrating on close readings of fictional work, however, I aim to show that, like other authors, Stevenson saw photographic vision as a threat to reading, law and art in his fiction. By focusing on close readings of fictional work in this monograph, I aim to extend the existing picture of the photographic

36 Ibid., 6.
37 Ibid., 6.
38 Ibid., 4.
39 Ibid., 4.
40 Owen Clayton, *Literature and Photography in Transition, 1850-1915* (London: Palgrave Macmillan, 2015), 4.
41 Ibid., 4.
42 Ibid., 165.

influence on fiction and add to existing scholarship by enabling another perspective to emerge, a perspective in which photography is not the prime influence on fiction, but is regarded as a form of representation from which fiction has to be sharply differentiated.

This monograph concentrates on explicit portrayals of photography and photographers in the fiction that I study, for example, the representation of Dr. Vimpany, the villainous photographer in Wilkie Collins' novel *Blind Love* (1890). I will investigate the relationship between photography and the law through constructions of reading in fiction, for example, how the reading of a will is related to ideas of photography in Charles Dickens' novel *Our Mutual Friend* (1865). This is because I will argue that photography is to be seen in the context of its relationship to constructions of law, reading and the reader represented in the fiction. The study therefore aims to illuminate how vision and reading are tied together and how visual codes are involved in how reading is experienced, conceptualised and carefully regulated. As such, the monograph will add to existing knowledge by showing how legal knowledge and methods of reading were a prime influence on fiction, its themes, how it was read and its readers.

Scholarship on the law's war against the image

Studies of legal visual culture, like my own, have emphasised the self-defining hostility of the law to certain images historically. Peter Goodrich argues that the English common law was founded in a rhetoric against the feminised image and 'idols of thought'.[43] I show that a similar strategy was taken up by the authors in this study who moved in legal circles in order to uphold a construction of the law against a photography perceived as feminine.

It has been recognised that the law's stake in such an identity-building enterprise is one of control and power, and, also, that the law discriminates between acceptable images and unacceptable ones. Thus, Costas Douzinas writes, 'The law understands the importance of the governance of images for the maintenance of the social bond and helps organise a regime of permitted images and forbidden idols which amounts to a complex legal administration of aesthetics and a related aesthetic organisation of law'.[44] This legal strategy is described as being of tantamount importance as it 'establishes the human subject', alongside law's own identity.[45] It is this building of control, power and identity in the law's war against photography that I will investigate most carefully here. I show that the construction of the law was synonymous with the construction of the identities and power of the political elite and their exclusion of the identities of perceived others.

Volker Boehme-Neßler elaborates why images such as photographs have historically frustrated the strategies producing the control and power of the law in his

43 Peter Goodrich, *Oedipus Lex: Psychoanalysis, History, Law* (Berkeley: University of California Press Berkeley, 1995).

44 Costas Douzinas, 'The Legality of the Image', *The Modern Law Review*, 63:6 (November 2000), 813.

45 Ibid., 830.

book *Pictorial Law* (2011). He suggests that language allows social control but images are not as conducive because of a number of factors. Visual communication creates 'effects in the recipients which were neither intended nor foreseeable' and 'images are less precise and have subsemantic side effects which are on the whole impossible to calculate'. He adds that 'images cannot express logical connections. Images cannot be assigned a single, unambiguous meaning: they are – to put it another way – non-notational. Whatever meaning an image has, depends on a whole bundle of different, not least cultural, auxiliary factors'.[46] Boehme-Neßler also notes that images pose a threat to traditional practices of legal interpretation such as the reading of the law which are fashioned to decipher texts. He writes that, 'images cannot be interpreted and understood using the same methods as words and text. The interpretation of visual legal communication is beyond the traditional legal canon of interpretation. Visual legal communication therefore needs to develop its own, new methods of interpretation'.[47] Here, I particularly emphasise why the image, the photograph, was historically seen as destroying traditional, dominant strategies of legal interpretation and reading after the advent of photography and what this reveals about the hidden aspects of such readings and those who read in such a way.

The difference between the representation of photography in writing and the adoption of photography outside of writing

In contrast to the negative portrayal in their fiction, many of the authors that I study in this monograph responded positively to the advent of photography outside of their writing. A number of them fraternised with photographers, or were enthusiastic amateur photographers themselves. Henry James chose the pictorialist photographer Alvin Langdon Coburn's 24 frontispieces for his collected works, *The Novels and Tales of Henry James* (1907–1909), which is more commonly known as *The New York Edition*. When Wilkie Collins published an edition of *The Woman in White* in one volume in April 1861, the novel was illustrated with a photographic portrait of the author. Later, in 1883, Collins dedicated his novel *Heart and Science* to his photographer friend, Napoleon Sarony. Sir Arthur Conan Doyle was himself a keen amateur photographer and published articles about his photographic expeditions in the *British Journal of Photography*. Because of such intersections between photography and fiction, it is not surprising that commentators have suggested that Victorian fiction and Victorian reading are modelled on the photograph and the viewing of photographs. As we have seen, Victorian fiction, particularly realist fiction, has been described as giving photography special privilege as a form of representation.

There, is, however, in the fiction I have studied from the mid-nineteenth century to the end of the 1920s, an incongruity between numerous authors' seemingly positive attitude towards photography outside of writing and their representation

46 Volker Boehme-Neßler, *Pictorial Law: Modern Law and the Power of Pictures* (London: Springer, 2011), 151.
47 Ibid., 183.

of photography within the fiction. Photography is consistently devalued in the writing of authors such as Henry James, Wilkie Collins and Sir Arthur Conan Doyle as well as other prominent writers such as Charles Dickens. In their works, writing as the dominant form of representation and its reading is sharply differentiated from the photographic image and protected from a type of literalist reading associated with photography which I will elaborate on further later in this introduction. The question is, why is there such an incongruity between the authors' personal attitudes to photography and the representation of photography in their writings? I suggest that the authors' reaction to photography in their fiction was outside of their conscious control as they were recruited unconsciously in the law's war against the image.

The fiction that I have studied appears to share a specific idea of truth and 'artistic truth' which it opposes to photographic truth. This idea of truth in fiction, I will argue, shapes its constructions of the law, reading and art. This conception of truth and 'artistic truth' has been described in recent scholarship as 'the truth of idealism'. As Josh Ellenbogen notes, from the beginning of the 1850s and until 1877, the blur in photography, which was contrary to the sharp and clean image since it eschewed fine detail and the clear delineation of features, as well as the untroubled representation of things as they were, had 'acquired a signifying capacity' and 'communicated its participation in a particular kind of project'.[48] Ellenbogen elaborates that this project, which pitted itself against a form of representation which aimed to 'mirror reality', was one of idealism which produced both art and 'truth'. He notes that in Francis Galton's 'scientific' composite photography and his construction of 'ideal types', which included racial types such as the Jew, there was a valorisation of the photographic blur which was seen as being both truthful and artistic. There was a circularity in Galton's discrimination: the blur was seen as truthful because it appeared artistic and appeared artistic because it was deemed truthful. Thus, Ellenbogen argues that Galton openly 'situates his project relative to the production of ideal imagery in both academic painting and established strands of art photography from the time'.[49] Both the centrality of the rejection of photography in fiction and the influential photographic movement called pictorialism, with its soft focus and its abstraction in conscious opposition to the sharpness and detail of the unfiltered photograph, were the ultimate artistic expressions of this idealism, which had been both long-standing and formative in traditional spheres of art such as painting and sculpture. Pictorialism itself has been described by Patrick Daum as a flight from 'brutal reality', which was seen as 'inartistic',[50] and in fiction similar ideas were espoused: that fiction was meant to portray something other than things as they were, that it was not meant to mirror reality. The veiling blur, which corrupted the purity and sharpness of the photographic medium, and

48 Josh Ellenbogen, *Reasoned and Unreasoned Images: The Photography of Bertillon, Galton, and Marey* (University Park: Pennsylvania State University Press, 2012), 132.

49 Ibid., 107.

50 Patrick Daum, 'Unity and Diversity in European Pictorialism', in Francis Ribemont and Patrick Daum (eds), *Impressionist Camera: Pictorial Photography in Europe, 1888-1918* (London: Merrell, 2006), 19.

idealistic art can therefore be seen as influential and formative for the history of photography of the period, whether artistic or scientific, such as in Galton's photographic experiments, and the larger history of fiction and the truth, too. Following Ellenbogen, I too contend that the critique of photography in the fiction I have studied goes alongside the soft focus and indistinct, blurry and obscured aesthetic of Victorian photographs and the photographic movement known as Pictorialism which aimed to veil reality; that it is framed by the larger conditions of idealism and idealist art and their ideas of 'artistic truth'. In Chapter 1, I will elaborate what the conditions of this shared ideal truth were; how it was related to ideas of legal truth; why photographic truth was consistently opposed to idealist truth; which group in society was unified under the banner of idealist truth and why.

As I aim to show, the widely shared and central critique of what photography symbolises in a range of Victorian and early twentieth-century fiction is hugely significant, influential and successful. It can be linked to the legal prohibition of photography and photo-realistic artwork from the courtroom in the 1920s. The critique of photography in fiction and its separation from the law therefore warrants special attention and study. My study of fiction is limited to the span of years from the invention of photography in 1839 to the early 1920s. This is because the 1930s mark a difference or even a radical break with prior traditions because of the difference in the reception of the photographic aesthetic in 'art-photography'. The 1930s are associated with the rise and acceptance of 'straight photography', which is characterised by detailed and sharply focused images and an effort to distinguish photography from painting. Straight photography has been described as 'a conscious rejection of the artistic styles of photography associated with the pictorialists and a turning back to the realistic tendencies that had defined photography in its earliest years'.[51] The straight photographers associated pictoralism with a 'misguided imitation of art' and rejected idealism in favour of a 'commitment to everyday life and the commonplace'.[52]

Legal reading and literalism

The authors I have chosen to study oppose an idealised 'legitimate' and 'legal' form of reading to a reading which is associated with photography. Indeed, ideas of law and legitimacy are closely associated with this reading, which is founded in legal legitimacy and legal interpretation. The authors appropriate this ideal of legal reading whereby laws are interpreted, constructed and deciphered from pieces of writing. These laws are then applied to situations in order to describe what happened and to assign the categories of blame, truth, falsity, legitimacy, illegitimacy, identity and ideas of criminality and innocence. I define readings as acts of construction and decipherment which construct truths and identities because this is how they are conceptualised in the fiction I have studied. The fiction connects the process of reading to subjectivity since types of reading, both illegitimate and legitimate, are

51 Peter Smith and Carolyn Lefley, *Rethinking Photography: Histories, Theories and Education* (London: Routledge, 2015), 93.
52 Ibid., 94.

tied to the identities of differing readers. Hence, outsiders are associated with the reading that is considered to go alongside photography while insiders are associated with an alternative reading. The fiction also connects the process of reading to the classifications which are inherent in rational thought: to the determination of right and wrong, both in terms of law and morality and in terms of truth and falsity. Reading is connected to the law in fiction because the law is constructed by readers through reading. Laws are enforced and transmitted through writing which has to be interpreted and constructed. However, the fiction disguises that this is what is happening and asserts that the law is 'natural' in some way, and this is drawn on by writers to assert fiction as naturally true and legitimate. This is because the material status of both law and fiction as writing is disavowed in order to bolster claims for their truthfulness outside of 'rhetorical constructions' and to limit the way in which they are both read. The law itself constructs readings and readers at the same time that it depends on them since in order to understand and apply laws, one has to enter into a particular framework of thinking with definite rules. It is therefore this framework and these rules that dictate what one's legal subjectivity, interpretations, constructions and decipherments are. The authors I have studied seize upon this idea because in addition to seeing reading as the discrimination of right and wrong, law and non-law, they insistently connect the identities of readers with competing forms of reading the law, as I will demonstrate.

That the process of reading the law is an act of creating identities is just one aspect of the larger idea that reading itself is the making of identity. While the nineteenth-century authors discussed here implicitly shared and constructed this idea, an explicit espousal of the position in literary studies was formulated much later. Dennis J. Sumara follows this idea of reading which he says derives from the thinking of hermeneutic writers such as Hans-Georg Gadamer.[53] Sumara subscribes to the notion that the 'the act of reading ought to be considered an important site for the contestation and negotiation of already slippery and shifting identities',[54] an idea which is particularly applicable to the representation of reading in the fiction examined in the following chapters. This is because the reading process is represented as inseparable from the creation of identities in these works, whether it can be seen to transform outsiders into insiders through reliance on an ideal and legitimated reading, or insiders into outsiders through reliance on excluded and marginalised readings which are made out to be both illegitimate and abhorrent.

The model of legal reading was chosen by authors to discipline reading through the construction of an ideal and its opposite because it was seen as the most privileged form of reading. This is because of the long history behind English law and the deference and respect given to legal thinking, which was regarded as one of the highest forms of rationality. In addition, most of the major authors investigated in this study were insiders to the legal reading as they all shared a significant amount

53 Hans-Georg Gadamer, *Truth and Method* (J. Weinsheimer & D. Marshall (trs), New York: Crossroad, 1990).

54 Dennis J. Sumara, 'Fictionalizing Acts: Reading and the Making of Identity', *Theory Into Practice*, 37:3 (Summer 1998), 206.

of legal knowledge and experience. In each case, the authors' awareness of legal readings preceded the writing of their works of fiction and was, therefore, likely to have been a formative influence. Rider Haggard's father was a barrister and Haggard too studied law and was called to the bar in 1884.[55] Henry James studied law at Harvard in 1861.[56] Similarly, Wilkie Collins read for the Bar and was admitted as a student of Lincoln's Inn on 17 May 1846.[57] Charles Dickens worked as a clerk to a solicitor after leaving school.[58] He also became a law reporter and transcribed cases in Doctors' Commons, the Court of Chancery and police courts.[59] In addition, authors such as Conan Doyle were not legally trained yet they assimilated the same ideas and language in the creation of detective fiction in which crime is countered with the power of the law, even if it is not the police which represent it.

These biographical facts provoke questions. This study asks why legal reading provides the model for reading and why it originates from a legal education and legal practice. Why are legal professionals so concerned to exclude photography and the reading it is associated with when they come to write fiction? Why do they associate this reading with photography and illegitimacy in the first place? Why are the construction of an ideal legal reading and the exclusion of photography so intimately bound up in the fiction of intimates of the legal reading *and* those outside of such intimacy? Why does the legal reading provide a model for the disciplining of the Victorian reader in fiction? I will aim to answer some of these questions in the following chapters.

The ideal legal reading which the authors mentioned above aim to construct through their writings can be situated in a larger complex of the control of reading in the period from the mid-nineteenth century to the end of the 1920s. Victorian fiction has already been shown to be obsessively concerned with correct forms of reading. Patrick Brantlinger's *The Reading Lesson: The Threat of Mass Literacy in Nineteenth-Century British Fiction* (1998) established this. Brantlinger shows that the mass consumption of the novel aroused anxiety and fears about reading as near-universal literacy was established in Victorian Britain. The question that arose was 'who could be sure that readers, especially those whom Arnold characterized as the "raw, unkindled masses", would not misinterpret even the safest books and put them to culture-subverting uses?'[60] It is in this context that 'novels and novel-reading were viewed, especially by novelists themselves, as both causes and symptoms of the rotting of minds and the decay of culture and society'.[61] Issues of the control of reading were foremost. Brantlinger writes for example that in 'the 1830s,

55 Christine L. Krueger, 'Henry Rider Haggard', *Encyclopedia of British Writers, 19th and 20th Centuries* (New York: Facts on File, 2003), 151.

56 Stuart Culver, 'Law', in David McWhirter (ed), *Henry James in Context* (Cambridge: Cambridge University Press, 2010), 180.

57 Lyn Pykett, *Wilkie Collins (Authors in Context)* (Oxford: Oxford University Press, 2009), 8.

58 G. K. Chesterton, *Charles Dickens* (Ware: Wordsworth Editions, 2007), 30.

59 David Sugarman, 'Law and Legal Institutions', in Paul Schlicke (ed), *The Oxford Companion to Charles Dickens* (Anniversary edn, Oxford: Oxford University Press, 2011), 324.

60 Patrick Brantlinger, *The Reading Lesson: The Threat of Mass Literacy in Nineteenth-Century British Fiction* (Bloomington and Indianapolis: Indiana University Press, 1998), 24.

61 Ibid., 24.

the debate about mass literacy shifted from whether the 'lower orders' should be taught to read and write at all to the questions of what they were reading, what they should read, and how to control their reading'.[62] Readings presented as correct readings were thought to shape the identity of readers and obliterate difference and insurrection:

> As later in Arnold, in both *Jane Eyre* and *Wuthering Heights*, the solution to social 'anarchy' and class conflict lies in right though not religious reading—that is, in a secular literacy that has the power to reshape the 'brutish' and dangerous working class after the 'respectably dressed', well-spoken, and non-violent image of the bourgeoisie.[63]

Brantlinger's monograph establishes the centrality of questions of right and wrong forms of reading and the integral place that fiction held in such formulations. Reading is a consciously political activity and closely related to notions of power: the preservation of the status quo or ideas of revolution. In this monograph I will investigate in depth how these political notions of reading and readers are enabled or constrained in the context of photography. In Chapter 3 of this monograph, I will concentrate in particular on how ideas of literalism and photography are wedded to ideas of both political and fictional representation.

The works of fiction analysed in this monograph connect photography with literalism, a form of reading which is therefore of the first relevance and importance to the complex I am analysing and whose outlines I will now sketch. Authors such as Charles Dickens, Henry James and Wilkie Collins associate literalist reading with the seemingly naïve belief that everything in a body of writing is somehow manifest, given, transparent and easily read rather than having to be laboriously and creatively deciphered. In contrast, the castigators of literalist reading asserted that there was something more valuable in writing beyond the visible, written words and what was explicitly expressed, an invisible 'spirit' which moved through a piece of writing.

This is striking because the nineteenth century has traditionally been defined as one where 'the literal reading' of the law in the form of statutes is dominant. For instance, Ian McLeod states that, 'there can be no doubt that, in the Nineteenth Century, the English courts were strongly inclined towards a literal approach to legislative interpretation'.[64] He ascribes this to the judges' deference to a democratically validated Parliament. However, at the same time, McLeod recognises the literal reading as a 'temporary aberration' in a proper historical view of the situation, suggesting that the purposive reading of the law was more established both before and after the period.[65] In any case, it appears that in responding to the literal reading of the time, the authors in this study were reacting to real legal debates about the interpretation

62 Ibid., 95.

63 Ibid., 120.

64 Ian McLeod, 'Literal and Purposive Techniques of Legislative Interpretation: Some European Community and English Common Law Perspective', *Brooklyn Journal of International Law*, 29 (2004), 1110.

65 Ibid.

and reading of the law, about real legal practices. Of course, it remains an open question as to how different legal interpretation was from the literal reading in reality. My focus is on how readings of the law were perceived as separate from and to be distinguished from such literal readings in fiction and I sense that in practice many of the authors studied here hypocritically denounced literal readings and that their alternative forms of 'freer' interpretation were not as 'deep' as they declared them to be. From my readings of fiction, it seems to me that the status of literal reading at the time was heavily contested as a dominant force in legal culture, perhaps a result of its perceived importance. This is apparent not just in the fiction I have studied, where literalist legal readings are presented as abhorrent (and in legal judgments too, as I will shortly argue), but also in legal manuals of interpretation at the time. Richard Posner suggests as much when he writes that the nineteenth century's legal interpretation consisted of a competition between 'narrow' (I read 'literalist') interpretation (which he writes is 'the stronger') and more flexible interpretation (which I read as 'non-literalist').[66] Fortunatus Dwarris' *A General Treatise on Statutes* (1875 [1830–31]) seems indicative of how legal interpretation and the literal reading is perceived. The author distinguishes literal interpretation from 'rational interpretation' which involves 'probable or rational conjectures'. He states that in cases of doubtful interpretation, a mixture of both literal and rational interpretation are to be employed.[67] Literal reading is therefore to be supplemented by non-literal strategies of decipherment. Dwarris also further limits the dominance of literal reading and states in his exposition of interpretation that 'the real intention, too, when collected with certainty, will always, in statutes, prevail over the literal sense of terms', that the 'whole context' will serve 'to enlarge or restrain literal meaning' and that the reader of the law should aim to avoid 'absurdity'.[68] Hence, even before what scholars have termed the transition to the purposive reading of the law in the twentieth century, legal interpretation defines itself in response to literal readings which are seen as misleading, false steps.

An illustration of how literalism is perceived as abhorrent in not just fiction, but also in legal decision making and the profession of the law, is the English case of *Salomon v A. Salomon & Co Ltd* (1895). Aaron Salomon, a sole trader, had decided to incorporate his business as a limited company. At the time, seven individuals had to subscribe as members of the company and Salomon's family filled the positions. Christopher Sutton has summarised the case that came before the Court of Appeal well:

> Aron Salomon, the Jewish immigrant, the outsider, came before the law in relation to a debt. He sought his literal, legal rights, that is, recognition of the simple fact that he had formed his company in strict accord with the law, and

66 Richard A. Posner, 'Legislation and Its Interpretation: A Primer', *Nebraska Law Review*, 68 (1989), 433.

67 Fortunatus Dwarris, *A General Treatise on Statutes: Their Rules of Construction, and the Proper Boundaries of Legislation and of Judicial Interpretation* (Albany: William Gould & Son, 1875), 135.

68 Ibid., 179, 197, 207.

> affirmation that the debt he was owed by the company, the corporate entity, was indeed owed to him as a private person.[69]

Salomon's case was eventually successful in the House of Lords ruling. However, in the Court of Appeal, Salomon became the 'target of vituperation' because of his literalist legal interpretation in setting up a limited company and because of his demand for his literal legal rights.[70] He was seen to interpret the letter of the law faultlessly and to be able to formulate his actions and claims for his rights on that reading, but he could not be seen as following the 'spirit' of the law. That is, he could not understand the rightful intention that was believed to exist outside of the realm of writing. Thus, at the same time that Salomon's strict adherence to legal forms was described as 'perfect',[71] as Hutton notes, the Court of Appeal 'described Salomon's law as: the "scheme", the "sham", the "mere device", the "perversion", "utter fiction", "myth", put together in such a "shrewd" and "ingenious" fashion by Aron Salomon under the "alias" of the company'.[72] Salomon's literalist interpretation of law was seen to pervert common sense. Lord Justice Lindley observed that:

> In a strict legal sense the business may have to be regarded as the business of the company; but if any jury were asked, *Whose business was it?* they would say Aron Salomon's, and they would be right, if they meant that the beneficial interest in the business was his.[73]

In this case, as in the fiction studied here, the literalist interpretation of law, and the suspect demand for literal legal rights, was associated with error, reduction and incompleteness since it was not seen by the judge to represent the legal situation and the crux of the matter correctly. In nineteenth-century literature, photography was figured in similar terms, particularly as it was seen, like literalism, to produce suspect and illegitimate 'copies' which 'resembled' the law, if they did not match it, as in the works of Wilkie Collins where photography is strongly associated with forgery. Literalism in the above example can also be seen as being limited by writing and obvious legal forms which seemingly do not allow space for the legal reader's imagination, thought, discernment or metaphorical and symbolic understandings. For if the strict legal reading was followed, as Lord Justice Lindley observes in the quote above, Salomon could not have done any wrong and legal judgment against him would have been impotent. This is the crucial point: *the literalist reading of the law destroys legal power and legal rule.* It subverts the strategies of control employed by legal interpreters. Literalism is thus akin to photography

69 Christopher Hutton, '"I Crave the Law": Salomon v Salomon, Uncanny Personhood and the Jews', in Marco Wan (ed), *Reading The Legal Case: Cross-Currents between Law and the Humanities* (New York: Routledge, 2012), 35.

70 Ibid., 35.

71 Lord Justice Lopes, Law Journal Reports 64 Law J. Rep. (n.s.) (1895), 693.

72 Hutton (n 69) 45.

73 Lindley LJ, Law Journal Reports 64, 692.

because both subvert legal power and control. Literalist reading was seen to efface legal discrimination and the subjectivity of individuals and to efface identity by limiting the operations of the mind and interpretation, just as it was seen to be a 'slavish' adherence to the letters on the page and to lack liberty and status. These criticisms are again akin to those made of photography, since photography was also seen as bypassing the operations of thoughtful composition and subjectivity by portraying 'literal' reality. The focus on the narrowness of literalism was developed through connecting it with detail, since Lord Justice Lopes said that: 'The incorporation of the company was perfect – the machinery by which it was formed was in every respect perfect, every detail has been observed'.[74] Literalist reading was seen as limited to details and to the minutiae of writing rather than showing an awareness of the broader and overall meaning of writing (and its relationship with other writing). Thus, Salomon's legal interpretation, the literalist reading, limited itself to one legal act when it should take into account several and the literalist legal reader is unable to understand the 'spirit of justice' that was believed to move through the totality of laws in a country, the intentions behind the framing of laws. Rather, the literalist becomes mired in a particular instance of a law which can seem to defeat the overall purpose and intention of legislation because of its obstinate and interfering, transfixed and material status as writing. Again, like literalism, photography itself is also linked with minute details which subvert the law as I show in my reading of the works of Henry James. Literalism and photography can be seen to occupy the same conceptual space as a suspect form of interpretation and representation.

The judges clearly saw themselves as non-literalist legal readers and aimed to differentiate their interpretation and reading of law from Salomon's, which Hutton shrewdly observes by comparing Salomon with Shylock in *The Merchant of Venice* who was also a literalist interpreter of law that demanded a literal legal right. Hutton writes, of both the play and the judgment:

> The drama that plays out pits a Christian evocation of the morality of mercy against a monstrous, artificial Other, consumed by desire for law. The Otherness of the Jew is identified with literalism, legalism and unnatural, uncanny personhood.[75]

The fact that Salomon was a Jew and was treated in such a harsh manner by the English court as a literalist legal reader is worthy of notice. It indicates how strongly a literalist reading was associated with the 'particular'. It was not just its connection to detail which made a literalist reading seem 'narrow', but its association with the ethnically 'other' who were seen as small 'tribes' that were opposed to a white, male character that was perceived as general, abstract, universal and omniscient.

In short, the literalist legal reading can be defined as one which, like Salomon's legal interpretation of English law, constructs the law, legal action and the formulation of legal rights in service of a self-interest which does not follow that of the

74 Lopes LJ (n 71) 693.
75 Hutton (n 69) 36.

political elite. The implication of the court's judgment in the Court of Appeal is that legal order exists as a 'spirit of justice' beyond the mediation of writing and the appearance of letters as visual marks, 'the body of legal writing'. This is because the judges had to look beyond the free standing law on the incorporation of Limited companies and consider the intention of the legislators and the purpose of laws to arrive at their judgment. The judges are therefore constructed as 'non-literalist' readers, even as telepathic readers that understand subjectivity, even when they are severely constrained by the letter of the laws and have to perform a literalist reading which pays meticulous attention to the body of legal writing. This 'non-literalist' reading disguises the subjectivity and anti-Semitic partiality of the position of the English judges at the same time that it effectively proves to observers that they reflect the English character. In addition, their obfuscation of the law through abstraction and idealisation, I argue, shores up the identities and status of lawmakers because they appear to have powers of reading beyond those of lay people and to have privileged access to legal truths. It is because, and only because of this, that Salomon as the Jewish and immigrant outsider has to be in the wrong in his following of English law while the English judges have to be right. The judges hold a similar position to the authors I have studied who have been involved in the law and they appear to have aimed to control reading and readers based on an idea of their superior acumen and experience in reading.

I believe that the analysis of fictional representations of the literalist reading of the law and its alternative are crucially important and lead to questions about the conceptualisation, truth status, authority and construction of the law and about the way in which the law preserves its status through the ways in which it is read and envisaged. I therefore believe that this monograph will make an important contribution to both English legal history, the English history of reading and literary history. Fictional representations of readings of the law provoke ideas about the relationships between fiction and law, law and art, and the construction of legal identities through depictions of differing readers of the law. The law in the fiction presents itself as unmediated, as removed from the written letter and the written body of laws. The law does so in order to present itself as abstract, universal, just, truthful and timeless, although it is clear that the idea of the law of the judges in the Court of Appeal in the Salomon case mirrored the invisible 'souls' of the lawmakers. I will argue that, as in the Salomon case, and in works such as Sir Arthur Conan Doyle's 'The Adventure of the Illustrious Client', which I discuss below, it is 'spirit' and 'character' which are seen as 'real' in relation to law. Conversely, I will argue that the body, associated with the photographic image and 'the body of legal writing', is systematically devalued as vain and false. The ideal legal reading used to determine legal solutions, I contend, is constructed via notions of the 'unwritten' and 'invisible' spirit of justice which legal insiders can 'read' and which actively opposes ideas of the body of legal writing. According to the fiction, real law is free from writing and media and bodily interference as I will show in this monograph as a whole.

I see underlying, if unspoken, ideals of legal invisibility as forming the framework of the legal reaction to Salomon's demand for his literal legal rights. In Chapter 2 of this monograph, I want to develop the idea that the 'anti-photographic' notion of legal truth and legal writing characterises a type of reading of law, one in which supposedly invisible things are 'read'. I will also relate this reading to the construction of identity. In so much fiction during the period, it is the reading of *things invisible* that is privileged and which is seen as the ideal reading of the law. The domain of invisibility excludes readers who are associated with photography from the realm of 'truth' and 'legal truth'. This reading sees invisible and intangible 'souls' and the invisible stuff of souls, such as thoughts and intentions and 'character', a crucial metaphor based on the textual. That is, inner thought and true being is understood as being a hidden type of writing, rather than an obvious and superficial photograph. This reading models the law, writing and truth on invisibility as well. I will demonstrate that this is the case through an analysis of Wilkie Collins' fiction in which individuals or 'souls' are being 'read' in Chapter 2.

In the three readings which follow, I will demonstrate how photography and literalism form an illegitimate couple in the imagination of the authors I discuss. These case studies are intended to introduce various aspects of my argument which will be followed through in more detail in the main chapters. Photography and literalism, I contend, are so strongly opposed that the foundations of reading, the law, and order are built on a system of differentiation between them. I will demonstrate how photography and literalist readings of the law are implicitly tied to the construction of the identities of perceived insiders and outsiders through ideas of ethnicity and gender. I will also show how such shared and largely unconscious constructions support and safeguard the subjectivity and interest of the political elite who the authors in this study defer and submit to, even when it is against their own self-interest and explicit political orientation in favour of rights for the lower-classes or for women. These three readings introduce the major theme that has preoccupied me in my research: how power is related to the law, photography, reading and the reader.

First reading: introducing literalism and the literalist and their association with photography, art and law

The end point of this monograph is 1925 when a legal act prohibiting photography in the court room came into operation. It was around this time that conservatism in thought had a resurgence and the war against literalism and photography was perceived to have a new urgency. A short story from this time gives ample evidence of and a revealing introduction to the long and widely shared chain of associations which had been established and attached to representations of photography, literalism and their alternative over the course of eighty years since the invention of photography. Sir Arthur Conan Doyle's short story, 'The Adventure of the Illustrious Client' (1924), is a rich text in which photography and literalism are coupled and posed as a threat to English identity. Baron Gruner is the philandering villain of the piece who 'collects women' and keeps a scandalous diary interlaced with photographic snapshots of his sexual conquests, evidence of his illegitimate desires outside the framework of the legal contract of marriage.[76] Sherlock Holmes is recruited to prevent the

76 Arthur Conan Doyle, 'The Adventure of the Illustrious Client', in *The Complete Sherlock Holmes* (London: Magpie Books Ltd, 1993), 990.

Baron's intended marriage to the English rose, Violet de Merville by retrieving the incriminating book which he terms a 'lust-diary'[77] and enabling it to be exhibited to her, thus proving the Baron to be a villain. The story, in which photography poses a threat to identity, suggests an act of fictional *reductio ad absurdum*. The Baron threatens to turn Violet not just into another photographic snapshot in his book, but also into a living and breathing photograph, an entity in which the image has usurped life. This appears to be the case since when Holmes meets Violet, he sees her as transformed by the Baron's love into 'a snow image on a mountain'.[78] The inference is that the Baron is able, whether literally or metaphorically, to substitute English womanhood with a monochromatic image and thus represent a unique threat to English identity. The Baron uses his powerful 'photographic vision' to take away Violet's identity and replace it with a photograph since he is associated in a number of ways with photography. One aspect of the photographic vision was that it was believed to see human beings as photographs or bodies and not as conscious individuals, since the camera could be seen as incapable of showing interiority, or human feelings and thoughts. George Eliot relied on this idea that the camera could only record what was 'external' and not internal thoughts and feelings when she remarked that Charles Dickens, like a camera, could 'copy Mrs. Plornish's colloquial style with the delicate accuracy of a sun picture', but that 'he scarcely ever passes from the humorous and external to the emotional and tragic, without becoming as transcendent in his unreality as he was a moment before in his artistic truthfulness'.[79] It is because of this perception that photography can only represent the external aspect of things and somehow effaces subjectivity that it is remarked that the cover of the Baron's book of photographic snapshots should say 'Souls I have ruined'.[80]

The characterisation of the Baron is an illuminating introduction to and prime example of how ideas of photography and literalism can be seen to mesh together with perceived outsiders in fiction in the period since the story seemingly invites a host of implicit comparisons between the two. The Baron is a stock type of the fiction studied, the literalist and perceived outsider, a figure whose characterisation I will sketch here but will be explored in full in the pages that follow. The Baron's photographic diary is the prime evidence that he is a literalist and because photography and literalism are so enmeshed in the fiction I have studied, I will refer to the type of literalism the diary indicates as 'photographic literalism' or 'photographic reading'. The diary is coupled with an idea of 'photographic literalism' which poses a threat to accepted and conventional reading practices and to the legal contract of marriage itself since it is the cherished collection of a man who, we find, has had relationships outside of marriage, such as the one with Kitty Winter, and is also rumoured to have killed a former wife. The book places photographic images of real women's bodies into the abstract and non-figurative realm of writing and reading rather than referring to 'souls' which are invisible and intangible, seemingly divorced

77 Ibid., 998.

78 Ibid., 991.

79 George Eliot, 'The Natural History of German Life', in *Selected Essays, Poems and Other Writings* (A. S. Byatt (ed), London: Penguin Classics, [1859] 2005), 107, 111.

80 Doyle (n 76) 990.

from materiality. The form of reading it provokes is deemed to be photographic because it is concerned with the representation of the physical nature of the body's qualities instead of the invisible properties of the 'soul' and internal consciousness manifested as thoughts and character. Rather than investigating internal consciousness, the diary is preoccupied with external appearances and physical sensation.

Conan Doyle's short story relies on the connections made between general reading and legal reading, the general reader and the legal reader. Both the general reader and the legal reader sit in the seat of 'judgment'; however, the legal reader is more explicitly concerned with questions of the law and legal writings. In the characteristic way of this type of fictional critique of photography and literalism, the form of literalism associated with the Baron's photographic book merges with an idea of the literalist reading of law. In the recounting of the Baron's criminal history, it is alleged, without any substantiation, that he has escaped a conviction for murdering his previous wife on the basis of a 'purely technical legal point'.[81] Holmes summarily dismisses the literalist reading as untruthful and inadequate since he is convinced that the Baron is the murderer. The reasons behind this contemptuous characterisation of literalism show how the construction of literalism in reading the law is shared across a range of fictions. I have defined the literalist legal reading as one which constructs the law, legal action and the formulation of legal rights in service of a self-interest which does not follow that of the political elite in my discussion of the Salomon case above. I have also noted how literalism is tied to the details of writing and is seen as a limited form of reading which is considered incapable of appreciating the broader context of laws. The foreign Baron, who the Englishmen prevent from marrying one of 'their' women, is the embodiment of such literalism. Firstly, if the reader follows Holmes' pre-emptory dismissal of it, literalism is seen as a wrong judgment. This literalist reading is thus the reverse of law: it is associated with injustice, since the murderer remains unpunished; and with slipperiness and odious deviousness rather than wisdom and imagination since the Baron has employed his wits in order to deceive all as to his innocence; and with falsity and lying since Holmes is convinced of the guilt of the Baron. A literalist reading is thus presented as a superficial, contrived and erroneous, untruthful reading which defeats the supposed 'spirit', or intention and purpose of justice which would appear to prohibit murder and punish the murderer. The further implication is that the literalist reading is wrong because of its limitations. Literalist reading seems to be considered a reductive and incomplete apprehension of reality since it cannot address the commission of the Baron's murder beyond the distracting medium of legal writing, the technical legal point. It is by remaining trapped to a reading within the framework of legal writing that justice cannot be done. Thus, literalist reading lights on a trifling, trivial point of technical and clearly secondary importance in order to subvert the broader punishment of sinful killing and the importance of life it appears to safeguard. In this reading which is tied to seemingly irrelevant details or particulars, the medium of the law and writing themselves become obtrusive, inflexible and rigid, circular or navel-gazing constructions trapped within their own self-regard, self-importance

81 Ibid., 985.

and minutiae without any connection to an outside. This is where the Baron's literalist photographic book and the literalist reading of the law that he is associated with are fundamentally connected: the 'body' of legal writing is, like the bodies of women, the object of fascination. In this case, the body of legal writing is the technical legal point which seemingly absolves the Baron of the crime committed but elsewhere legal writing can take the form of statutes, wills, legal documents and writing which can take on the status of legal evidence. The literalist Baron can only derive authority and meaning from the body of written law and its materiality, just as he is seduced by bodily form and can only see the legal contract of marriage as a union of bodies and not 'souls'. The literalist thus becomes associated with all that is considered bodily in the range of fiction presented in this study since he or she cannot be separated from seeing the body in everything that he or she does and by being a seeing body. The literalist is seen as limited in perception by both the body and vision. This connection with the body includes important and surprising categories as alternative forms of 'truth' to the accepted law of the non-literalists such as the natural sciences which are formed on observation. Lastly, literalist reading is not only tied to trivial particulars, but is also particularistic since it cannot claim to be in the interests of a justice perceived as abstract and universal, but is solely in the narrow interests of the Baron. Literalism is therefore associated not just with photography but with the politics of perceived outsiders which lay claim to law and legal representation, such as the politics of foreigners. As the literal reading practised by the Baron suggests, such literalist outsiders do not defer to the supposed truth and universality of the law but use it opportunistically and instrumentally. They simply see the law as a medium which furthers self-interest and allows actions to be legitimated. What is worrying to political elites is not the lack of legal knowledge which such literalists possess but their excessive knowledge of law and their shrewdness in how it can be turned to their advantage.

The literalist reading of the stock figure of the Baron is presented in the same terms in which photography is denounced in a range of nineteenth century fiction and art criticism, terms explored in the Chapter 1 of this monograph. Photography, as such, in the words of the photographer John Leighton in addressing the Royal Photographic Society in 1853, could be held to be 'too literal'.[82] That is, both literalist reading and photography are seen as partial, narrow and constrained forms tied to the superficial, to the immediate event of a reading or seeing and to the details or particulars rather than to broader 'truths'. Thus, Leighton stated that 'minute detail is the attribute of the sun-picture'.[83] Both literalist reading and photography are regarded as tied to the body: either the physical body of individuals or the body of legal writing. This was because photography was strongly associated with portraiture. For instance, in an article in 1863 in the *Atlantic*, entitled 'Doings of the Sunbeam', Oliver Wendell Holmes remarked that 'Card-portraits … as everybody knows, have become the social currency, the sentimental "Green-backs"

82 John Leighton, 'On Photography as a Means or an End', *The Photographic Journal* (21 June 1853), 74.
83 Ibid.

of civilization'.[84] The photographic portrait was seen as ubiquitous and as 'necessary' to social functioning as money. Chapter 3 focuses on fiction to foreground the idea of how constructions of photography as false, narrow and tied to the body are related to how the truth of a law perceived as abstract and universal is formulated.

Because literalism and photography are conflated by writers, I have concentrated on the connections between them in order to illuminate precisely why and how they are seen to pose such a threat to the law in the fiction. The law that literalists produce through their reading is considered by authors such as Conan Doyle and Wilkie Collins to be a semblance of the law rather than the real thing. Thus, the Baron's unconvincing verdict of 'not guilty' which derives from a literalist reading, and his body-first conception of the legal contract of marriage, in which it is not souls that are recognised and united but bodies that are joined together in lust, are considered semblances of a legal ruling and a legal contract. In the works of a number of authors in the period, such as Robert Louis Stevenson's *The Wrecker* (1892), these semblances of law are constructed in the same negative terms as the photographic copy. The literalist's law is not considered to carry truth but, irrespectively, *appears* to be the literal legal truth anyway. It forms part of the body of law and is therefore like the literal and visual body without the corresponding representation of a 'soul' in the Baron's photographic snapshots and 'lust diary'.[85] This is where literalism and photography are intimately connected: both are considered to produce grossly limited photographic copies of the law, or mere likenesses of the law. Such photographic copies of the law are ghostly and hollow doubles and imposters, representations of law without its character or virtue. The ghostly double of law haunts the pages of the authors considered here and is countered in a particularly explicit fashion in the writings of Wilkie Collins as the threat of a fatal resemblance to identity which will be demonstrated in Chapter 2.

Literalism is, I argue, best conceived as a radical alternative to the ideal legal reading which supports the system of deference and power in operation. As such an understanding of literalism and the standards it is measured against is crucially important. Representations of literalism and its alternative relate to power and its transmission in the society and culture of the time. They show the asymmetry of power relations and the major points of resistance and submission to the perspective and interest of the political elite. Critics of literal legal reading separate photography and the law not because they wish to protect the law in a non-partisan way. Legal identity is so heavily guarded because it is so politically valuable to the political elite and is considered one of the prime sites of giving meaning and form to personhood and belonging. Law becomes a ghostly double of itself only because perceived outsiders like the foreign Baron are able to gain access to it and reform it through a reading perceived as literalist. They subvert the authority and authorship of the ruling elite to create laws as an outcome of their contestations of the legal system and thus usurp the position that the elite hold as 'authors' who control what the system of law is and how it is articulated. Tellingly, the Baron is a

84 Oliver Wendell Holmes, 'The Doings of the Sunbeam', *Soundings from the Atlantic* (Boston: Ticknor and Fields, 1864), 255.

85 Doyle (n 76) 998.

photographic 'author' since his diary combines photographs with writing. He is an alternative author to the political elite who has the power to change reading and therefore the interpretation of the laws. The Baron can construct laws and rule over the people by doing so since in this country there is 'the rule of law'. This is evident in the short story through the characterisation of Kitty Winter, who has been one of the photographic subjects of the Baron and whose photographic snapshot is in the Baron's book. Kitty is persuaded by the Baron to accept the photographic book when she discovers it by accident and to forgive the Baron for possessing it and to continue her relationship with him, irrespective of his deviance. Kitty thus acquiesces in supporting the literalist reading in the diary and being treated like a body and being reduced to a photograph. This submission to literalism and being treated like a body ultimately leads Kitty to occupy the status of a 'fallen woman', a mere body and nothing else. For it is heavily insinuated that Kitty has subsequently become a prostitute since she frequents the lowest haunts of London and must somehow support herself as an independent woman despite her tarnished reputation as having been the Baron's woman. Photography and literalism ultimately lead Kitty to become open and amenable to the desires of all comers as a prostitute in financial straits since she should have ended her relationship with the Baron over it like Violet (who cannot see herself as a body). The photograph and the literalist reading that the Baron's diary supports are thus linked to ideas of the prostitution of law and its non-discriminating availability and pliability to the wider public. This is why literalism and photography really matter: they are forms of representation associated with the power, will and voice not of the rulers, but the ruled, a form of power grounded in a more publicly justifiable form of legitimacy than the rule that was in operation at the time. Therefore, the connections between the masses, literalism and photography as their popular form of representation leads to this idea: the law is ultimately to be separated from the photograph and literalism because if it weren't then it would be readily accessible to the masses and not enclosed by the political elite. Instead, the political elite would have to succumb to the laws and desires of others and become 'passive' readers and not writers of the law. In their terms, they would become readers of the photographic imposter that masquerades as law – a law that is not of their making and their desires but still carries legitimacy and symbolic weight, that appears to be the law.

Significantly, the Baron's vision is presented as not only as an attack on the law, but also as an attack on idealism and art. Sherlock Holmes describes Violet, who is in danger of being corrupted by the Baron, in terms of an idealistic art object out of a painting:

> She is beautiful, but with the ethereal other-world beauty of some fanatic whose thoughts are set on high. I have seen such faces in the pictures of the old masters of the Middle Ages.[86]

The Baron's threat therefore goes beyond the disruption of accepted reading practices to subvert art viewing practices and also involves the idea of the conversion

86 Ibid., 991.

of not just the law, but also an art object into a photographic snapshot. Literalism and photography are opposed to reading, art and the law, a constant series of oppositions in the fiction analysed in this monograph. Chapter 1 situates ideas of literalism and reading of the law in fiction from the mid-nineteenth century to the end of the 1920s within the vocabulary and conceptual framework of art and art criticism. This is because art terms are an important component of how reading the law and readers of the law are represented in the fiction that I have studied. The works I study consistently draw attention to artists, art, the viewing of art and even art criticism itself in relation to photography and reading. Art and the law have power as they force a particular perspective and order on things and nature. For the purposes of reducing ambiguity and the application of terms, the law has to decide on a suitable definition of acts, intentions and terms amidst contending definitions and can be seen to be reductive. The law also incorporates the unspoken political orientation of the judge which affects the construction of terms. Similarly, the idealistic art which informs my analysis presents a view of the world which seeks to claim freedom from an expression of a political position, despite the particularistic vantage point that informs its construction. In order to understand how this power is constructed and maintained in the period, I will emphasise the similarity of art and the law in their shared framework of idealism. If reading the law is related to vision, I wish to demonstrate how completely it relies on idealism, art terms and art thinking and artistic truth rather than ideas of photography and photographic truth, which, as we have seen, challenges the readings of a number of recent critics such as Nancy Armstrong. Understanding how Victorian art terms and art criticism oppose photography and actively exclude it allows us to see how and why fictional accounts of reading the law and fictional readers of the law in the latter half of the nineteenth century do likewise, since shared terms are used.

In 'The Adventure of the Illustrious Client', the literalist reading of law, and art, is countered by a proposed alternative. It will be my aim to outline and analyse this as I believe it also appears in other works. I have termed this reading 'the ideal reading of law' for reasons which I will discuss below. This monograph sees this alternative as the central and accepted, authorised form of reading in much fiction between the mid-nineteenth century and the 1920s. The outlines of this reading emerge when the legal reading of the Baron is countered in a contest of readings. This reading emerges through implication and insinuation, through subliminal tactics of contrast. It is the aim of this monograph to reconstruct the features of this 'reading in hiding' by stressing its contrast to representations of literalism. The triumphant, idealist reading of the law is associated with the viewing of art and the reading of art scholarship in the story. This tying together of the law and art, legal reading and art viewing is an integral strategy in a range of fiction. It is Watson who embodies the alternative to the literalist reader and reading in 'The Adventure of the Illustrious Client'. Holmes orders Watson to learn everything that he can about Chinese pottery in the course of twenty-four hours in order to distract the Baron with the viewing and discussion of an art object. Holmes will then steal the photographic book from the Baron's study while he is distracted from guarding his treasure of literalism and photography.

While it might at first appear that Watson is mimicking the literalist reading of the Baron through Holmes' instruction, and countering him with his own weapons, we soon find that this is not the case. Watson's attempt at literalist reading fails, showing that an Englishman cannot read in this manner. Watson's 'knowledge' of pottery is never actually called on because he and the Baron do not actually talk about it. There is no open clash of readings. This would be too explicit since the counter form of reading to literalism has to be insinuated and thus insidiously suggested to the reader of the short story. We never see what Watson's counter form of reading consists of since Holmes emerges with the photographic book in his hand to interrupt the scene. The point is that the literalist reading in the photographic book is to be seized and exploited by representatives of law and order while the reading of insiders remains concealed and implicit: the unspoken rules of this reading are to remain clandestine and thus unchallenged and unrecognised guides to thought.

Watson's reading of Chinese art is compared quite explicitly to the reading of a barrister and thus art viewing and the reading of the law are conflated. As Watson notes:

> It is said that the barrister who crams up a case with such care that he can examine an expert witness upon the Monday has forgotten all his forced knowledge before the Saturday. Certainly I should not like now to pose as an authority upon ceramics. And yet all that evening, and all that night with a short interval for rest, and all next morning, I was sucking in knowledge and committing names to memory.[87]

The English barrister's reading, the legal reading, is attacked through what is called, in the legally suggestive terms, a 'cross-examination'[88] by a villainous reading and the supposedly slavish, foreign catechism it calls for, since the Baron asks Watson:

> what do you know of the Emperor Shomu and how do you associate him with the Shoso-in near Nara? Dear me, does that puzzle you? Tell me a little about the Nonhern Wei dynasty and its place in the history of ceramics.[89]

The Baron's legal reading, as evidenced by his cross-examination, is predictably literalist and photographic since it puts the historical details or particulars at the forefront. The Baron also expects Watson to have what we can term 'a photographic memory' of the history of Chinese ceramics, a term which first appeared in the 1870s and 1880s.[90] As Kate Flint writes, the idea of photographic memory could carry negative connotations. Flint cites the example of the British psychiatrist Henry Maudsley. In his 1876 revised version of the *Physiology of Mind*, Maudsley described a man who could read a text and then repeat it, backwards.

87 Ibid., 995.
88 Ibid., 997.
89 Ibid.
90 Kate Flint, 'Photographic Memory', *Romanticism and Victorianism on the Net*, 53 (2009).

Maudsley turned to the idea of photographic memory to describe the phenomenon, writing that the case seemed to be one 'in which the person seems to read a photographic copy of former impressions with his mind's eye'.[91] However, Flint states that:

> Maudsley's prime examples of people with 'photographic memories'—one who was an 'imbecile in the Earlswood asylum for idiots' who could accurately repeat a page of a book that he had read a year earlier, without understanding a word of it, and an 'epileptic youth, morally imbecile', who would repeat a leading article in a newspaper having read it once—are distinguished by the fact that they lack comprehension of the details that they so meticulously regurgitate.[92]

Maudsley invoked the idea of 'judgment', with its legal connotations, when he speculated on the cognitive reasons for a photographic memory that was limited to an apprehension of the details. He wrote that a mind which is capable of such a feat:

> is prevented by the very excellence of its power of apprehending and recalling separate facts from rising to that discernment of their higher relations which is involved in reasoning and judgment, and so stays in a function which should be the foundation of its further development; or that, being by some natural defect prevented from rising to the higher sphere of comprehension of relations, it applies all its energies to the apprehension of details.[93]

For Maudsley, then, the photographic memory which clung to details was implicitly connected with forms of thought which were considered inferior to ideas of legal judgment and reasoning. Watson, however, is deemed capable of rising to this higher level. Like the English barrister who ultimately forgets all the facts in the previous comparison cited above, Watson cannot and does not read photographically and with a photographic memory (although unlike the barrister he cannot even remember them on the occasion that he needs them). Details elude him. Furthermore, the Baron tells Watson and us, the readers, that Watson has not read the one book which would have told him the true value of the art object, a book that the Baron has written himself. Watson, the Englishman and insider, occupies a position of telling and wilful ignorance in respect to the Baron's own meticulous and patient, fact-based, contextual and historical scholarship.[94] In the chapters of this monograph, I will show how this lack or forgetting of historical awareness, of history, contextualisation and knowledge supports the idealisation of law and art in

91 Henry Maudsley, *The Physiology of Mind: Being the First Part of a Third Edition, Revised Enlarged and in Great Part Rewritten, of 'The Physiology and Pathology of Mind'* (New York: D. Appleton, 1876 [1878]), 517.

92 Flint (n 90).

93 Maudsley (n 91) 518.

94 Ibid., 997.

their construction of things and individuals as abstract, discrete and timeless entities. Such constructions shore up the position of the dominant group in society because they are manufactured so as to eliminate resistance to the elite's portrayal and following of a truth and reality presented as abstract and universal even though they rely on the actual, unfair conditions of existence.

Second reading: literalism, literalists and the work of gendering in fiction

One of the most important dimensions of 'the photographically literalist' reading is its consistent association with women. Accordingly, gender is a crucial theme of this monograph: the gendering of photography, law and art plays a vital role in the fiction investigated in this monograph. The way in which ideas of photographic literalism interact with the processes of assigning gender, while simultaneously constructing ideas of law, is illustrated in H. Rider Haggard's novel *Mr Meeson's Will* (1888). The novel could be read as a parable of how law is formed from and against ideas of photography and literalism, which are related to the female body, and then is subsequently legitimised in relation to these ideas.

Before the publication of *Mr. Meeson's Will*, Haggard had united fiction, art, the law and truth as a realm of masculinity which excluded photography, women and their bodies in his literary criticism. In the article 'About Fiction', published in 1887 in the *Contemporary Review*, Haggard attacked the 'naturalistic school of writing' which originated in France and which he called an 'accursed thing'.[95] He stated that its aim was to '[p]aint the mortal shame of nature with the living hues of art'. The form and reproduction of the naked and immoral woman was everywhere present in such fictions: '[h]ere are no silks and satins to impede our vision of the flesh and blood beneath'.[96] In *Mr. Meeson's Will*, therefore, Haggard can be seen to attack naturalism and a type of writing which he sees as photographic in intent and character. Haggard invoked the terms of art, the law and the 'idealised truth' in the summation of his argument in *The Contemporary Review*, turning to visual metaphors when talking about the seemingly differing field of fiction:

> Art in the purity of its idealized truth should resemble some perfect Grecian statue. It should be cold but naked, and looking thereon men should be led to think of naught but beauty. Here, however, we attire Art in every sort of dress, some of them suggestive enough in their own way, but for the most part in a pinafore. The difference between literary Art, as the present writer submits it ought to be, and the Naturalistic Art of France is the difference between the Venus of Milo and an obscene photograph taken from life. It seems probable that the English-speaking people will in course of time have to choose between the two.[97]

95 H. Rider Haggard, 'About Fiction', *Contemporary Review*, 51 (February 1887), 176.
96 Ibid.
97 Ibid., 179.

For Haggard, the photograph and the naked form of a woman were both associated with the French foreigner and sexual degeneration. They were considered as the other of 'the truth', art and beauty. Through ideas of obscenity, the photograph was also linked with the other of the law. Haggard's ideas can be seen as derived from Immanuel Kant's *Critique of Aesthetic Judgement* (1790). Lynda Nead indicates that Kant had had a formative influence on Haggard's society and I argue that Haggard can be seen as mirroring a Kantian position.[98] Like Kant, Haggard aims to separate bodily or sensuous pleasure from aesthetic pleasure which is associated with 'the "higher" faculty of contemplation'.[99]

In Haggard's novel, *Mr. Meeson's Will*, the law and legal reading both have to be separated from the female body and the contemplation of the female body since a photograph of a tattoo becomes legally read as a will, after some contestation. The novel therefore ranks legal reasoning above that which is to do with matter and the sensuous, both of which are associated with the bodies of women. As in much of the fiction that is presented in this monograph, a constructed idea of femininity plays a role of prime importance in assigning and arranging other identities and sites of alterity around ideas of literalism and law reform. *Mr. Meeson's Will* was just one instance of a general and well established attitude of misogyny which underlay ideas of law and legitimacy. The novel begins with a contractual dispute between Augusta Smithers, a popular writer of novels, and her exploitative publisher, Mr Meeson, who insists on keeping the author to the letter of the contract despite the equitable alternative to reward her properly for her success. He tells Augusta that, despite the spectacular sales of her novel, there is 'no ground for your coming to ask more money than you agreed to accept'.[100] This first scene is of a literalist legal reading that is constrained and unjust and it results in the disinheritance of Mr Meeson's nephew, Eustace, who takes the writer's side against the publisher. From the first, the novel is concerned with literalism and the reading of the law and with women and their subjectivity through the figure of a woman writer intruding upon the masculinised sphere of writing and authorship, both fictional and legal. At first, the woman appears to be against literalism but we subsequently find that she is as representative of it as the exploitative publisher.

This first scene where literalism triumphs against an equitable reading is followed by the writer's attempt to escape Meeson's literalist reading of the contract. This results in her emigration. However, Mr Meeson coincidentally accompanies Augusta on her voyage and there is no easy escape from literalism and the literalist. There is then a shipwreck. It is when she is marooned with Mr Meeson on a remote island that Augusta Smithers becomes a reformer of the law. She tells Mr Meeson that his disinheritance of his nephew is 'wicked' and then suggests that he 'alter' the existing will.[101] Mr Meeson immediately accepts Augusta's advice. In the absence of conventional writing materials, Augusta then encourages Mr Meeson,

98 Lynda Nead, *The Female Nude: Art, Obscenity and Sexuality* (London and New York: Routledge, 2001).
99 Ibid., 23–24.
100 H. Rider Haggard, *Mr. Meeson's Will* (London: Spencer Blackett, 1888), 27.
101 Ibid., 127.

the publishing scoundrel and literalist, to have a new will tattooed onto her own back so that his nephew, Eustace, may regain the inheritance of which he was dispossessed. For we find that Augusta has fallen in love with the dispossessed victim who took her side.[102] At the moment of authoring the amended will, in a revealing paradox, Augusta becomes a supremely literalist 'reader' as the will is tattooed onto her back and she becomes the passive receptacle of a body of legal writing, indeed, becoming the body of legal writing herself. To force the point home, Haggard actually refers to the tattoo as 'the body of the will'.[103] Although photography will be associated with the will in more explicit fashion later in the novel, Augusta 'reads' like a photographic plate or a mirror in the tattooing process. The will is itself a 'photographic' colour and like a photograph since the tattooing is done with cuttlefish ink.[104] Cuttlefish ink played a role in producing the sepia colour of nineteenth-century photography from the 1860s.[105] The words in photographic sepia therefore appear on the 'illiterate' surface of Augusta's body which can't recognise them as writing but 'sees' and reflects them as images. The tattooing, which is only accepted as a legitimate legal form and will at the end of the novel, is productively ambiguous: it carries the connotation of female illiteracy since Augusta can't read the will herself, it being on her back. However, Augusta's 'blindness' as a woman reader is also finally valued as the will does become law in spite of its associations with the photograph and the female body. The fiction appears to portray the act of law reform as though it reflected a legal triumph on the part of an early feminist against one of the political elite in power. Thus, the weaker and marginalised party, in the form of a woman, gains the upper hand by using her body, which is the basis of her female identity, and is able to express her will in law through it. The law reformer, Augusta, finally endures the indignity of being offered as evidence in a trial over the will's validity in the form of photographs of her exposed body. The will, or the law, and writing itself thus become a photograph through the agency of both the woman law reformer and the literalist reader of the law, Mr Meeson, who combine forces and intents. The woman allows her own body to become merged with and bear the body of a legal writing through a metaphorical reading and through the inescapability of her association with literalism.

However, the form of the photographically literalist law is also associated with other identities and sites of alterity, including the lower classes. These groups in society are classed and devalued in the same terms as women literalists since they are perceived as outsiders by the political elite, as the ruled rather than the rulers and therefore unworthy of holding the reins of power. The inspiration for Augusta's scheme is telling. She sees the tattoos of the lower-class sailors who are characterised as drunks and do not speak standard English and the idea for her tattoo begins there. The will and the legal writing not only mimic the bodies of the lower classes, the will is also executed by the coarse sailor Bill. Mr Meeson is present while the

102 Ibid., 136.
103 Ibid., 137.
104 Ibid., 132.
105 David Taylor, *Foundation Course Black and White Photography* (East Sussex: AE Publications, 2015), 102.

tattoo is being done and Bill tattoos while maintaining contact with the hand of the testator Mr Meeson who is too weakened by illness to write himself and who only signs the document in a somewhat feeble manner. Thus, legal authorship is problematised in the writing of the will as there is multiple and not single authorship: the will and the legal writing are the conception of the woman author Augusta, but it is also authored by the drunken sailor Bill at the same time that it is authored by Mr Meeson. Thus, the rich, upper-class man's law is severely adulterated in its construction and expression, presumably because he had become a literalist before when he kept Augusta to the terms of an exploitative legal contract. The novel has to reinstate Mr Meeson as the centre of authority and legal authorship in order to demonstrate that he has finally come back into the fold of the non-literalist readers. The anxiety is not only that insiders will become seduced by literalist readings, but also that other authors will become writers of the law outside of the ranks of the ruling elite through literalism. There is a racial construction, too. The resultant tattoo corrupts the white skin of Augusta and makes it a 'photographic' sepia, or brown colour, since this is the colour of the cuttlefish's ink which is used, supposedly 'spoiling' its beauty forever, a constant refrain in the novel. Thus, Lady Holmhurst, a minor character, tells Augusta that she 'should have to be very much in love before I would spoil myself in that fashion for any man'.[106] The figure of the woman therefore acts as a coordination point. It is a place where the figures of radically different authors and those alien to the political elite such as literalists, the lower classes and the non-white unite. Perceived outsiders to the political elite, organised by the consciousness of a woman and through ideas of literalism, are instrumental in writing this form of law. It is apparent that because of their different origin and identity from those in power, the attempts of perceived outsiders to produce laws are seen as 'contaminating' the legal institution with 'foreign' elements and their difference. These literalist outsiders bring into being the dream of difference: an alternative, radically transformed law and legal identity which would fundamentally alter the character and subjectivity of the legal readers in the establishment.

Gender is foremost in the construction and organisation of a photographic legal writing in the novel as it is in general in the fiction that I investigate. It is Augusta's idea to make the new will and the idea for the tattoo/will is also hers. As Lady Holmhurst, Augusta's special friend, insists, Augusta's idea stems not from any 'abstract' sense of justice, but, we infer, from a woman's feeling and 'love', her desire, since '[n]o girl would allow herself to be tattooed in the interest of abstract justice'.[107] Mr Meeson himself emphasises the gendered nature of Augusta's thought by exclaiming '[w]hoever would have thought of such a thing except for a woman?'[108] Perceived outsiders to the political elite are seen as being susceptible to women and their organising consciousness and subjectivity.

In the legal satire in *Mr Meeson's Will*, Augusta becomes photographic evidence. She is 'filed' as a photographic copy at the Registry. Because the photograph of the

106 Haggard, *Mr. Meeson's Will* (n 100) 181.
107 Ibid., 191.
108 Ibid., 131.

writing becomes a legal document and forms part of the legal archive, anxieties over the photograph and its relationship to women emerge. Indeed, the filing is thought to be impossible because of this relationship between gender and law: Eustace says, 'You can't file a lady; it's impossible!'[109] The photographer is avaricious and begins to sell copies of the photograph to the public as a mild form of pornography. The photographer is compared implicitly with the literalist and publisher Mr Meeson. Mr Meeson was a rank materialist who saw writing as a commodity and who aimed to keep Augusta, like his other authors, to the strict terms of an exploitative legal contract because of his avarice. The photographer also uses a strict literal interpretation of law to argue that his selfish exploitation of Augusta is justified, just as Mr Meeson did. He argues that the initial contract to take the photographs does not bear any stated terms which say that his additional selling of the photographs is illegitimate. As Haggard writes:

> The man admitted outright that he had put the photographs upon the market, saying that he had never stipulated not to do so, and that he could not afford to throw away five or six hundred pounds when a chance of making them came in his way.[110]

The photographer thus selfishly defeats the purpose and intention of the contract which was intended for purely legal purposes in the same way that Mr Meeson disrupts ideas of fair pay and reward through a literalist reading in which everything has to be stated outright otherwise it is said not to apply.

The photograph enters the register of 'truth' via the newspaper, as an illustration alongside the text.[111] The photograph and literalism appear to be the chosen form of representation and reading of women, the lower class and ethnic minorities. They thus pose a serious threat to political elites. As an alternative conception, and as a dream of difference, the law of perceived outsiders appears to subvert the law, order, 'truth' and conventional reading practices as they are seized upon by the lower classes and are represented in the mass reading and circulation of the newspaper. This alternative law is the optimist and reformer's desire: a body of transformed and transformative legal writing that, like a perfect image, is immediately and openly available and transparent to all of the people and represents them, irrespective of gender, race or class. Through the larger metaphor of exposure, since Augusta exposes herself for the legal writing to become visible, and law is tied to the body of its first author and initiator, this law becomes open, diverse and democratic. The identities involved in making the will are explicitly linked to the laws that are created as their formative influences and the law is made openly with supreme self-confidence in its legitimacy. However, in order that the legal document, the will, not be published as the pornographic photograph, the photographer who took the picture of the tattoo across Augusta's shoulders is eventually held in constructive contempt of court and the sale of the photographs is

109 Ibid., 203.
110 Ibid., 220.
111 Ibid., 217–218.

prohibited.[112] Haggard refers to the incident as 'the unlawful dissemination of photographs',[113] stressing its illegal character. The reason why the circulation of the photograph is in contempt of court is not given and one could infer several reasons. I will outline in my third reading below why I believe that photography is associated with 'contempt' of court and the law of the ruling elite.

As an alternative site of law and legal readings, the pornographic photograph of Augusta's shoulders and the body of legal writing threatens to be published everywhere, including in shop windows and newspapers.[114] The photographs seem to reproduce the woman endlessly and to create a massive photographic album with the one message: woman as bodily form. The photographic reproduction is represented as a limitless succession of copies which detracts from the unique status of the tattoo as legal document, thus destroying the 'aura' of the law, a term I have borrowed from Walter Benjamin's influential 1936 essay, 'The Work of Art in the Age of Mechanical Reproduction' in which he describes how aura was associated with place and privilege in Western painting and which (photographic) reproduction threatened.[115] The *corpus vile* and tattoo is also to take the place of the letter of the law as the interest and the message. Legal writing is transformed into a series of visual marks that are not read, but seen as exposed images since the interest is not in reading the writing, but in the location of the writing on the woman's body. This fact upsets the status and seriousness of the legal document, the will. 'Photographic literalism' therefore appears to threaten the foundations of order, reading and law in the novel through their intimate associations with women and the semblance of law.

Third reading: fiction and the prohibition of photography from the courtroom in 1925

There is a significant legal example where the complex of related terms I analyse can be seen to mesh and work together in order to control reading. The Criminal justice Act 1925 legally institutionalised and codified the prior work of fiction which separated photography from the law, art and reading. It is the most visible point of the work of controlling reading through the foil of photography. Section 41(1) of the Criminal justice Act 1925 provides:

> No person shall
>
> (a) take or attempt to take in any court any photograph, or with a view to publication make or attempt to make in any court any portrait or sketch of any person being a judge of the court or a juror or a witness in or a party to any proceedings before the court, whether civil or criminal; or
>
> (b) publish any photograph portrait or sketch taken or made in contravention of the foregoing provisions of this section or any reproduction thereof.

112 Ibid., 220.

113 Ibid., 220.

114 Ibid., 219.

115 Walter Benjamin, 'The Work of Art in the Age of Mechanical Reproduction', in Hannah Arendt (ed), *Illuminations* (London: Fontana, 1968), 214–218.

Section 41(2)(c) extends the prohibition to any photograph, portrait or sketch taken or made 'in the building or in the precincts of the building in which the court is held'.

Legal scholarship has often attributed this ban on photography in the courtroom to a short-term reaction to the newspaper coverage of the Seddon trial of 1912, where Frederick Seddon and his wife were tried for the murder of Eliza Barrow.[116] At the end of this trial, on 15 March, one photograph which had been taken secretively appeared in *The Daily Mirror*. This showed Frederick Seddon, having been found guilty, being sentenced to death by Mr Justice Bucknill at the Old Bailey, with his chaplain at his side. The photograph led to questions to the Prime Minister in the House of Commons and to a promise from the Home Secretary to change the law.[117] The photograph continued to be cited in parliamentary debates in support of the ban on photography over a decade later. It was mentioned by Lord Darling when the prohibition of photography in court was being considered in the House of Lords in 1924:

> There was a dreadful case some time ago, in which a photograph was taken at the Old Bailey of a Judge passing sentence of death. That photograph was published—a most shocking thing to have taken, or to have published, dreadful for the Judge, dreadful for everybody concerned in the case. Of course, the Judge knew nothing of it, could not do anything to prevent it, and could not punish the person who had done it.[118]

On the face of it, the photograph appears innocuous, as the statute appears to be couched in neutral language free of anxieties. However, in an inseparable fashion, both the photograph and what it represented could be seen to have been deemed so 'dreadful' because they could be associated with ideas of legal reform and legal revolution and the statute can be seen as a reaction to a severe crisis of legitimacy in law. The decision in the Seddon trial had demonstrably aroused the passionate sentiments of the public. As Geoffrey Howse notes, there was 'an enormous public outcry at his trial's verdict; and a petition bearing more than 250,000 signatures claiming [Seddon's] innocence'.[119] The photograph which showed the judge's decision in the act of being spoken was therefore supremely provocative and contextualised in a contest of ideas about law and fairness where judges were seen as disconnected from the common sentiment and thought and the people's justice was set against the justice of the judges. It could be tied to a critical outsider's view of English law. In particular, the photograph was controversial because the death penalty which it quite literally depicted in the act of being pronounced had grown particularly untenable and was considered by many as sadistic and barbaric. Thus, the literalism of the photograph challenged the real meaning of capital punishment as being about abstractions and ideas of justice and

116 Daniel Stepniak, 'British Justice: not Suitable for Public Viewing?', in *Criminal Visions: Media Representations of Crime and Justice*, Paul Mason, ed. (Cullompton, Devon: Willan Publishing, 2003), 255.

117 *House of Commons Debates* (18 March 1912), Vol. 35, column 1529 (Mr MacCallum Scott).

118 *House of Lords Debates* (26 February 1924) vol 26, columns 313–314 (Lord Darling).

119 Geoffrey Howse, *Murder and Mayhem in North London* (Barnsley: Wharncliffe Books, 2010), 78.

showed it as the act of killing an actual human being. It can therefore be seen that a combination of the photographic form and a legal outsider's vision appeared to merge as a challenge to the existing legal institution and dominant ideas of legal truth.

If a historically contextualised reading which takes into account criticisms of the law is applied, the inflammatory Seddon photograph, I argue, is best understood in its own time as championing a literal form of legal truth and rendering law more open to the people's criticisms and to those of perceived outsiders. It is the combination of photographic form and the subject matter that produced an incendiary product which horrified members of parliament since the photograph threatened the base upon which their power was built.

The law in the statute that was formulated in response to the Seddon photograph, I contend, was built on an exclusion of the photograph and the politics of exposure from the register of truth in the newspaper and mass reading practices. The law represented a strategy of excluding photography as an outsider's view of the law, a view which could influence the public's ideas and reading of the law. Although it did so by insinuation and suggestion, like the fiction explored in this monograph, the prohibition was constructed in the spirit of obscuring truth and hiding identities, on spreading wilful ignorance about law and quelling the legal literacy of the masses, on circulating shared deceptions and mystifications and fictions about law and its sources of authority and legitimacy. Linda Mulcahy has recently made a similar argument, seeing the 1925 prohibition as 'an effort to re-impose social order and retain the mystery of law' while 'preserving the interests of the legal, political and social elite, including judges, against a backdrop of fears about an increasingly disrespectful populace'.[120] For while the law could insistently and loudly declare what it was not, and even while it controlled representations, it could never openly and definitely say what it was. For this was to remain implicit as an unrecognised, carefully fenced guide to thought. Thus, whether the Seddon photograph was seen as inflaming the public's ideas of alternative justice or allowing them to be amplified and magnified in a concrete image, the subsequent legal prohibition carries the message that the law cannot be photographically represented and that the exposure of the law is forbidden. The prohibition attests that the law cannot be fixed in a 'body' of writing, like the newspaper, or be tied to the body of the judge. The prohibition can also be read as part of an eschewal of the alternative conceptions of existing law and justice that could be associated with the people and the legal reformer's perspective in Seddon's trial, and it is precisely the legal reformers who, like photographers, are associated with literalism in a range of fiction. In this, the legal prohibition can be seen to form a continuum with the fiction I have described.

Section 41(1) of the Criminal Justice Act 1925 reflects the combination of art viewing and reading to control reading practices and the conceptualisation of law. The Section extends its prohibition to *photographic* or photo-realistic drawing in the court: portrait drawing that is tied to immediate vision, resemblance between

120 Linda Mulcahy, 'Revolting consumers: a revisionist account of the 1925 ban on photography in English and Welsh courts and its implications for debate about who is able to produce, manage and consume images of the trial', *International Journal of Law in Context*, 14 (2018) 559.

reality and representation, the body and to the event and to the details. It prohibits the making of 'any portrait or sketch of any person being a judge of the court or a juror or a witness in or a party to any proceedings before the court, whether civil or criminal'. This restriction resulted in drawings produced by specialist artists who made written notes during the trial and then did the drawing from memory once outside the court. The prohibition thus supported idealism, and imaginative reconstruction rather than imitation and drawing from 'nature'. It supported artwork based on writing and thus reading rather than the immediacy of vision because reading was deemed to be more amenable to strategies of control than seeing.

In both the law and in fiction, then, I have seen a conceptual triangle that links together the law, art and reading in response to photography. It seems to me that the reader and the art viewer are produced out of this complex. I have specifically concentrated on this complex to answer the following question: how law, vision and reading are related to each other after the advent of photography until the 1920s. In the following chapters, I will unpack the constructions and associations behind each of the above terms to show how they are systemised and relate to each other through ideas of literalism and idealism. I aim to show why and how photography was consistently devalued and opposed to law and a conventional legal reading as 'the truth' and how this devaluation formed the basis of an entire system of thought and power.

References

Armstrong, Nancy. *Fiction In The Age Of Photography: The Legacy Of British Realism*. Cambridge, Massachusetts and London, England: Harvard University Press, 2002.

Benjamin, Walter. "The Work of Art in the Age of Mechanical Reproduction." In *Illuminations*, edited by Hannah Arendt, 214–218. London: Fontana, 1968.

Bentham, Jeremy. *Panopticon; or, The Inspection-House*. London: T. Payne, 1791.

Boehme-Neßler, Volker. *Pictorial Law: Modern Law and the Power of Pictures*. London: Springer, 2011.

Brantlinger, Patrick. *The Reading Lesson: The Threat of Mass Literacy in Nineteenth-Century British Fiction*. Bloomington and Indianapolis: Indiana University Press, 1998.

Brontë, Charlotte. *The Letters of Charlotte Brontë*, vol. 2: 1848-1851, edited by Margaret Smith. Oxford: Clarendon Press, 2000.

Clayton, Owen. *Literature and Photography in Transition, 1850-1915*. London: Palgrave Macmillan, 2015.

Crary, Jonathan. *Techniques of the Observer: On Vision and Modernity in the Nineteenth Century*. Cambridge, Massachusetts: MIT Press, 1992.

Culver, Stuart. "Law." In *Henry James in Context*, edited by David McWhirter, 180–191. Cambridge: Cambridge University Press, 2010.

Lord Darling. Speech to the House of Lords, 26 February 1924. *House of Lords Debates*, Vol. 56, columns 313–314. https://api.parliament.uk/historic-hansard/lords/1924/feb/26/criminal-justice-bill-hl#column_313

Daum, Patrick. "Unity and Diversity in European Pictorialism." In *Impressionist Camera: Pictorial Photography in Europe, 1888-1918*, edited by Francis Ribemont and *Patrick Daum*, 15-30. London: Merrell, 2006.

Douzinas, Costas. "The Legality of the Image." *The Modern Law Review*, Vol. 63, No. 6 (Nov., 2000), 813–830.

Doyle, Arthur Conan. "The Adventure of the Illustrious Client." In *The Complete Sherlock Holmes*. London: Magpie Books Ltd, 1993. 984–999.

Dwarris, Fortunatus. *A General Treatise on Statutes: Their Rules of Construction, and the Proper Boundaries of Legislation and of Judicial Interpretation*. Albany: William Gould & Son, 1875.

Eliot, George. "The Natural History of German Life." In *Selected Essays, Poems and Other Writings*, edited by A. S. Byatt, 107–139. London: Penguin Classics, [1859] 2005.

Ellenbogen, Josh. *Reasoned and Unreasoned Images: The Photography of Bertillon, Galton, and Marey*. University Park: *Pennsylvania State* University *Press*, 2012.

Finn, Jonathan Mathew. *Capturing the Criminal Image: From Mug Shot to Surveillance Society*. Minnesota: University of Minnesota Press, 2009.

Flint, Kate. "Photographic Memory", *Romanticism and Victorianism on the Net* 53 (2009) https://www.erudit.org/en/journals/ravon/2009-n53-ravon2916/029898ar/

Foucault, Michel. "Where Is the Law, And What Does It Do?" In *Maurice Blanchot: The Thought from Outside*, translated by Brian Massumi, 33–40. New York: Zone Books, 1987.

Foucault, Michel. *Discipline and Punish: The Birth of the Prison*. Translated by Alan Sheridan. New York: Vintage Books, 1995.

Gadamer, Hans-Georg. *Truth and Method*. Translated by J. Weinsheimer & D. Marshall. New York: Crossroad, 1990.

Goodrich, Peter. *Oedipus Lex: Psychoanalysis, History, Law*. Berkeley: University of California Press Berkeley, 1995.

Haggard, H. Rider. "About Fiction." *Contemporary Review* 51 (February 1887): 172–180.

Haggard, H. Rider. *Mr Meeson's Will*. London: Spencer Blackett, 1888.

Holmes, Oliver Wendell. "The Doings of the Sunbeam." In *Soundings from the Atlantic*, 228–281. Boston: Ticknor and Fields, 1864.

Howse, Geoffrey. *Murder and Mayhem in North London*. South Yorkshire: Wharncliffe Books: 2010.

Hutton, Christopher. "'I Crave the Law': Salomon v Salomon, Uncanny Personhood and the Jews." In *Reading The Legal Case: Cross-Currents Between Law and The Humanities*, edited by Marco Wan, 29–46. New York: Routledge, 2012.

Krueger, Christine L. "Henry Rider Haggard." In *Encyclopedia of British Writers, 19th and 20th Centuries*, edited by George Stade, Karen Karbiener and Christine L. Krueger, 151–152. New York: Facts On File, 2003.

Law Journal Reports 64 Law J. Rep. (n.s.) (1895), 693.

Leighton, John. "On Photography as a Means or an End." *The Photographic Journal* (21 June 1853): 74–75.

Maudsley, Henry. *The Physiology of Mind: Being the First Part of a Third Edition, Revised Enlarged and in Great Part Rewritten, of "The Physiology and Pathology of Mind"*. New York: D. Appleton, 1876 [1878].

MacCallum, Scott. Speech to the House of Commons, 18 March 1912. *House of Commons Debates*, Vol. 35, column 1529. https://hansard.parliament.uk/commons/1912-03-18/debates/83ef70ec-6d0a-46aa-ab54-735eb65aa675/CommonsChamber

McLeod, Ian. "Literal and Purposive Techniques of Legislative Interpretation: Some European Community and English Common Law Perspective". *29 Brooklyn Journal of International Law* (2004), 1109–1134.

Mulcahy, Linda. "Revolting consumers: a revisionist account of the 1925 ban on photography in English and Welsh courts and its implications for debate about who is able to produce, manage and consume images of the trial," *International Journal of Law in Context* (2018), 14, 559–580.

Nead, Linda. *The Female Nude: Art, Obscenity and Sexuality*. London and New York: Routledge, 2001.

Novak, Daniel A. *Realism, Photography and Nineteenth-Century Fiction*. Cambridge, Cambridge University Press, 2008.

Posner, Richard A. "Legislation and Its Interpretation: A Primer". 68 *Nebraska Law Review* (1989), 431–453.

Pykett, Lyn. *Wilkie Collins (Authors in Context)*. Oxford: Oxford University Press, 2009.

Rabb, Jane M. *Literature and Photography Interactions 1840 – 1990: A Critical Anthology*. Albuquerque: University of New Mexico Press, 1995.

Sampson, Edward C. "Thomas Hardy-Justice of the Peace." *Colby Library Quarterly*, Volume 13, no. 4, (December 1977): 263–274.

Sekula, Alan. "The Body and the Archive," *October 39* (1986): 4 – 64.

Smith, Peter and Lefley, Carolyn. *Rethinking Photography: Histories, Theories and Education*. London: Routledge, 2015.

Stepniak, Daniel. "British Justice: not Suitable for Public Viewing?" In *Criminal Visions: Media Representations of Crime and Justice*, edited by Paul Mason, 254–277. Cullompton, Devon, UK: Willan Publishing, 2003.

Sumara, Dennis J. "Fictionalizing Acts: Reading and the Making of Identity." *Theory Into Practice*, Vol. 37, No. 3, Literary Theory in the High School English Classroom (Summer, 1998): 203–210.

Tagg, John (1988) *The Burden of Representation: Essays on Photographies and Histories* The Macmillan Press Ltd: London.

Taylor, David. *Foundation Course Black And White Photography*. East Sussex: AE Publications, 2015.

Turner, J. M. W. *Light and Colour (Goethe's Theory) – the Morning after the Deluge - Moses Writing the Book of Genesis*, 1843. Oil paint on canvas, 787 x 787 mm. Tate Gallery.

1 Representation of photography, literalist reading and 'the absence of higher truths' in art

In this chapter, I aim to outline how photography was linked to literalism and literalist reading in art criticism in a strategy intended to produce, simultaneously, art viewers and readers. As I aim to show, fiction shared this strategy. Focusing on John Ruskin's writings, although I also discuss other art critics, I aim to show exactly how his tying together of literalism and photography and his position that they were limited in terms of artistic truth influenced fiction and consequently produced both intended readers and art viewers. It is my intention to show how Ruskin's formulations were productively exploited by fiction drawing on his own statements about the conceptual relationship between power, the law and reading, which he understood as enmeshed and mutually reinforcing categories.

Fine art, art criticism and photography

I first want to provide a general background to John Ruskin's ideas about photography and artistic truth in order to allow his formulations to be seen as part of a larger context from which they drew meaning. I will explain why they were seen as so persuasive by writers of fiction, since they endorsed a position that was accepted and shared by influential voices. My first aim is therefore to demonstrate that photography was seen as lacking in art status by certain art critics and that this, although it was by no means universal, was a strong tradition. This is evident in the categorisation of artistic endeavour in the Great Exhibition of the works of Industry of All Nations at Crystal Palace in 1851. This was the first occasion on which photographs from around the world were exhibited together. Photography was included in class X (instruments, clock making, surgical, musical, philosophical), and in the department of the 'machines and instruments' in a relatively narrow space.[1] The Great Exhibition Jury agreed that, 'Photography may be said to be too faithfully exact in its results, for the purposes of art'.[2] Photography was seen as 'too literal' a form of representation to be considered art.

1 Helene Bocard, s.v. 'Great Exhibition of the Works of Industry of All Nations, Crystal Palace, Hyde Park (1851)' in John Hannavy (ed), *The Encyclopedia of Nineteenth-Century Photography* (New York: Routledge, 2013).

2 Royal Commissioners, *Reports by the Juries on the Subjects in the Thirty Classes into which the Exhibition was Divided* (London: Spicer Brothers and W. Clowes and Sons, 1852), 600.

DOI: 10.4324/9781003173854-2

Underlying the categorisation of photography as a form of literalism was the idea that the photograph could not convey the highest forms of truth, such as artistic truth because it was deemed as an imitative and therefore derivative form of art incapable of accommodating true imagination and idealism, with its emphasis on broadness and generality. The photograph was seen as severely limited. The Victorian artist Henry O'Neil commented that, '[w]hen photography came first into notice, we were all fascinated by the marvellous accuracy with which every detail of form was rendered, and, with the new-born wonder of children, we forgot the absence of higher truths'.[3] O'Neil was conveying an idea which, as I will show, can be seen in other criticism of the photograph, which maintained that it could only be considered an inferior and limited form of truth because it did not convey human and spiritual 'truths' which the imagination could perceive.

In fact, in some quarters, photography was perceived as a significant threat to the art establishment in the period. Charles Landseer, the elder brother of the animal painter Edwin, nicknamed it 'foe-to-graphic art'.[4] The way in which photography and portrait painting were seen to oppose each other is emblematic of how photography was seen as threatening the living of the artist by taking away his custom. Whereas paintings were expensive, photography was a relatively cheap medium that gave a greater number of people a way of preserving the memory of their loved ones in an affordable way. Photography was therefore commonly said to have ruined miniature painting and to have taken away the livelihood of the male artist.[5] This perceived threat of photography to art and the art establishment appeared to have instigated much of the denouncement of photography in art criticism.

The 'hatred' of the photographic and the questioning of its aesthetic status in terms of truth are evident in a brief but revealing digression on 'photographic sculpture' by the art historian and poet Francis Turner Palgrave in an essay in which he considered the art of sculpture. François Willème had recently invented and patented what was called 'photosculpture', 'a form of photographically derived sculpture with only minimal need for handiwork'.[6] It was a cheap means of reproducing statues based on photographing originals from a number of different positions. Palgrave railed against those who utilised the new technology of producing statues through photographic processes in his *Essays on Art* in 1867. Palgrave remarked 'on the ludicrous impossibility of effecting anything in sculpture that can in the very least deserve the name, by any mere mechanical process, be the means ever so ingenious'. He believed that the public 'patronise the invention … from the petty passion for novelty' and went on to claim that:

> A true likeness is something caught from the mind of one man by the mind of another; and this cannot be done by twenty times twenty cameras, all

3 Quoted in Julia Thomas, *Victorian Narrative Painting* (London: Tate Publishing, 2000), 52.

4 Ibid.

5 Anonymous, 'Visits to Noteworthy Studios: Mr. Sarony's Studio at Scarborough', *Photographic News* (6 March 1868), 10–11.

6 Robert A. Sobieszek, 'Sculpture as the Sum of Its Profiles: François Willème and Photosculpture in France, 1859-1868,' *The Art Bulletin*, 62: 4 (December 1980), 618.

> working together. In the nature of things, 'Photo-Sculpture' is a sham art. And every sham art, as English manufacturers are beginning to discover, is the death of a genuine art. 'These are things,' as old Blake said of something similar, 'that we artists HATE.' And all true lovers of art will hate them likewise.[7]

For Palgrave, the photographic image was soulless and false since it needed to be distinguished from a 'true likeness'. It was also false because it is incompatible with the 'genuine' or 'true' art of sculpture and can only masquerade as that art form in the form of 'sham'. Thus, while the photographic image had the appearance of 'truth', it was believed to be 'untrue'. Palgrave suggested that photography was the reproduction of the surface rather than the intimation of depth which he invoked through the idea of telepathy at the beginning of the quote. For Palgrave, it led to both the decline and degradation of sculpture. Thus, photography was linked to the subversive and ephemeral truth of representing things in the world rather than the representation of the mind and subjectivity, a connection that was important in other art criticism of the time. For Palgrave and others like him, the photograph did not convey eternal and unchanging truth which was the 'artistic truth' of 'the soul'.

Palgrave's essay relied on implicit notions of and divisions between two constructed visual communities which he invoked through the last line of the quote above, when he included himself among artists and lovers of art who hated photographic sculpture. First, there was the harmonious and unified artistic community which was cognisant of artistic truth and which 'hated' the photographic – the artists and art lovers who Palgrave classed himself among. Secondly – but much more implicitly – there was the degraded community which was constructed around the desire for the photographic and worldly representation. These were 'those who are [not] accessible to higher motives than the lust for cheap art or a novel kind of article'.[8] Palgrave's criticism of photography was that it was untouched by human vision and thought. Palgrave refers to an idea of telepathy to describe how a 'true' artist catches the likeness of another, and does not refer to sight or vision in describing the process, which perhaps seems counter-intuitive, but suggests a comparison between the camera and the mind of the artist rather than the eye. The latter does not rely on 'sight' so much as 'insight'.

John Ruskin: photography and artistic truth

Thus far, it has been my aim to show how photography was constructed as non-art in certain traditions of art criticism, or even as a threat to it. I have suggested that critics such as Palgrave had an investment in differentiating photography from the hand of the artist because they feared that photography could ultimately supplant art as the dominant form of representation. If it did, it would thus take away the privilege of representing artistic truth through traditional forms of art like painting and sculpture. These larger ideas and anxieties, I contend, provide the context for understanding how photography was devalued and dismissed as a form of artistic

7 Francis Turner Palgrave, *Essays on Art* (New York: Hurd & Houghton, 1867), 279.
8 Ibid., 267.

truth in the writings of John Ruskin. I will discuss and concentrate on Ruskin's work in terms of the relationships created between photography, reading and art for a number of reasons. First, Ruskin was the pre-eminent art critic of his time and his theorising was hugely influential. In particular, his ideas codified a complex of thought which is worked out in detail in the fiction I have studied. This is because Ruskin wrote about both art and reading and explicitly invoked ideas of literalism and literalist readings when discussing each topic. He framed general principles about how both art and 'true' reading were to be distinguished from what he saw as the literalism of photography and a literalist reading. His writings therefore not only introduce but also illuminate the connections drawn between photography, literalism, art and reading. In fact, as I aim to show below, Ruskin also drew on ideas of power and legal truth to elaborate his points. Therefore his work is a crucial source for my own argument which links ideas of art, law, photography and reading in order to understand what kind of reader and reading fiction aimed to produce, and how such constructions legitimated the structures of power of the political elite from the invention of photography to the nineteen-twenties. This exploration of how reading was related to power is important to my research because I hope that one of its unique claims for attention is to cast light on forgotten and unrecognised historical guides and controls of thought and being. I believe the recognition and understanding of such guides and controls will allow us to understand the nature of our own present through an understanding of our situation in regards to the historical situation I am describing.

I will first elaborate how Ruskin saw the photograph as incapable of representing artistic truth because of its perceived literalism. This idea, that the photograph is associated with literalist reading, and that it is untruthful, appears to be crucial to the fiction I have studied. The fiction appears to share and productively exploit the terms in which Ruskin criticised the literalism of the photograph: that it was deemed untruthful, deceptive and misleading. A detailed study of how Ruskin related the literalism of the photograph to ideas of truth and deception will, therefore, offer a helpful context to my analysis of the role of photography in fiction.

Ruskin often used photography to 'preserve' architecture commissioned to be demolished. As the critic Michael Harvey argues, Ruskin's belief in the value of the photographic architectural record is his most consistent attitude towards photography. Harvey writes that throughout his life, Ruskin was continually dispatching assistants to purchase, commission or take photographs and make sketches of buildings he thought of as valuable and vulnerable.[9] However, Ruskin's writings also consistently couple the photographic and the natural and both are problematised throughout his criticism. On the one hand, Ruskin supported the veracity of the photographic image in practice. On the other hand, he was unable in his writings to allow photography to intrude upon the sphere of fine art as a form of representation and truth. Ruskin therefore stands among those critics of photography discussed in this monograph who were not averse to the use of the medium and its capacity for documentation but nevertheless could not allow it to be seen as a superior form of

9 Michael Harvey, 'Ruskin and Photography', *Oxford Art Journal*, 7: 2 (1984), 25, 27.

truth and representation. Ruskin initially celebrated the advent of photography, but even in 1846, in a letter to a W. H. Harrison, at the same time as he praised the daguerreotype, he asserted that:

> My drawings are truth to the very letter - too literal, perhaps; so says my father, so says not the Daguerreotype, for it beats me grievously. I have allied myself with it; sith it may no better be, and have brought away some precious records from Florence. It is certainly the most marvellous invention of the century; given us, I think, just in time to save some evidence from the great public of wreckers. As regards art, I wish it had never been discovered, it will make the eye too fastidious to accept mere handling.[10]

Ruskin writes that in the contest of 'literally' representing the truth, it is the photograph that is the victor. It is upon seeing so that he allies himself with it. But even while the photograph's ability to document or record appearances is useful in saving 'evidence', with its legal connotations, or for making 'records', Ruskin criticises the 'literality' of photography by saying that it 'may no better be' or that its virtues are limited. The strong connotation is that there is something wrong with photography and literalism. The idea is carried forward by the statement that photography and literalism are somehow ruinous for art and the acceptance of the handling of other media. Ruskin writes that photography will make the eye 'too fastidious', that is, that photography will make the viewer overly attentive to and preoccupied with matters of accuracy and detail. It was thus a denunciation of literalism that lay behind all of Ruskin's formulations regarding the relationship between art and photography. I will discuss Ruskin's idea of literalism in more detail below, but will first outline why Ruskin saw the photograph as false as an art form. By 1870, in his inaugural Slade lectures at Oxford, published in the same year as *Lectures on Art*, in the lecture on 'Light' Ruskin was emphatic in his denunciation of photography, stressing its mechanical nature, which he saw as opposed to the human intelligence and imagination of the artist. Ruskin also commented on the falsity of photographic 'truth'. He wrote that:

> [p]hotographs supersede no single quality nor use of fine art, and have so much in common with Nature that they even share her temper of parsimony, and will themselves give you nothing valuable that you do not work for. They supersede no good art for the definition of art is 'human labour regulated by human design' and this design, or evidence of active intellect in choice and arrangement, is the essential part of the work … you will not care for photographs of landscape. They are not true, though they seem so. They are merely spoiled nature.[11]

10 John Ruskin, *The Complete Works of John Ruskin, vol 3* (E. T. Cook and Alexander Wedderburn (eds), London: George Allen, 1903), 210.

11 John Ruskin, *The Complete Works of John Ruskin, vol. 20* (E. T. Cook and Alexander Wedderburn (eds), London: George Allen, 1903), 165.

In Ruskin's conception, the photograph conveys a strictly limited 'truth' although it again has the appearance of it and, significantly, it is associated with nature itself. Indeed, Ruskin's conclusion is that photographs are 'merely spoiled nature', because they appear to be the thing itself but are not. In this view, photographs are, therefore, incapable of reflecting the 'truth' of the natural world. Ruskin as the informed critic and the true knower gets past this veil of surface appearance to understand the inferior position which photography holds in relation to art and artistic truth. His idea that the photograph is false contains within it the implicit contrast with the 'truth' and evidence of the 'human spirit', the religious idea of the 'soul', selfhood and the expression of identity in painting and art. Thus, Ruskin writes in the concluding remarks of the third volume of *The Stones of Venice* (1853):

> All art is great, and good, and true, only so far as it is distinctively the work of *manhood* in its entire and highest sense; that is to say, not the work of limbs and fingers, but of the soul, aided, according to her necessities, by the inferior powers; and therefore distinguished in essence from all products of those inferior powers unhelped by the soul. For as a photograph is not a work of art, though it requires certain delicate manipulations of paper and acid, and subtle calculations of time, in order to bring out a good result; so, neither would a drawing *like* a photograph, made directly from nature, be a work of art, although it would imply many delicate manipulations of the pencil and subtle calculations of effects of colour and shade.[12]

Artistic truth is therefore associated with the expression of the spirit (itself strongly suggested to be implicitly male). Ruskin's denunciation of photography quite significantly asserts that art is possible 'though the eyeball be sightless'.[13] This invocation of blindness is of great significance as I will show in the following chapters, in particular in my exploration of how Henry James cast blindness as normative in Chapter 3. Thus, the machine-made photographic image, which Ruskin associated with nature because of its material production, was thought of as unmediated by the male human mind and was therefore grossly limited and superficial. This idea that the photograph was lacking in human truth figured in the fiction I have studied quite prominently and was often exploited to denounce photography, and particularly its capacity to bear legal truth. This is evident in Wilkie Collins' association of photography with what was perceived as the dehumanising discourse of science which I will discuss in Chapter 2.

In *The Art of England* (1883) Ruskin wrote on the topic of portraiture that 'Depth of expression' is 'unattainable by photography'.[14] He also used ideas of photography to devalue art which did not match his expectations. When Ruskin considered John Brett's 1858 landscape *Val d'Aosta*, which is a highly realistic

12 John Ruskin, *The Complete Works of John Ruskin, vol 11* (E. T. Cook and Alexander Wedderburn (eds), London: George Allen, 1903), 201–203.

13 Ibid., 201–203.

14 John Ruskin, *The Complete Works of John Ruskin, vol 33* (E. T. Cook and Alexander Wedderburn (eds), London: George Allen, 1903), 302.

landscape painting and full of incredibly fine detail, he criticised it for being 'too photographic', writing that Brett 'took to mere photography of physical landscape, and gradually lost both precision and sentiment'.[15] Significantly, the painting was seen as a 'direct' copy of nature and divested of humanity, since Ruskin wrote that, 'I never saw the mirror so held up to Nature; but it is Mirror's work, not Man's'.[16] In both narrative art and fiction, the literalism of photography was also consistently associated with the mirror and its passive reflection, and with copying, such as in the work of Wilkie Collins where photography is associated with forgery.

Thus far, I have aimed to show how Ruskin saw photography as a limited form of truth and have suggested that he saw it as divested of humanity and human truth. I now aim to develop what standard of truth Ruskin judged the photograph by, as this form of artistic truth appears to have been shared by writers of fiction. His idea of 'artistic truth' can be seen to shape the idea of the legal truth and the reading of the law in the fiction that I will analyse later. Ruskin's own ideas about what constituted 'truth' in art and how art is related to nature are evident since 'truth' is the great theme of his work. In the first volume of *Modern Painters* Ruskin wrote that: 'The word Truth, as applied to art signifies the faithful statement, either to the mind or senses, of any fact of nature'.[17] However, nature is secondary and partial: 'the truth of nature is a part of the truth of God.'[18] The 'truth' of the patriarchal figure is the ultimate form of truth. 'Truth' itself is to be distinguished from mere (photographic) imitation since 'there is a moral as well as material truth, — a truth of impression as well as of form, — of thought as well as of matter'.[19] Imitation is inferior because of its materialism, which is contrasted with an idea of unconditional truth, and a lack of generalisation: 'truth is a term of universal application, but imitation is limited to that narrow field of art which takes cognizance only of material things.'[20] Thus, Ruskin writes that:

> As you will never get from real linen cloth, by copying it ever so faithfully, the drapery of a noble statue, so you will never get from real mountains, copy them never so faithfully, the forms of noble landscape. Anything more beautiful than the photographs of the Valley of Chamouni, now in your printsellers' windows, cannot be conceived. For geographical and geological purposes they are worth anything; for art purposes, worth—a good deal less than zero. You may learn much from them, and will mislearn more. But in Turner's 'Valley of Chamouni' the mountains have not a fold too much, nor too little. There are no such mountains at Chamouni: they are the ghosts of eternal mountains, such as have been, and shall be, for evermore.[21]

15 John Ruskin, *The Complete Works of John Ruskin, vol 14* (E. T. Cook and Alexander Wedderburn (eds), London: George Allen, 1903), 238.
16 Ibid., 237.
17 Ruskin, *The Complete Works of John Ruskin, vol 3* (n 10) 104.
18 Ibid., 141.
19 Ibid., 104.
20 Ibid., 104.
21 John Ruskin, *The Complete Works of John Ruskin, vol 22* (E. T. Cook and Alexander Wedderburn (eds), London: George Allen, 1903), 220.

For Ruskin, 'truth' is everlasting and unchanging and distinct from fickle matter and the event of copying. Truth is also about conveying inner 'essence' rather than appearance, a particularly important idea which influenced fiction like Wilkie Collins' detective novels in which there is more to matters 'than meets the eye', such as in *The Moonstone* (1868), where false appearances lead to an incorrect impression and judgement of an act of burglary committed for what is presented as benign purposes of love and protection. Indeed, Ruskin views photographic imitation as valueless in its own right. He asserts that natural phenomena are only to be subjects in landscape 'in their direct relation to humanity. [...] Rocks and water and air may no more be painted for their own sakes, than the armour carved without the warrior'.[22] Nature is not important enough in its own right, only so far as it has a relation to humanity. The notion of artistic 'truth' is carefully delineated in the fourth volume of *Modern Painters* as the supreme truth which is superior to the 'truth' of the sciences and mathematics. It is the 'truth' of the imagination – to be differentiated from the degraded and 'deceptive' forms of imitation – which reflects 'divine' truth, or mirrors the mind of the Christian God, the supreme figure of the patriarch:

> So that I am more and more convinced of what I had to state respecting the imagination, now many years ago, viz., that its true force lies in its marvellous insight and foresight,—that it is, instead of a false and deceptive faculty, exactly the most accurate and truth-telling faculty which the human mind possesses; and all the more truth-telling, because in its work, the vanity and individualism of the man himself are crushed, and he becomes a mere instrument or mirror, used by a higher power for the reflection to others of a truth which no effort of his could ever have ascertained; so that all mathematical, and arithmetical, and generally scientific truth, is, in comparison, truth of the husk and surface, hard and shallow; and only the imaginative truth is precious.[23]

Ruskin thus states that the imagination is the bearer of truth and the imagination itself is the product of unintentional and divine revelation. The relationship between the idea of supreme truth and nature may therefore be inferred. Art is only 'truthful' in that it partakes of the supreme 'truth' of the Christian God, but this gives it superiority in relation to scientific 'truth', which aims to delineate nature. Other representations of nature, such as the scientific, are only of the 'surface'. They are not insightful, but associated with the degraded forms of vision which includes the imitative and the photographic, which are represented as superficial. Ruskin's ideas of representation and the imagination of the artist heavily influenced writers of fiction who denounced photography along with realism in their works in the same terms. One instance is Henry James' short story 'The Real Thing' (1892), where photography is associated with realist or literalist portrait painting and the corruption of the artistic vision and reading of an illustrator of books.

22 John Ruskin, *The Complete Works of John Ruskin, vol 12* (E. T. Cook and Alexander Wedderburn (eds), London: George Allen, 1903), 17.

23 John Ruskin, *The Complete Works of John Ruskin, vol 6* (E. T. Cook and Alexander Wedderburn (eds), ondon: George Allen, 1903), 44–45.

In summary, the two orders of truth that compete in Ruskin's account are the intangible, eternal and invisible, or the artistic and the non-photographic, and the fleeting, bodily and visible, or the photographic: the religious and the scientific. There are two mirrors in opposition to one another which reflect the visible and the invisible, for the artist must not passively mirror nature but passively mirror the mind of the Christian God, although this passivity is presented as an active creation. Fiction, as I will show, takes hold of these notions in order to characterise and obsessively to present the legal truth as superior to a degraded 'mirror-like' photographic truth. One instance is Wilkie Collins' novel *The Moonstone*, which I have alluded to above: the scene which seems to subvert of ideas of innocence and guilt is witnessed by Rachel by looking into a mirror. She is associated with photography in various ways in the novel, as I aim to show in Chapter 3.

Having discussed Ruskin's idea of how superior truth was to be distinguished from photographic and literalist truth, I now aim to show how he constructed concealment and obscurity in expression as a superior means of artistic communication. Such a form of artistic expression could clearly stand as a form of representation distinguished from photography with its clarity and details. This valorisation of concealment and obscurity is important to understand because the fiction that I have studied exploited such a mode of communication in order to insinuate ideas and connections and to construct unrecognised guides to thought in order to control readers. As I will show in my discussion of *The Wrecker* (1892) below, fiction exploited concealment, one of the most crucial strategies for representing the powerful, to valorise and support the power of the political elites. Obscurity was seen to communicate suitably the identities of the powerful. Ruskin's criticism leads to the valorisation of 'obscurity' which is evident in the work of his hero, Turner. For Ruskin, obscurity in representation can be contrasted to his idea of photography, which was that it was a direct, unfiltered, unmediated form of representation. He writes:

> in all the great *painters*, properly so called, a peculiar melting and mystery about the pencilling, sometimes called softness, sometimes freedom, sometimes breadth; but in reality a most subtle confusion of colours and forms, obtained either by the apparently careless stroke of the brush, or by careful retouching with tenderest labour; but always obtained in one way or another; so that though, when compared with work that has no meaning, all great work is *distinct*, —compared with work that has narrow and stubborn meaning, all great work is *in*distinct; and if we find, on examining any picture closely, that it is all clearly to be made out, it cannot be, as painting, first-rate. There is no exception to this rule. EXCELLENCE OF THE HIGHEST KIND, WITHOUT OBSCURITY, CANNOT EXIST.[24]

Ruskin, the literalism of photography, hidden truth and the power of reading

I have so far suggested that Ruskin's formulations codified a system of thought in relation to an 'anti-photographic' artistic 'truth'. Ruskin's ideas were both hugely influential and explicitly stated larger, underlying and shared currents in thought regarding the

24 Ibid., 81.

nature of artistic truth, expression and representation. Such ideas were therefore poised to influence creativity and its expression in writers and artists considerably. A similar framework of thinking is repeated in other criticism of the time, such as in Oscar Wilde's essay 'The Decay of Lying – An Observation' (1891), which also saw art as a 'veil' over nature, or an obscuring of literal fact.[25] Other voices included the lesser known Philip Gilbert Hamerton's 1871 work of scholarship on art theory, which explicitly deals with the relationship between photography and painting amidst general ideas of art and the ideal in painting, and even literature, which is entitled *Thoughts About Art*. Hamerton summarised his own conclusions on the relationship between photography and painting by asserting that:

> Photography and painting are for ever independent of each other, and there is no manner of rivalry possible between them. Each has its own path.
>
> Painting does not need the help of photography, and in practice can be little served by it, except for occasional reference.
>
> Because painting deals with truths not attainable by photography, as the relations of light and color, and the imaginative interpretation as opposed to the literal imitation of nature.[26]

I have suggested that art as a domain of meaning in Ruskin's writing was seen as an attempt to mirror the mind of the supreme patriarchal figure which was thought of as 'the truth', a truth that is purportedly universal and eternal. I have tried to show how Ruskin perceived the literalism of photography as untruthful in great detail because such ideas, I suggest, can be seen to influence heavily the fiction I will study in the following chapters. I now aim directly to address Ruskin's ideas about literalism and its relationship to truthful reading as these can further elaborate why and how accepted practices of reading were formed in opposition to ideas of literalism. Ruskin's ideas cast a light on the perceived relation between vision and reading, which is part of my larger investigation of the connection between vision, the law and reading. The way in which vision and power are tied together in Ruskin's formulations is important for my analysis of how literalism and non-literalist readings threatened or supported the monopoly of power of the political elite.

Ruskin addressed the idea of literal representation in art in *The Stones of Venice* (1851). He characterised literalism in painting as:

> a literal and painstaking imitation of the externals of Nature, as in the works of the Dutch school, against whom I had to prove that the truths thus sought were but a small part of the truth of Nature, and that there were higher and more occult kinds of truth which could not be rendered but by some sacrifice of imitative accuracy, and which Turner had by such sacrifice succeeded in rendering for the first time in the history of art.[27]

25 Oscar Wilde, 'The Decay of Lying,' in *Intentions* (New York: Brentano's, [1891], 1905), 31.
26 Philip Gilbert Hamerton, *Thoughts About Art* (Boston: Roberts Brothers, 1871), 143.
27 John Ruskin, *The Complete Works of John Ruskin, vol 11* (E. T. Cook and Alexander Wedderburn (eds), London: George Allen, 1903), XX.

Ruskin therefore constructed the idea of literalism as that which was preoccupied with external appearance rather than an implicit 'internal substance', and with an inferior and limited form of truth which was only evident to the 'uninitiated', since he referred to higher 'occult kinds of truth'. The adjective 'occult' has an implication of concealment and veiling since the verb 'to occult' means to interfere with the view of a person by introducing a barrier between them and the thing and because of the Latin origins of the word ('classical Latin *occultāre* to hide, conceal, also in astronomical sense, frequentative of *occulere* to cover up, hide, conceal'.[28]). Through implicit contrast, literalism is thus associated with unfiltered or unconcealed vision: this is why it was so strongly associated with photography which was seen as an unmediated form of representation.

If photography was associated with literalism and a literal writing out of nature and the truth, then the suggestion is that it is produced for the literalist reader, or for literalism in reading. Thus, if Ruskin's agenda was to control readers, this could be done through offering an alternative to literalism which was held up as much more valuable. Such an interpretation is supported by Ruskin's own characterisation of reading and literalism in his lecture on 'King's Treasuries' (1864), later published in *Sesame and Lilies* (1865). The way that Ruskin defined ideal reading in this lecture stood in contrast to his characterisation of literalism as concerned with the 'external' and with direct vision. Ruskin suggested that true writing had a secret, internal (perhaps invisible) dimension which the reader was supposed to access. Thus, Ruskin stated at the outset of the lecture that 'I want to speak to you about the treasures hidden in books; and about the way we find them, and the way we lose them'.[29] There is no tangible or apparent treasure in a book, so Ruskin was indicating a treasure that was invisible to the eyes. Ruskin characterised the practice of true reading as an attempt to dig up this hidden or concealed treasure.[30] Reading was thus presented as a labour intensive activity while a book was presented as something with a depth beyond superficial vision and internal or 'deep' value. Meaning could not be immediately accessible and reading was tantamount to an initiation. As Ruskin wrote:

> And be sure, also, if the author is worth anything, that you will not get at his meaning all at once; —nay, that at his whole meaning you will not for a long time arrive in any wise. Not that he does not say what he means, and in strong words too; but he cannot say it all; and what is more strange, *will* not, but in a hidden way and in parables, in order that he may be sure you want it.[31]

Thus, Ruskin's idea of reading was set against an idea of reading that sees writing as immediate, apparent, easily accessible, open to all.

28 *Oxford Dictionaries, s.v.* 'occult' (last accessed 20 November 2018) http://www.oed.com/view/Entry/130167?rskey=OmpjsS&result=2#eid.

29 John Ruskin, *The Complete Works of John Ruskin, vol 18* (E. T. Cook and Alexander Wedderburn (eds), London: George Allen, 1903), 54.

30 Ibid., 63–64.

31 Ibid.

For Ruskin, the 'true book' was modelled on scripture. When he was defining what a true book was, he wrote: 'That is his writing; it is, in his small human way, and with whatever degree of true inspiration is in him, his inscription, or scripture. That is a— Book'.[32] Thus, there were underlying ideas of masculinity, patriarchy and power in Ruskin's conception. The true book was modelled on the word of the Christian God, the supreme patriarchal figure and an entity considered the most powerful. Man imitated the Christian God and his power in creating 'the true book'. In terms of truth, the true book was to be distinguished from 'books of the hour' and 'firm fact-telling', which Ruskin characterised as 'merely letters or newspapers in good print'. In fact, Ruskin also differentiated the true book from mere (literal) description. As he wrote:

> So, though bound up in a volume, the long letter which gives you so pleasant an account of the inns, and roads, and weather, last year at such a place, or which tells you that amusing story, or gives you the real circumstances of such and such events, however valuable for occasional reference, may not be, in the real sense of the word, a book at all, nor, in the real sense, to be – read.[33]

Thus, Ruskin's idea of true writing, which emerges from contrast, is that such writing is 'eternal', unconditional, not factual. Such writing is also non-descriptive and does not involve telling the 'real circumstances' of events. That is, true writing eschews most of the claims that are associated with ideas of the truth and it is true as a result of this. This is the idea of the truth for a reader like Ruskin: if it expresses patriarchal will, desire and law, only then is it really true, no matter how (and, in fact, because it is) divorced from actual conditions in society and forms of knowledge.

It is in this context that we can interpret Ruskin's explicit comments about literalist reading in the course of his lecture, which is opposed to true reading and which cannot see true books (Bibles) as valuable. Ruskin changed the word 'books' into 'bibles' in the following Biblical passage to illustrate his point:

> How wholesome it would be for the many simple persons who worship the Letter of God's Word instead of its Spirit, (just as other idolaters worship His picture instead of His presence,) if, in such places (for instance) as Acts xix. 19, we retained the Greek expression, instead of translating it, and they had to read – Many of them also which used curious arts, brought their bibles together, and burnt them before all men; and they counted the price of them, and found it fifty thousand pieces of silver![34]

The passage suggests that Ruskin's idea of the literalist reader is of someone that cannot see the invisible and hidden value or treasure in a true book, the mystical 'spirit' of the supreme patriarchal spirit. Like an idolater, such a person can only see the external appearance of the 'picture' of the powerful patriarch rather than feel the power of his

32 Ibid., 59.
33 Ibid.
34 Ibid., 67.

'presence'. The literalist uses what appears to be the inferior sense of sight instead of faith and deference or submission. That is, they do not fully accept a larger power over themselves and feel this power's superiority in the core of their being. Such a literalist cannot 'dig' deep down into the book and can only think in terms of material value or in terms of pieces of silver rather than in terms of intangible 'value' and 'treasure'. In fact, this emphasis on materialism reveals that Ruskin's idea of the literalist relates to his idea of women, an idea which is important to emphasise since it can be clearly seen to be developed in the context of literalism in the fiction that I discuss below as well as the other fiction I have studied. Ruskin declared at the outset of his lecture that it was above all mothers who saw education as a commodity and a means of advancement in life rather than having 'abstract' value in its own right.[35] As he wrote, 'I am always struck by the precedence which the idea of a —position in life takes above all other thoughts in the parents' – more especially in the mothers' – minds'.[36] What was troubling about these mothers was that they taught their children to compete for equal representation in the professions through reading and education and thus advance in life. Ruskin does not state outright that he sees the women's position as an attack on his own privilege, station in life and economic class, but I suggest that this is the best interpretation of his work.

Ruskin on the relationship between reading, the law and power

So far in this chapter I have discussed ways in which Ruskin constructed literalist reading in opposition to a reading which found or dug for a hidden truth and treasure below the surface of the text. I have emphasised the patriarchal dimensions of this reading. I now wish to show that Ruskin applied his ideas to the reading of law and to the power of giving laws. Ruskin himself can be seen to supply an interpretation of how his ideas about reading supported power and the status quo, a theme of great significance, I argue, in understanding the fiction I have studied.

I will first examine how Ruskin applied his ideas about art viewing and truthful reading to a reading of the law itself. The authors I have studied presented the reading of the law in the same fashion, which is why it is of importance to stress the point. Ruskin saw the photograph as not being able to convey full legal truth, or as a limited, corruption of truth. As he wrote:

> Photographs have an imitable mechanical refinement, and their legal evidence is of great use if you knew how to cross-examine them. They are popularly supposed to be 'true,' and, at their worst, they are so, in the sense in which an echo is true to a conversation of which it omits the most important syllables and reduplicates the rest. But this truth of mere transcript has nothing to do with Art properly so called; and will never supersede it. Delicate art of design, or of selected truth, can only be presented to the general public by true line engraving.[37]

35 Ibid., 54.
36 Ibid.
37 John Ruskin, *The Complete Works of John Ruskin, vol 19* (E. T. Cook and Alexander Wedderburn (eds), London: George Allen, 1903), 150.

This passage can be understood by referring to Ruskin's intent simultaneously to produce both art viewers and readers and the finding of 'hidden' truth. In emphasising his own 'visual literacy' and aesthetic refinement, at the same time as limiting the application of photography to legal questions, he turned to both art and the literacy of the lawyer to assume the position of the knowledgeable and informed subject. Art and legal knowledge are associated together in an idea of correct reading and cross-examination. Ruskin constructed the photograph as lacking in truth, discourse, representation and meaning which the experienced lawyer/art critic can 'fill in' over and beyond mere vision. Ruskin, the legal reader, himself reads what is missing, blank, invisible. The legal reader imaginatively constructs meaning and truth out of the incomplete artefact. This is akin to the reading which Ruskin valorised, which found hidden or concealed truth. Thus, Ruskin not only aimed to produce at the same time, both art viewers and readers, but also relied on an idea of a legal reader to model them on.

In *Of Queens' Gardens* (1865), Ruskin invoked the idea of a conceptual and mutually sustaining triangular relationship between law, reading and power. The purpose of reading was seen as that which enabled leadership and the rule of the law. As he wrote:

> I wish you to see that both well-directed moral training and well-chosen reading lead to the possession of a power over the ill-guided and illiterate, which is, according to the measure of it, in the truest, which is, according to the measure of it, in the truest sense, kingly; conferring indeed the purest kingship that can exist among men: too many other kingships (however distinguished by visible insignia or material power) being either spectral, or tyrannous; — spectral—that is to say, aspects and shadows only of royalty, hollow as death, and which only the—likeness of a kingly crown have on or else—tyrannous—that is to say, substituting their own will for the law of justice and love by which all true kings rule.[38]

Ruskin further emphasised that true kingship was founded not just on an ideal of justice, but also on the basis of an 'eternal law':

> A king's majesty or—state, then, and the right of his kingdom to be called a state, depends on the movelessness of both: —without tremor, without quiver of balance; established and enthroned upon a foundation of eternal law which nothing can alter, nor overthrow.[39]

The knowledge of the law was therefore closely associated with reading in Ruskin's formulations, just as it was integrated with power. As Ruskin stated, he believed that

> all literature and all education are only useful so far as they tend to confirm this calm, beneficent, and therefore kingly, power—first, over ourselves, and, through ourselves, over all around us.[40]

38 John Ruskin, *The Complete Works of John Ruskin, vol 18* (n 29) 109–110.
39 Ibid.
40 Ibid.

The ultimate aim of books, presumably including the category of fiction, was to produce power through reading and to promulgate adherence to 'the eternal law' which Ruskin believed in. This formulation codified the implicit aims of the fiction I have studied. One of the aims of this chapter is to show how Ruskin's formulation represented an exact and contemporary interpretation of the larger, general purpose of fiction and its construction of reading and readers of a hidden and non-literalist truth. This is so that accepted reading can be reimagined as a strategy of control, just as much as it can be seen as an expression and reinforcement of power and the asymmetry of power in society.

The representation of women: exploring art's gendered idea of photography's literalism and reading the law

In this chapter, I have tried to show how Ruskin attempted to differentiate art from a photographic or literalist reproduction of reality. I have also aimed to indicate how he distinguished true reading from literalist reading. Both the reader and the artistic viewer, according to Ruskin, were to differentiate their reading from literalism. Ruskin also invoked ideas of law and legal reading to elaborate his points. Ruskin's work therefore sheds light on the larger construction of reading, art viewing and the production of readers and how such constructions work together to manufacture a relationship between law, vision and reading. He also explicitly raised the question of power and how it provides a way of seeing how his constructions were used to legitimate conventional authority and the status quo, as well as how they can illuminate the unique status and agenda of fiction. I now aim to show how Ruskin's influential ideas were worked out in practice in fiction.

In this chapter, I have explored how Ruskin's denunciation of photography and literalist reading are enmeshed in ideals of artistic truth and patriarchal authority. I have examined how ideas of gender form an important component of the constructions of literalism, reading and art viewing. I will now more closely analyse the representation of literalist reading and photography in fiction in terms of gender and class coordinates. This is because I see Ruskin's ideas which linked correct reading with the expression of power and rule to have been consistently worked out in the narratives I have studied by associating alternative or literalist forms of reading with groups outside of the political elite, particularly women and the poor. Gender plays a particularly important role, as I have already aimed to establish in the introduction to this monograph. Ruskin's views on art are themselves implicitly gendered. In regards to female vision, Ruskin often asserted that women could not be seen as artists and therefore separated art from the vision of women, reserving these domains exclusively for men. In a letter of 1858 to a Miss Sinnett, he wrote that:

> I am quite delighted with your sketches, they are full of exquisite perception and feeling. You *must* resolve to be quite a great paint*ress*; the feminine termination does not exist, there never having been such a being as yet as a lady who could paint. Try and be the first.[41]

41 John Ruskin, *The Complete Works of John Ruskin, vol 14* (n 15) 308.

The letter clearly states that Ruskin thought that no woman had ever been an artist. In 1875, Ruskin went further to attest that 'I have always said that no woman could paint'.[42] Ruskin's ideas about art and truth can be seen as part of a larger movement which privileged constructions of male vision over constructions of female vision. In these constructions, male vision is associated with artistic discrimination and idealism while female vision is excluded from these ideas alongside constructions of photography. In addition, I have above suggested that Ruskin explicitly associated mothers with literalism. The reason for this is that as the title of *Kings' Treasuries*, which I have discussed above, suggested, reading, power and the public sphere were seen as being for men (*Queens' Gardens* stated that the place of women was the domestic sphere).

Art, reading and photography in fiction

Robert Louis Stevenson and Lloyd Osbourne's *The Wrecker* (1892) can be seen to build on Ruskin's formulations about the relationships between photography, art and reading in its elaboration and emphasis, in particular, of how law and art are tied together against photography and literalism. This work is illustrative of the fiction I have studied, in particular, because art is clearly associated with the privileged in society in the novel and also because the path to art and the realm of aesthetics for the art viewer is established through reading and a concealment of the crimes of political elites. Thus, false legitimation of the position of the political elites and the non-literal application of legal reading to their activities leads to the status of true reader and true art viewer, just as in the other fiction I have studied. In short, I suggest that the novel illuminates in detail how reading, the law, art and power form a complex in precisely the way that Ruskin suggests. In addition, the novel can be seen to rely heavily on ideas of gendering in setting out its ideas and can thus characterise how exactly conditions of power, legitimacy and reading relied on perceived differences between men and women. As a member of the Scottish Bar, Stevenson exploited the relationships between the domains and professional identities of art, law and fiction.[43]

I will first introduce how the novel ties together photography and reading as a diversion of the artistic mind and the true reader. The hero of *The Wrecker*, Loudon Dodd, wants to become an artist against the wishes of his business-minded father. However, Dodd is diverted from his artistic aims by a photographer turned businessman, by the name of Jim Pinkerton. Pinkerton is presented as both photographer and poor reader, since his relationship with the Bible is founded on a doubt which emerges from photographic vision, or which comes from the authority of a photographer. As the authors write:

42 Ibid.

43 Stevenson studied law at the University of Edinburgh from 1871 to 1875. He was called to the Scottish bar in 1875. See Jennifer Speake (ed), *Literature of Travel and Exploration: R to Z, Index* (New York, London: Taylor & Francis, 2003), 'Biography, 1152.

> A travelling tintype photographer picked him up, like a haw out of a hedgerow, on a wayside in New Jersey; took a fancy to the urchin; carried him on with him in his wandering life; taught him all he knew himself — to take tin-types (as well as I can make out) and doubt the Scriptures; and died at last in Ohio at the corner of a road.[44]

It is indicative that Pinkerton's teacher is portrayed as ignorant since he only knows how to photograph and to doubt the Scriptures, since that is 'all he knew himself'. Pinkerton himself refers to his tin-type days as a period of illiteracy.[45] Later, he says that he is a 'galoot about literature', a clear confession that he is a type of reader that reads incorrectly since the word 'galoot' means an idiot.[46] In fact, Pinkerton indicates how literalist photographic reading and his own materialism are related to the 'spirit' of scripture in a pun about alcoholic spirits. Pinkerton tells Loudon that 'you don't seem to catch on to business principles! The prime cost of the spirit is literally nothing'.[47] Pinkerton therefore makes Ruskin's point that the literalist who has been corrupted by photography can only see things in material, tangible terms and cannot see the spiritual, which is thought of as God-like, immaterial and intangible.

The novel attempts to distance Loudon from Pinkerton and his photographic reading. The separation between photographic, literalist reading and an interpretation of the law is developed in Dodd's concealment of a financially motivated murder by a group of men led by Norris Carthew, a member of the political elite. A group of men sailing on the *Currency Lass* are stranded and waiting for rescue. The crew of the *Flying Scud* appears, but its captain, Captain Trent, demands that 'the Currency Lasses', who are named after the ship they sailed in, give him all their wealth in return for safe passage to San Francisco.[48] One of Norris Carthew's men, a 'Currency Lass', then kills Captain Trent. There is a resulting fight in which Carthew and his men kill the whole of the crew of the *Flying Scud*. The men conceal their crime in order to prevent arrest and scandal and conceal their identities through impersonation by pretending to be the crew of the *Flying Scud*, thus losing their female identity as the 'Currency Lasses'. Carthew also vows to buy the *Flying Scud* in order to conceal the crime – and any suggestion as to their being women rather than men – forever. Carthew and the men conceal the fact that they are literally criminals and could be represented as women. In terms of being judged according to a 'literal' interpretation of law, they would be punished and their characters would be ruined. However, the novel justifies the crime and excuses it, even though Loudon finds out the truth of the matter, since Carthew is not seen as a criminal and gets away with his deception. Loudon, the hero, colludes in the concealment. The novel therefore supports a differing, non-literalist notion of law for Carthew, a member of the political elite and integrates this with the support of his masculinity over a perceived femininity which has to be rigorously excluded.

44 Robert Louis Stevenson and Lloyd Osbourne, *The Wrecker* (New York: Charles Scribner's Sons, 1895), 53.
45 Ibid., 231.
46 Ibid., 177.
47 Ibid., 128.
48 Ibid., 477, 504.

However, photography threatens to expose the crime and the men's attempts to maintain their masculinity and not be seen as the 'Currency Lasses'. Pinkerton, who is associated with the reading of photography, buys the 'wreck' of the *Flying Scud* and threatens to expose all and sundry and their deceptions to the world. The purchase of the *Flying Scud* by Pinkerton and his partner is presented as a form of commercial violence against art, since Dodd has to tear out a page of his sketch-book in order to write his intended partnership with Pinkerton in the purchase at the auction.[49] The purchase is also associated with the madness of photographic vision, in a pun playing on the connotation of speculation with vision since it is a 'mad speculation' by Pinkerton.[50] The wreck serves as an implicit metaphor for 'photographic' evidence of crime. This is because it is associated with the 'photo-graphic' miniature. It is described by Dodd as 'our miniature craft'. Dodd also writes that '[t]he dear little ship presented a horrid picture of confusion', stressing its association with denigrated images.[51] Concealment is therefore associated not just with male identity, but with the work of gendering. It is suggested that the literalism of photography can only support literalist readings of the law, a reading of the law to the letter.

The story of Dodd's artistic liberation is bound up with the concealing of the crime and the identities of Carthew and his men, his support of non-literalist law. Dodd gives protection to a member of the political elite from the literal law and maintains the masculinity of the men so that they are not seen as 'Currency Lasses'. If the purchase of the *Flying Scud* can expose identities and the crimes of the political elite through photographic 'speculation' and photography's perceived literalism in the figure of Pinkerton, with his photographic education, Dodd does not take up the opportunity. Dodd finally achieves his aim of freeing himself from Pinkerton's photographic reading and his world of commerce and materialism through his support of the deception of the political elite.

Throughout the novel, Pinkerton's literalist reading and vision threaten to overturn and master Dodd's artistic reading and vision and pit him against Carthew, the member of the political elite, through an interpretation of the law. The novel does not explicitly develop the connections between artistic viewing and reading in the figure of Dodd, but does suggest them implicitly. When Dodd visits his father's memorial, he states, 'I could now judge their taste in monuments; their taste in literature, methought, I could imagine, and I refrained from drawing near enough to read the terms of the inscription'.[52] Dodd thus asserts that he senses what sort of a reader emerges from an expression of art such as a monument. That is, as an art viewer of the moment, he can ascertain the inferior form of reading on which it is based, a reading which he avoids being part of, since it will also be evident in the writing of the inscription, from the hand of the poor readers. I have argued that Dodd is almost led by Pinkerton's acquisition of the *Flying Scud* to reveal the story of murder and put Carthew in the position of a recognised criminal, a position

49 Ibid., 186.
50 Ibid., 208.
51 Ibid., 238.
52 Ibid., 116.

against the law. It can also be seen that Dodd conceals the knowledge of the crime so that he can have a mutually beneficial friendship with the privileged, which gives him financial independence. The legitimacy of the political elite is therefore maintained in the novel through concealment and deception.

I now wish to concentrate in greater detail on the theme of reading in the novel, since the production and regulation of reading and readers is the focus of my monograph. Reading is further implicated in the way that Dodd comes to his relationship with Carthew, the way that he comes to command his support and attains status as a free aesthete. Dodd gets to Carthew and the realm of aestheticism away from Pinkerton through a reading conducted over and beyond images, that is, by ignoring or suppressing images in favour of writing, in contrast to a 'photographic reading'. Earlier on, Dodd threatens to develop a photographic reading when he associates himself with Pinkerton. As Dodd narrates, his vision became like a camera when it came to reading names and, through names, identities:

> A negative of a street scene, taken unconsciously when I was absorbed in other thoughts, rose in my memory with not a feature blurred: a view, from Bellairs's door as we were coming down, of muddy roadway, passing drays, matted telegraph wires, a Chinaboy with a basket on his head, and (almost opposite) a corner grocery with the name of Dickson in great gilt letters.[53]

However, Dodd later relinquishes the photographic reading, which sees letters as images and their external, surface appearance and sees them in terms of business, like the grocer's sign. It is this reading which figures as a path towards a relationship with Carthew and access to a situation where Dodd can live a life as an aesthete. This reading is outlined in a scene in which letters figure alongside pictures. Dodd reads individual letters on individual stamps in a Mr. Denman's stamp album and puts them together into a new whole in order to arrive at an understanding of Carthew's location. As he narrates:

> In Mr. Denman's exchanges, as in those of little Agnes, the same peculiarity was to be remarked, an undue preponderance of that despicably common stamp, the French twenty-five centimes. And here joining them in stealthy review, I found the C and the CH; then something of an A just following; and then a terminal Y. Here was almost the whole name spelled out to me; it seemed familiar, too; and yet for some time I could not bridge the imperfection. Then I came upon another stamp, in which an L was legible before the Y, and in a moment the word leaped up complete. Chailly, that was the name; Chailly-en-Biere, the post town of Barbizon—ah, there was the very place for any man to hide himself—there was the very place for Mr. Norris [Carthew], who had rambled over England making sketches—the very place for Goddedaal, who had left a palette-knife on board the *Flying Scud*.[54]

53 Ibid., 210.
54 Ibid., 420–421.

Dodd does not read the letter like a literalist. It is an imaginative reading above the individual letter. It is an inspired reconstitution. The subjects of the individual stamp, I believe, are peace and commerce personified.[55] The stamp appears to suggest Pinkerton's mix of photography and commerce, since photographs, as I have indicated in the introduction, were heavily associated with the representation of the human figure.

Dodd's non-literalist reading accords with his earlier attempt to get at the truth of the mystery around the ship through photographs when the image frustrated discovery. When searching the *Flying Scud*, Dodd is presented with a series of photographs. The photographs convey an idea of the evidence of a photographic archive, with annotated names of photographic subjects. The men are presented as the crew, with their names written as labels. However, Dodd's own recollection of the men does not tally with the individuals represented in the photograph and 'the writing of photography'. The photograph represents the disparity between names and persons and identities, reading and vision, full of unrecognisable and unidentifiable persons. It only qualifies as truth and the legal path towards unearthing the crime when it is seen as a representation of falsity and evidence of concealed identity by the artistic observer and through art, via Dodd's sketchbook. For Carthew and his crew have impersonated the members of the *Flying Scud*, which is revealed by comparing the photograph with the personal recollection of the artist and the sketchbook.

In other words, the reader of photographic writing has to ignore literal representation and interpret things in a non-literalist manner. It is the artistic viewer's interpretation of reality and persons which is trustworthy, not the literalist's. The artist, in the form of Dodd, is in the privileged position of truth. The photograph, read literally, puts false and misleading relationships between names and persons, writing and identities. In it, identities are too apparent and self-evident. However, identities, the novel shows, are concealed. It is the recognition that identities are concealed that is the mark of the artistic observer and which grants him entry to a situation as an aesthete in the novel. The photograph with apparent identities would otherwise be a barrier to the entry of aestheticism. When Dodd sees and reads photographically and literally, in a manner tied to the photograph, he cannot arrive at a solution of the mystery.[56] The photograph deceives him and misdirects him, preventing him from his union with Carthew. Dodd has to use his sketchbook and artistic vision to supplement and overtake the photograph to discover that the men in the photograph are mysterious strangers, the key to unravelling the mystery and uniting with Carthew who enables him to become an 'independent' aesthete who is untroubled by money matters. It is an art which distrusts photography and its literalism that is key to the correct reading and interpretation of the law. It is art that is the key to finding out the proper relationship between images, identities, names and persons and which leads to the political elite and their patronage of the situation of an aesthete. The artistic vision cannot see the political elite as criminals:

55 https://colnect.com/en/stamps/stamp/25495-Peace_and_commerce_Type_Sage-Peace_and_Commerce-France (last accessed 22 November 2018).

56 Ibid., 297–299.

it must legitimate them and conceal their crimes at the same time as differentiating them from women (as the Currency Lasses).

I have so far tried to show how literalism, art and the law are tied together in the novel and how Ruskin's ideas have been worked out to legitimate the political elite through the idea of concealment. Concealment and concealed identities, as they are differentiated from photographic appearance, are of paramount importance in understanding the complex that I am studying in this monograph and the legitimation of the status quo. In summary, *The Wrecker* presents photography and literalist readings as corruptions of the legal truth and the true interpretation of a law which favours the self-interest of the political elite. This reflects how Ruskin saw photography and literalism as countering the power of patriarchy in the form of kingship. *The Wrecker* alludes to literalist reading as a devaluation of spirit and actually suggests that the legally authorised identity of the political elite distinguishes them from women in the form of 'the Currency Lasses'. Thus, 'legal representation' and the non-literalist reading are both involved in the work of gendering at the same time as assigning legitimacy and authorised identities. They assign notions of right and wrong as well as male and female identity.

Conclusion

My discussion of *The Wrecker* illustrates the way that the fiction studied in this monograph was heavily influenced by Ruskin's position on artistic truth and his characterisation of photography and literalist reading. Like Ruskin, the fiction aimed to produce simultaneously artistic viewers and readers. As I aim to show, in Chapters 2 and 3 of this monograph, fiction can also be seen to model legal truth on artistic truth. In Ruskin's writings, the literal reading is seen to produce photographic truth, or the semblance of the law, an alternative to both scripture and the legal truth. The ideal reading is seen to produce legal truth and true law since it controls the interpretation of what law is: the expression of the will of the patriarchal figure and his ordering of the world, individuals, property and relationships. Such a reading, which supports power and the status quo, which is indeed understood as allowing that power to find expression, can access the hidden spirit of the law which is not accessible to 'outsiders'. In specific art criticism and fiction, the formation of law, legal truth, legal knowing and legal reading is implicated in such ideas and continuous with them. There seems to be an important conceptual triangle between art, the law and fiction which seems to have been unrecognised and which I feel deserves further, detailed attention and investigation since it has exerted such a powerful hold on the historical imagination. In the next chapter, I will elaborate how fiction uses Ruskin's ideas to further characterise the legal truth and proper reading and aim to make a path through the conceptual triangle which links together art, fiction and the law to produce art viewers, readers and, in particular, readers of the law.

2 Photography's 'fatal resemblances'

Reading the invisibility of individuality and truth in the work of Wilkie Collins

Introduction

In this chapter, I wish to show how reading is influenced by constructions of identity and legal truth which define themselves against the idea of the photographic representation of likeness or resemblance. That is, I wish to further characterise an acceptable reading which is seen as the finding of individuality in writing. The fiction I have studied utilises an individualising and atomising power over its subjects, preventing the formation of group identities and thus rival forms of power, as I will show. This is a significant area of study since the writers I look at in this monograph conflated ideas of identity and reading, so a study of the inter-relations between each of these illuminates one of the larger aims of fiction, which was to express a particular idea of individuality in writing and to control and shape readers' views on this model of personhood. Discussing this larger individualising aim of fiction, Nancy Armstrong in *How Novels Think: The Limits of Individualism from 1719-1900* (2006) has written:

> the history of the novel and the history of the modern subject are, quite literally, one and the same. The British novel provides the test case. It came into being, I believe, as writers sought to formulate a kind of subject that had not yet existed in writing. Once formulated in fiction, however, this subject proved uniquely capable of reproducing itself not only in authors but also in readers, in other novels, and across British culture in law, medicine, moral and political philosophy, biography, history and other forms of writing that took the individual as their most basic unit.[1]

This chapter analyses the depiction of reading in fiction as it emerges from the ideas of individuality and visual resemblances in the work of Wilkie Collins. In Collins' fiction, as I will show below, the idea of a photograph as a 'likeness' is challenged. That is, the photograph's visual resemblance of the individual, or its

1 Nancy Armstrong, *How Novels Think: The Limits of Individualism from 1719-1900* (Colombia: Columbia University Press, 2006), 3.

DOI: 10.4324/9781003173854-3

'likeness', is seen as inappropriate and misleading for ascertaining both individuality and legal truth. In fact, I will further contend, the photographic likeness is seen as a fraud on identity which is likened to both the murder of the individual and an act of forgery, or exploitation of their identity. Collins therefore outlines a picture of likeness as a 'fatal resemblance'.[2] This is perhaps most evident in his novel *Blind Love* (1890), where a character feigns death by falsely appearing in a photograph as a corpse so as to commit an insurance fraud. I will aim to show that in order to maintain the uniqueness of both individuality and the legal truth, Collins' fiction not only constructs them both as invisible, or hidden and concealed, but also accordingly groups the truth claims of photography with forms of truth considered superficial and literalist, such as the natural sciences, which are based on 'observation' and finding visual resemblances between things.

Drawing on previous scholarship, I will first show how Wilkie Collins' ideas about the natural sciences, photography and the law can be brought together in order to analyse his work. I will then show that the concepts of resemblances and individuality are the ones which tie together these seemingly disparate constructions in his writing. I will then establish that the depiction of acceptable reading in Collins' writing is set against the procedure of finding visual resemblances between individuals and show how precisely reading is seen as the finding of both individual identity and the legal truth, which are both seen as hidden or concealed. Finally, I will situate this reading of identity in its political context and show precisely how it interacts with the asymmetry of power in society. I will argue that this form of reading is set against the formation of truths through the finding of resemblances which are closely associated with groups and group or 'identity politics'. In contrast, I see the idea of reading Collins' work as associated with the individuating and isolating forms of 'personal politics' and their truth claims.

Wilkie Collins, truth and photography

Collins' perspective on photography, the law and truth has been investigated before and I will first set out such accounts before going on to show how my study of his work builds upon this existing knowledge. Elizabeth Anderman writes that *The Moonstone* (1868), *The Law and the Lady* (1875) and *Blind Love* (1883) 'play with the idea of the pencil of nature in order to highlight the ambiguities of representation. The photographs are novelistic details that trouble questions of identity and representation'.[3] Anderman also writes that:

2 Wilkie Collins, *The Woman in White* (London: Chatto & Windus, [1859] 1896), 389; Wilkie Collins, *Armadale* (New York: Harper & Brother Publishers, 1874), 49.

3 Elizabeth Anderman, 'No Reality Here: Sensation Novels and Photography', in *Picturing the Language of Images*, Nancy Pedri, Laurence Petit, ed. (Cambridge: Cambridge Scholars Publishing, 2014), 298.

> a second look at the references to photography reveals that they comment on the ambiguity of details and the arbitrary and constructed nature of 'truth'. The references to photography simultaneously obscure and reveal the central mysteries; they destabilize ideas of truth and normality by playing with anonymity.[4]

Anderman notes that in the work of Collins, '[t]he photograph is a symbol of the natural sciences, which does not necessarily show the details of life but destroys them by reducing them to their composite parts'.[5]

Anderman's account is useful, particularly in the way that she sees photography in Collins' fiction as paired with natural science and the loss of identity in terms of anonymity. However, she does not consider the relationship between the law, reading and photography in the work of Collins, nor does she touch on the importance of resemblance in his references to photography. I see the interrelationships between these concepts as crucial to the meaning of Collins' work. As I will argue in this chapter, it is not the threat of anonymity that conveys the idea of a loss of identity via photography, but rather that of the individual being made to resemble a double that is out to usurp and exploit his or her identity. In the novel *Blind Love* which I have mentioned above, for instance, the sham presentation of death in the photograph by the character Lord Harry is the culmination of a photographic scheme to substitute a bodily double for himself in the insurance fraud.

Robert Dingley has argued that ideas of the legal truth contend with ideas of photographic truth in Collins' work, writing that Collins' novel *Blind Love* aims to discredit photographic evidence.[6] Dingley also suggests that in:

> Collins' almost exemplary rejection of photographic testimony, realistic fiction seeks to identify and define its own superior epistemology by contrast to distance its own purchase on truth from that of mechanical reproduction.[7]

I follow and build on Dingley's idea that fiction was invested in showing that its truth was very different to the truth of photography, however, contrary to Dingley, I aim to show that fiction cultivated its truth status by a focus on acceptable forms of reading. Furthermore, I suggest that Dingley is silent on the association of the photographic with the analytical processes of natural history in Collins' work, depictions of individuality and resemblances which appear to me to be significantly inter-related. I see Collins as bolstering the claims of the law and legal truth in relation to those of natural history and science and argue that this distinguishes

4 Ibid., 299.

5 Ibid., 303.

6 Robert Dingley, 'The Unreliable Camera: Photography as Evidence in Mid-Victorian Fiction', *Victorian Review*, 27:2 (2001), 46.

7 Ibid., 49.

not only the character and form of the law but also the reading of it that is promoted.[8]

Wilkie Collins' constructions of reading and individuality in his work rely on photography's assumed coupling with science. His work is particularly worthy of analysis and revealing of the construction of legal truth in fiction because I am positing, as part of my interpretation, that he is acting as a member of an unofficial and non-formalised group which accepts and validates a certain type of truth and therefore his work reflects a group identity and perspective of these types of 'knowers'. Certainly, at the time Collins was writing, photography was used in scientific circles as evidence. As Jennifer Tucker has noted, although the public circulation of scientific photographs 'was smaller than that of other types of photographs (portraits, for example,), scientific pictures had a disproportionate hold on people's concept of what photography was'.[9] The reasons why are clear in Collins' work as I aim to show. He saw photography as the occupation of a detached, anti-social and inhumane scientist. Collins exaggerated the coupling of photography and science in order to denounce both as inferior forms of truth that threatened the legal truth. Thus, he could amplify the threat of these combined forms of truth and see them as fundamentally corrosive of the legal identity of the English.

As I will argue below, Collins united ideas of both legal knowledge and artistic discrimination in constructing a response to photography. He thus relied on intellectual currents in art and art criticism which aimed at marginalising the sciences and photography in relation to art's own 'truth' or truth-telling authority. Such ideas are in evidence in the reactions to the early introduction of photographic illustration in scientific books. The pioneers who did use photography in scientific publications were criticised for lacking taste and discrimination. When

8 I will briefly mention that I am approaching the subject of false and illegitimate doubling in relation to photography in Collins' work. My ideas are distinguished from previous research in this area because of the focus on photography and its relationship to the law. For an analysis of Collins' double in terms of the representation of women and 'female identity', see Nathalie Abi-Ezzi, *The Double in the Fiction of R. L. Stevenson, Wilkie Collins and Daphne Du Maurier* (Bern: Peter Lang, 2003). She sees Collins' doubles as subversive of patriarchal truth but does not investigate representations of truth in his work in detail. Other critics have analysed individual novels such as *Poor Miss Finch* and *The Woman in White* in terms of twins, doubles, likeness and difference. Irene Tucker sees anatomical science as informing the investigation of bodily likeness through the sickness of women in *The Woman in White*. She usefully notes that a limit on the observation of the opaque internal body influences Collins' thinking. Irene Tucker, 'Paranoid Imagining: Wilkie Collins, the Rugeley Poisoner, and the Invisibility of Novelistic Exphrasis,' in Irene Tucker, *The Moment of Racial Sight: A History* (Chicago and London: The University of Chicago Press, 2012), 75–118. Wieland Schwanebeck notes how scientific ideas of twins and hereditary influenced *Poor Miss Finch* and the larger 'binary sense-making operations' of detective or detective-like novels in the period. Wieland Schwanebeck, "It's Never Twins?'—It's Always Twins: *The Notting Hill Mystery* (1865) and the Specter of Twinship in Early Detective Fiction', *CLUES: A Journal of Detection*, 36: 1 (Spring 2018), 58–68.

9 Jennifer Tucker, *Nature Exposed: Photography as Eyewitness in Victorian Science* (Baltimore: The John Hopkins University Press, 2005), 8.

Charles Darwin published *The Expression of the Emotions in Man and Animals* in 1872, with an 'unprecedented' inclusion of 'real' photographs in a popular scientific book,[10] reviewers questioned his choice of illustrating the book with photographs as opposed to works of art. The anonymous reviewer in the *Athenaeum*, speaking of the staged photographs by Oscar Rejlander, compared the photographs critically with art, of which he assumes Darwin has 'imperfect knowledge':

> Mr. Darwin declares that painters can hardly portray suspicion, jealousy, envy, &c., except by the aid of accessories which tell the tale. Surely this is a mistake, due to an imperfect knowledge of what Art has done. Painting, it is not too much to say, can do whatever acting can; and that acting can satisfy our author and produce what he considers satisfactory illustrations of the emotions, is shown by his liking for Mr. Rejlander, who, as Mr. Darwin expressly says, 'acted' the required emotions, or got others to act them.[11]

The photographic 'performances' are, in the reviewer's opinion, 'almost sure to mislead anyone who puts much faith in them'.[12] As he states, echoing the previous criticism of Rejlander's art-photography work as non-artistic: 'These photographs are sufficient to illustrate Mr. Darwin's meaning; but they have no higher value'.[13] It is the fine arts that are able to remedy the lack in the photograph, the reviewer argues. They are considered to be a much better source for the illustrations of emotional expression. Ideas of interpretation and visual literacy are implicit in such constructions. As Jonathan Smith comments, the reviewer's perception of Darwin is that '[h]is reliance on photography and acting – and bad acting at that – exposed his visual illiteracy, his lack of aesthetic refinement and taste'.[14] The construction of Darwin the scientist as an outsider to the visual order of art indicates that there is a community of insiders who realise 'what Art has done' and who have access to the 'truth' in art to which the outsider does not have access.

As in the courtroom and policing, photography was increasingly accepted in scientific circles as a matter of practice as the nineteenth century progressed, although even in such disciplines, in areas such as botanical illustration, the dominance of art and of painting remained unchallenged. However, works of fiction at the time that Collins was writing exclude the eye of science and photography in order to ensure that the importance of culture to understandings of vision and the self remained dominant and unchallenged. In the short story by M. D. Conway, 'My Lost Art' (1862), a man goes insane when he takes daguerreotypes of Jupiter, magnifies them and then begins to believe that he sees men residing on the planet.

10 Phillip Prodger, s.v. 'Darwin, Charles Robert', in John Hannavy (ED), *Encyclopedia of Nineteenth Century Photography* (Taylor & Francis: New York and London, 2008).

11 Anonymous, 'The Expression of the Emotions in Man and the Animals', *The Athenaeum*, 2351 (16 November 1872), 632.

12 Ibid., 632.

13 Ibid.

14 Jonathan Smith, *Charles Darwin and Victorian Visual Culture* (Cambridge: Cambridge University Press, 2006), 229.

It is indicative that the vision of the heavenly body proceeds from a form of minute and reductive photographic reading which is exercised on the planet through a magnifying process.[15] The process also aims to make visible that which is 'invisible' to the naked eye. Photography here, as a form of looking which ultimately leads to madness, intrudes on the invisible and heavenly realm to divest it of religious meaning. Similarly, Collins saw real individuality as invisible and concealed and therefore saw a photographic representation of it as fraudulent (and mad – see my discussion of the mad Dexter's collection of scientific photographs in *The Law and The Lady* (1875) below).

Wilkie Collins exploited the coupling of photography and science to manufacture representations of individuality, the legal truth and reading in his fiction. As I will show, he did so by denouncing the ability of the photograph to represent or find likenesses or resemblances.

Individuality, the identity photograph and the law

Since I am investigating the constructions of individuality and identity in relation to photography in this chapter, ideas of the identity photograph are relevant to my analysis and figure in each of Collins' works I study. I therefore first wish to introduce existing scholarship on the identity photograph, so that I can demonstrate how I am building and extending existing scholarship on the representation of the identity photograph in fiction. I then wish to contextualise Collins' writings by showing what relationship identity photographs have to larger thought and law in the period so that his writings can be seen as integrated with a larger understanding of the relationship between photography and the self.

The Victorian identity photograph has been studied by a number of scholars. In her introduction to the historical status of the 'identity photograph', Karen Strassler outlines the general tenor of thought on the subject.[16] She writes that studies 'have typically focused […] on its use as a technology of power and surveillance. Rarely the object of study in its own right, the identity photograph's history tends to be subsumed within accounts of the optic technologies of modern states and their archival regimes'.[17] Strassler locates the work of John Tagg and Alan Sekula on the identity photograph within this general framework. She notes that Tagg associates the identity photograph with an emergent modality of ruling which is characterised by a 'proliferating system of documentation' that generated 'new forms of knowledge about state subjects',[18] while Sekula sees 'the broader archival imagining of society in the late nineteenth century'[19] achieved through 'honorific'

15 M. D. Conway, 'My Lost Art', *The Atlantic Monthly* 10 (1862), 230–231.

16 Karen Strassler, 'Ethnography and the National Identity Photograph', in Tanya Sheehan (ed), *Photography, History, Difference* (Lebanon, NH: Dartmouth College Press, 2014), 151–171.

17 Ibid., 163.

18 John Tagg, *The Burden of Representation: Essays on Photographies and Histories* (Amherst: University of Massachusetts Press, 1988), 63–64; see also John Tagg, *The Disciplinary Frame: Photographic Truths and the Capture of Meaning* (Minneapolis: University of Minnesota Press, 2009), esp. Chapter 1.

19 Strassler (n 16) 163.

and 'repressive' modes of portraiture.[20] Strassler points out how repetitively and reductively this association between the identity photograph and repressive power is made. Thus scholarship sees the identity photograph 'a means for identifying and controlling those 'others' – the criminal, the insane, the poor, the colonized – deemed dangerous and unruly by the state'.[21] The identity photograph is seen as implicated in the construction of 'order' and ordering practices as well as 'the truth'. In studies of colonialism, for example, the identity photograph is illustrative of the 'enumerative and classificatory' rationality of colonial regimes,[22] their dehumanising gaze toward the colonized, and the construction of a positivist 'regime of photographic truth'[23] to which subjects submit.

Like Strassler, I am sceptical of these accounts of how the Victorian identity photograph was used because I have seen fiction, like that of Collins, as challenging the equation of photography with individuality and identity. In fact, recent scholarship has begun to challenge the existing picture. Significantly, work on the interaction between Victorian fiction and photography has also been a recent challenger of the monolithic picture painted. Thus, Daniel Novak notes that in some fiction, photographs were understood to be interchangeable and that in 'A Counterfeit Presentiment' (1858) in *Household Words* a literary celebrity was told that he could substitute his own picture with that of another person under his name. This leads him to state that:

> while a variety of critics have powerfully addressed how photography's association with realism helped to define criminality, gender identity, and even national identity, the fact that the Victorians thought of photography as a medium with the potential to efface particularity and individuality severely complicates our understanding of realism's political mobilization.[24]

In my readings of his novels, I will aim to show that, as in 'A Counterfeit Presentiment', Collins consistently saw photographs as interchangeable representations of individuals such as in *Blind Love,* which I have mentioned above, or *The Woman in White,* where the photograph was associated with substituting one character's identity for another. Furthermore, he denounced photography because he saw this interchangeability as illegitimate: he linked it with insurance fraud in *Blind Love.* I will thus build on Novak's point to show in particular how Wilkie Collins saw the photograph as effacing individual identity because of its very representation of likeness and show how he built his own constructions of identity and reading about it. However, it is important to emphasise the point that Novak makes, that Collins is to be seen as part of a larger grouping of individuals.

20 Allan Sekula, 'The Body and the Archive', *October* 39 (1986): 3–64.

21 Strassler (n 16) 163.

22 Ibid., 163.

23 Jean-François Werner, 'Photography and Industrialization in Contemporary Africa: An Ivoirian Case-Study,' *Visual Anthropology*, 14 (2001), 251–268.

24 Daniel A. Novak, *Realism, Photography, and Nineteenth-Century Fiction* (Cambridge: Cambridge University Press, 2008), 5.

As I will aim to show, Collins saw the photograph's effacement of identity as illegitimate, a subversion of legal truth. Collins was exploiting underlying currents in legal thought in the construction of his fiction. It is hardly coincidental that the inability of the photograph to bear identity is evident in legal constructions too. In the 1895 case of *Frith v Frith and Paice*, a photograph of a divorce petitioner's wife was not admitted. It was stated by the judge that in matrimonial cases, except under very special circumstances, the Court will not act upon identification by a photograph only. [25] The legal wariness of investing identity in the photograph is also evident earlier in the reporting of a case from 1879 in the *Central Law Journal* from an account in *The Law Times*. In the trial of a prisoner at the last Middlesex Sessions, the indictment contained an allegation of a previous conviction for felony, and in support of that allegation, evidence was received of a photograph taken, as it was alleged, of the prisoner whilst undergoing his previous sentence. As the report states:

> This photograph was submitted to the jury, but as it represented him without moustaches, which he now had, they had considerable doubt as to his identity, but when the foreman asked the prisoner to stand facing them, they were satisfied, and they immediately returned a verdict that he was the same man.[26]

The report goes on to state that the admission of a photograph under such circumstances appears to be a novelty, and 'one which may lead to serious and untoward consequences. It is certainly a new class of evidence, and one, the admission of which deserves very mature consideration'.[27]

Thus, I argue, Collins work is to be seen not as an individual interpretation of the dissonance between individuality, identity and photography, but as the affirmation of a shared set of beliefs regarding the relationships between them. His work, as I will show, is thus a rich source of material about individuality but also how reading is constructed out of the proposition that likeness cannot represent personhood. In particular, I will aim to demonstrate towards the end of this chapter that Collins is a particularly rich source of material regarding the political implications of the individualising forms of reading that he intended his readers to take up.

The relationship between scientific photography and the murder of the individual: copying and 'fatal resemblances'

As I will show, in many of his novels, as in *Blind Love* which I have briefly introduced above, the attribute that Wilkie Collins most associated with photography was its ability to render likenesses, or to represent a resemblance to the individual. Collins saw the photographic likeness as effacing identity. I contend that Collins' fiction criticised photography as the bearer of resemblances in order to contest the

25 *Frith v Frith and Paice*. The Law Reports of the Incorporated Council of Law Reporting: Courts of Probate, Divorce, and Admiralty, and on Appeal Therefrom in the Court of Appeal; Also Decisions in the Ecclesiastical Courts. 74. Probate Division. 19 Dec. 1895. Print.

26 2, *Central Law Journal* (16 July 1875), 462.

27 Ibid.

status of photography as an alternative form of representation. That is, he attempted to counter what he saw as the strongest attribute of photography and to suggest that this aspect of the form of representation was itself illegitimate by enlisting the help of ideas of the law. Collins' fiction is constructed in such a way as to demonstrate that photographic resemblance could never represent individuality. I wish to demonstrate how and why the representation of resemblances was depicted as contrary to both the law and to claims of what constituted a unique and specific identity, particularly through ideas of the scientific photograph. I will do so through a reading of details concerning photography in *Armadale* (1866), since a key theme of the novel is the idea of resemblance and how it troubles individuality and because it features scientific photography in what I see as a particularly significant detail. I discuss this novel not because it features or concentrates on the representation of photography at any great length (photography instead features through significant details), but because I believe a reading of it allows a linking of the way actual or nominal resemblances are conceptually linked to photography. Setting out Collins' ideas on these topics will allow me to argue in the following sections of the chapter that Collins' ideas about photographic likeness or resemblance significantly influenced his constructions of the ideas of identity, reading, truth and the law which he depicted as counter-forms to what he saw as the photographic representation and its representation of individuality.

I want to first establish how photography is understood as related to the illegitimate representation of resemblances in *Armadale*. The denouncement of photography in Collins' fiction relies on the fact that the photograph was seen as a likeness or a resemblance of the individual. Furthermore, Collins, as I will show, particularly criticised the scientific photograph which he saw as finding resemblances between groups of people. In accordance with these ideas *Armadale* suggests implicit associations between photography as a depiction of likeness or resemblance and forgery as an attempt at resembling individuality in writing which work together to harm what is understood as a unique and truly individual identity. The female villain, Lydia Gwilt, is first introduced as a copyist, or a forger.[28] That is, she assumes someone else's identity in writing to imitate or resemble her and presents the copy and the imitation as valid. Finding resemblance and promoting resemblances in a form of representation such as writing in order to exploit them is itself seen as a fundamentally illegitimate act. Furthermore, Lydia's forging of a letter furthers a scheme on the part of a certain Inglesby to exploit the name Allan Armadale which resembles that of another man, to the detriment of that Allan Armadale. Because of the forgery, and Lydia's use of resemblances, Inglesby marries the woman who has been promised to the other Armadale through an illegitimate use of resemblances. That is, Lydia not only commits a fraud on identity herself, by assuming the identity of another, but she provides invaluable assistance in another fraud on identity, a fraud which harms the original who is resembled and imitated. Resemblance and imitation is thus seen to lead to the injury of the one that is imitated. By imitating or attempting to resemble a person, Collins suggests, something is taken away from

28 Collins, *Armadale* (n 2), 31.

that person: their fundamental rights are open to usurpation. The finding and exploiting of resemblances between individuals threatens their identity. This idea is a constant in each of his novels.

Lydia herself is described as having an 'imitative dexterity' that is also described as 'wicked'.[29] Imitation is thus presented as illegitimate and sinful. What is worth emphasising is that Lydia's attempt at resembling the identity of another relies on visual resemblances: her writing has to visually resemble that of her victim's. This is why it is particularly visual resemblances that are seen as problematic and why, as I will show below, photographic representation, which takes likenesses or resemblances, is also problematised in the novel and seen as opposed to the true representation of identity.

Like photography, it is implied that Lydia the forger takes over the identity of an individual and exploits it on the basis of likeness or visual resemblance. In fact, Collins can be seen to implicitly associate photography and the forger, because he characterises them in the same terms. Significantly, Lydia is described thus: 'No creature more innately deceitful and more innately pitiless ever walked this earth'.[30] It is this lack of pity which also characterises photography. Collins says of a young woman called Miss Milroy, that:

> The dreadful justice of photography would have had no mercy on her; and the sculptors of classical Greece would have bowed her regretfully out of their studios. Admitting all this, and more, the girdle round Miss Milroy's waist was the girdle of Venus nevertheless; and the pass-key that opens the general heart was the key she carried, if ever a girl possessed it yet. Before Allan had picked up his second handful of flowers, Allan was in love with her.[31]

The pitiless justice of photography is therefore unable to represent Miss Milroy the individual, who is described as being beautiful in real life. Just like photography, in fact, Lydia sees Miss Milroy as having faults and she criticises her appearance which she explicitly measures against her own, saying that:

> Am I handsome enough, to-day? Well, yes; handsome enough to be a match for a little dowdy, awkward, freckled creature, who ought to be perched on a form at school, and strapped to a backboard to straighten her crooked shoulders.[32]

Therefore, the forger and photography are not only described in the same terms, but also both see individuals in the same way, mercilessly. They are united in their lack of compassion and human feeling and their emphasis on visual appearances.

What is important for the purposes of my analysis is to show how the forger and photography are consistently tied to an idea of murder in the novel. That is, forgery

29 Ibid., 31.
30 Ibid.
31 Ibid., 173.
32 Ibid., 420.

and photography are associated with the active killing of the individual, since Lydia is not only a forger but heavily suggested by Collins to be a prior murderer (who has escaped conviction) and whose murder attempt on the hero is foiled. Thus, photography and the finding of likenesses and resemblances can be seen as an intended obliteration of the individual. In order to pursue this current in the novel, I first suggest that 'the dreadful justice of photography' in the above quote works through implying an idea of execution, or rather, murder, which is particularly suggested by the adjective 'dreadful'. I argue that this is the case, because photography was frequently associated with the idea of execution. Daniel Novak writes that 'some critics have noted that Victorian journalism often relied on gothic tropes of torture, execution, and the 'black arts' in order to represent the process of photography'.[33] For instance, in an article on the subject of photography in the popular journal, *Household Words* in 1853, a photographer says of his photographic portraits that 'they have all been executed here. If you mount farther up you also may be taken'.[34] In *Armadale*, because the justice of photography is dreadful and merciless, it appears to be illegitimate, although it pretends to be the law. The idea that is invoked is that this illegitimacy is because of a literalist reading of the law, a mechanical application of a punishment. Mercy is something that changes the severe adherence to the letter of the law and supplies another punishment or even leniency. What is worth noting is that Lydia also intends the execution of Miss Milroy in the same way that photography itself does. Lydia states that 'Half the musical girls in England ought to have their fingers chopped off in the interests of society, and, if I had my way, Miss Milroy's fingers should be executed first'.[35] Photography and Lydia are both seen as the representative of a pitiless law associated with literalist reading.

This relationship between photography and illegitimate execution is echoed later. Towards the end of the novel, Collins aims to show that forgery or copying and the exploitation of visual resemblances leads to a murder of the individual since Lydia plots to kill Armadale. The murder is itself part of a plan to exploit resemblances and it can thus be seen how the idea of resemblances between individuals is again seen, as in the beginning of the novel, as introducing chaos into society and the law and also how Collins ties it to photography. Lydia has married the son of Inglesby, who also shares the name Allan Armadale but has taken the assumed name of Ozias Midwinter instead. Lydia wishes to murder the Armadale that is not her husband so that she can subsequently exploit the resemblances in the shared name to suggest that as Mrs. Allan Armadale she was married to him so that she can become rich. The key motivation of the plan of murder is to find and exploit resemblances between individuals. As Collins stated towards the beginning of the novel, resemblances are seen as 'fatal' to identity and understood in terms of the murder of the individual:

33 Novak (n 24) 38.

34 Anonymous, 'Photography,' *Household Words*, VII (19 March 1853), 55.

35 Wilkie Collins, *Armadale* (n 2), 285.

> Again, in the second generation, there are two Allan Armadales as there were in the first. After working its deadly mischief with the fathers, the fatal resemblance of names has descended to work its deadly mischief with the sons.[36]

The intended murder is presented as the logical outcome of the exploitation of resemblances between the individual and others in a way that does away with that individual's specificity and uniqueness. The point that Collins seems to be making is that the act of finding resemblances between individuals exploits individuals without paying due respect to their individuality. Finding resemblances and likenesses and presenting them, like photography, is seen to obliterate what is unique about the individual. The imitative art of photography is furthermore seen as an illegitimate exploitation of individuality. Collins therefore denounced what he saw as the key attribute of photography: its ability to represent resemblance or likeness. He used the law and ideas of heinous crime and murder to cast it as illegitimate.

In fact, a telling detail reveals a further intention behind Lydia's plan. Lydia herself is described as someone who lacks true individuality precisely because she resembles other individuals. Lydia is said to resemble all other criminal women and 'liars' by a lawyer in the novel and only has a 'surface' individuality. As he states,

> Whatever other difference there might be among them, I got, in time, to notice, among those who were particularly wicked and unquestionably guilty, one point in which they all resembled each other. Tall and short, old and young, handsome and ugly, they all had a secret self-possession that nothing could shake. On the surface they were as different as possible. Some of them were in a state of indignation; some of them were drowned in tears; some of them were full of pious confidence; and some of them were resolved to commit suicide before the night was out. But only put your finger suddenly on the weak point in the story told by any one of them, and there was an end of her rage, or her tears, or her piety, or her despair; and out came the genuine woman, in full possession of all her resources, with a neat little lie that exactly suited the circumstances of the case.[37]

Lydia herself then lacks what is considered to be truly individual: what is perceived of as unique, special, rare. She reveals this precisely in the course of expressing human emotion through tears, showing that she lacks real humanity. Lydia's finding and exploiting of resemblances therefore has to be seen as an expression of her personhood and her attempt to fashion the world in her own image, a world in which there is no individuality. It is significant that she herself will be known as Mrs. Allan Armadale. As in her forgery of the letter, through mere resemblance to the individual, she will effectively assume his identity, despite not having any real individuality herself.

It is here that one can see, in a significant detail, how photography, science and confused resemblances between individuals form a conceptual triangle which is

36 Ibid., 49.
37 Ibid., 363.

the culmination of Lydia's finding and promoting of resemblances and her murderous impulses. The detail, I argue, is to be seen in the light of the novel's concentration on the idea of resemblance and also in relation to Collins' other representations of scientific photography, such as the detail that the mad Dexter in *The Law and the Lady* (1875) is characterised by keeping a similar collection of photographs. That detail formed an important component of Elizabeth Anderman's research. As she writes, the mad villain of the piece, Dexter, keeps scientific photographs of the mad, seeing a resemblance between people whose states of mind are beyond surface appearance of portraiture and whose portrayal cannot be generalised.[38] Anderman notes that the photographs are examples of human anatomy too and represent the analytic disciplines of dissection and the natural sciences, particularly as they are displayed alongside horrifying human skeletons and human skins.[39] Anderman writes that they could refer to Dexter's madness because the mad in the photographs reflect his madness.[40] I agree and suggest that in this detail, too, the idea of visual resemblances is a working out and representation of the organisation of Dexter's mind. Dexter sees in terms of visual resemblances between individuals. To him, the heroine Valeria resembles the first wife of her husband whose suicide letter Dexter attempted to destroy, leading to the legally indeterminate status of her husband's guilt in her death.[41]

In *Armadale*, the scientific photography is kept by Doctor Downward, the supervisor of a lunatic asylum, who suggests the details of the murder. Collins describes the collection of the Doctor's scientific photographs in his private surgery in the following terms:

> Above the fire-place hung a collection of photographic portraits of men and women, inclosed [sic] in two large frames hanging side by side with a space between them. The left-hand frame illustrated the effects of nervous suffering as seen in the face; the right-hand frame exhibited the ravages of insanity from the same point of view; while the space between was occupied by an elegantly illuminated scroll, bearing inscribed on it the time-honored motto, 'Prevention is better than Cure'.[42]

The scientific photographs represent individuals as they appear to resemble each other. The individuals are seen as representatives of type and disease rather than personality. Scientific photography, it is emphasised, is reductively the representation of resemblances between individuals. Furthermore, scientific photography attempts to represent hidden or otherwise invisible mental states in the form of the body. It attempts to make visible what is invisible and at the core of identity and to conceptualise it in terms of visual resemblances, which seems reductive and false. What is most worrying is that mental states are seen to be shared across a group and

38 Ibid., 253.
39 Anderman (n 3) 305.
40 Ibid., 306.
41 Ibid., 219.
42 Ibid., 578.

to resemble one another so that the uniqueness and specificity of individual thought is lost. Individuals are thus represented in the scientific photograph, and grouped together in terms of visual resemblances, but they lose their individual identity which is made up of invisible and unique thought. The photograph purports to render as external what is internal and integral but it is seen as unable to convey it and as a false representation of personhood. In the photographs, individuals are exploited in order to present the idea that there is no identity outside of resemblance to others. The scientific photograph is the externalisation of the minds of both Doctor Downward and Lydia because they join forces to attempt murder on the hero. That is, the scientific photograph is associated with both the man of science who suggests the means of murder to Lydia through a chemicals and poisonous gas and Lydia the forger who actually uses the chemistry to attempt the murder in actuality. Of course, photography itself was associated with chemistry, too. Thus, Lydia is the agent who carries out the scientific murder, Doctor Downward as the man of science is the mind behind the scientific murder, the cold planner. Because the scientific photograph represents resemblances, it is seen as an illegitimate template to impose on reality and individuals, an illegitimate organisation of people and society.

The link between scientific photography, the murder of individuality and resemblances is maintained throughout Collins' works and can be seen to figure in his last novel, *Blind Love* (1890). Dr Vimpany, the villain, convinces the Irishman Lord Harry to leave aside his newspaper business, and to participate instead in an insurance fraud which involves photography. In his capacity as a doctor, with a stress on his standing in the world of science, Dr Vimpany then acquires a sickly body double or 'likeness' of Lord Harry and attempts to confuse the identity of the one with the other, to make the world submit to a 'fatal resemblance'. When the likeness between the two men disappears as the health of the body double unexpectedly improves, Dr Vimpany kills and buries the body double, Oxbye. He then stages a deathbed photograph of Lord Harry to represent the death (or to 'murder' the individual) in order to perpetrate the fraud on the insurance office. It is significant that the dead man, Oxbye, who Dr Vimpany first attempted to exploit, is, among other things, a copyist, a mere imitator (indeed, his occupations are said to lead to his malady).[43] The idea of a photographic fraud on identity is linked to an implicit idea of forgery and the forger.

Constructing a reading of individuality and legal truth against the threat of resemblance

I have aimed to show that for Collins, then, the very fact that photography represented a likeness or resemblance of the individual was seen as illegitimate because he saw it as promoting a notion of selfhood which he did not agree with and which he saw as opposed to the concept of individuality. Collins thought that individuality was unique, specific and original, as well as invisible or hidden. He

43 Wilkie Collins, *Blind Love* (Piccadilly: Chatto & Windus [1888] 1890), 206.

therefore aimed to show that a photographic copy of individuality which claimed to represent an individual and his or her character, and his or her internal and hidden states of mind was not only impossible but an assault and misrepresentation of individuality. I now wish to show how Collins used such ideas to construct an idea of reading. Collins, as I will aim to show, explicitly saw and emphasised the fact that reading was the finding of identity or individuality and also that reading in itself demonstrated the legitimate identity of the reader. Collins' work therefore illuminates how and why the authors I have studied consistently connected reading with identity and were afraid of the ways that photography could transform the identity of readers. Collins, as I will demonstrate, appeared to construct reading as the finding of identities – either those that were legitimate and were to provide models for the self, or those that were illegitimate and were to be excluded.

In *The Woman in White* (1860) the finding of identity through reading is set against a context of threatening photographic resemblances which confuse and harm ideas of individuality and identity. I will therefore first establish this context of resemblances before outlining how the finding of individuality is set in relation to it. The most obvious example of the threat of resemblance is that Count Fosco who, along with Laura Fairlie's husband, Percival Glyde, aims to exploit visual resemblances between Laura and her double, Anne Catherick. Laura's consignment to the status of 'living image' through 'fatal resemblance' is figured as a symbolic death, since Anne dies in Count Fosco's captivity and Laura is forced to take the place of the deceased woman.[44] Laura seems to be 'put to death' by Count Fosco's vision which finds and exploits resemblances. This vision, while pretending to point out identity, seems to kill the subject rather than to represent her. This is why it is a 'fatal resemblance'. Count Fosco represents the scientific vision since he is a chemist who dabbles in medicine and has been able to preserve a body after death. When Marian falls sick, he boasts of his 'vast knowledge of chemistry, and [his] luminous experience of the more subtle resources which medical and magnetic science have placed at the disposal of mankind'.[45]

Photography is not only implicitly alluded to, but also explicitly connected with the man of science's fraud on identity. Laura's uncle, Mr Fairlie, is described as creating photographic copies:

> His last caprice has led him to keep two photographers incessantly employed in producing sun-pictures of all the treasures and curiosities in his possession. One complete copy of the collection of the photographs is to be presented to the Mechanics' Institution of Carlisle, mounted on the finest cardboard, with ostentatious red-letter inscriptions underneath.[46]

Through photographic resemblance, Frederick Fairlie's photographic copies of art seem to confuse the distinctions between photography and art, the copy and the original, the true and the alternative. The corruption between copy and original is

44 Wilkie Collins, *The Woman in White* (London: Chatto & Windus [1859] 1896), 389.
45 Ibid., 301.
46 Ibid., 175.

itself presented as an advantage. For example, the photographic copy of the Rembrandt etching is a copy that celebrates another copy which is distinguished by a printer's blot and even named after it, to the disadvantage of the unknown and anonymous subject matter.[47] It is thus the alternative that is given special status, not the true, just as Laura's individuality is replaced by the identity of Anne. This confusion between art and its copies and their relative artistic merits is experienced at a linguistic level by Mr Fairlie himself, as he writes:

> At the end of June, or the beginning of July, then, I was reclining in my customary state, surrounded by the various objects of Art which I have collected about me to improve the taste of the barbarous people in my neighbourhood. That is to say, I had the photographs of my pictures, and prints, and coins, and so forth, all about me, which I intend, one of these days, to present (the photographs, I mean, if the clumsy English language will let me mean anything) to present to the institution at Carlisle (horrid place!), with a view to improving the tastes of the members (Goths and Vandals to a man).[48]

Mr Fairlie's photographic ambitions are such: his merging of art and photograph, copy and original, his intention to educate the public through photographs, which are implied to be 'false copies', without the spirit of the originals. Such photographic ambitions form a continuum between him and the villains of the piece, whose plan is to put Laura in the place of her likeness, making use of the resemblance between the two. Indeed, photographic reproductions of art provide the backdrop to the events that will subsequently emerge. It is in such a setting that Mr Fairlie refuses to exert himself in his capacity as Laura's legal guardian, despite promptings from Marian and his lawyer. It is against the background of photographic reproductions that Mr Fairlie passively allows the actor Count Fosco and the impersonator Percival Glyde to carry out their sinister machinations of swapping Laura's identity with her likeness and consigning her to existence as the 'living image' which Walter had feared so much. Again, it is this setting of photographic reproductions of art which sees Laura turned away from her own home as an imposter, as reality is confused with deception. Count Fosco and Frederick Fairlie negotiate and determine the conditions of the photographic substitution of Laura for Anne in the room surrounded by the photographic copies of artworks.

I have thus established the context of threatening resemblances in the novel in relation to which determinations of identity and truth through reading can be situated. I now wish to examine how reading and the finding of the truth of identity is conditioned by this context of resemblances. In the novel, the artist-hero, Walter Hartright, representative of the masculine, idealised visual community, acts out of 'the motive of serving the cause of Laura and the cause of Truth' in order to destroy the photographic system of fatal resemblances which results in an alternative, unacceptable form of legal identity and legal truth.[49] The legal truth is that which

47 Ibid.
48 Ibid., 303.
49 Ibid., 534.

determines which identities are valid or legitimate and those which are illegitimate. Thus, Laura, who is the 'original' in the photographic fraud on identity is a legitimate individual, because she is herself, while Anne, her double, is illegitimate, not only because she is presented as Laura, but also because she is actually a child born out of wedlock. The ending of the novel restores the victim of the photographic conspiracy against 'Truth' in the form of fatal resemblance, Laura, to recognition in her birthplace. As I will show, Walter's finding of the truth of identity and the finding of legal truth is conducted through a form of reading which is set against the idea of resemblance and accordingly organised and conditioned by the ideas of resemblance.

First, however, I want to show how the photographic image of Anne Catherick and its resemblance is itself constructed as a threat to reading, that is, reading as the finding of individuality. This is because it is important to show that ideas of acceptable reading in Collins' work respond and react to the threat of photographic resemblance directly. That this is the case is evident in the scene where Walter tells Marian Halcombe of his moonlit adventure where he met Anne for the first time and enlists her help in understanding the encounter. The two turn to a letter in order to find out the identity of the mysterious woman. But in the drawing-room as Marian and the drawing master read through a letter in an attempt to rehabilitate the mystery of the woman in white, the photographic image constantly insists and intrudes in order to silence the reading and the attempt to reconcile the image into familiarity with the word. Both Marian and Walter see Laura Fairlie passing and repassing the opening on to the terrace – a glass door frame – walking slowly from end to end of the terrace monochromatically in the full radiance of the moon in her white muslin dress. Marian halts her reading on the appearance of Laura and only resumes it when she is out of sight. When Walter and Marian at last realise that they are confronted by a photographic likeness, a 'living image', Marian drops the letter, abandoning her role as a reader. At this, Walter's reaction turns quickly to one of fear and foreboding. He tells Marian of the likeness between Laura and the woman in white:

> I see it—more unwillingly than I can say. To associate that forlorn, friendless, lost woman, even by an accidental likeness only, with Miss Fairlie, seems like casting a shadow on the future of the bright creature who stands looking at us now. Let me lose the impression again as soon as possible. Call her in, out of the dreary moonlight—pray call her in![50]

Walter's practical response to the photographic image and its substitution of reality through likeness or resemblance is to try to exclude it and Marian is surprised at his superstitious fears which seem out of keeping with the times and modernity. However, the course of the novel is to suggest that Walter's reactions, those of a drawing master whose father was a drawing master and who therefore represents a

50 Ibid., 50.

long-standing patriarchal, artistic tradition, are justified. Resemblance is seen as a fundamental threat to reading.

Having shown that likeness or resemblance is explicitly shown as being a direct threat to reading in the novel, I want to show how an acceptable form of reading is fashioned as directly oppositional to likenesses or resemblances. Walter is a drawing master, and his artistic vision and reading exposes the 'Truth', or the legal truth of identities in the novel. Firstly, when Count Fosco attempts to confuse the identity of Laura with that of Anne, Walter is one of the few individuals who is able to discern the difference. Walter cannot confuse the photographic copy with the original, or the visual resemblance with the uniqueness of identity. He cannot acquiesce in the effective 'murder' of Laura through the 'fatal resemblance', since she is thought of as dead by Mr Fairlie and others. Walter's artistic vision and reading is demonstrated in an obvious act of reading in the novel. Walter is able to discern the identity and thus find the individuality of Percival Glyde who was Count Fosco's partner in his photographic fraud on identity through an act of reading. He aims to find out who Percival Glyde really is and turns to a marriage register and its legal copy to do so. Walter's reading and his finding of identity and individuality through it, I contend, is the reading of things invisible and hidden since it relies on the reading of a blank space as well as of identity which Collins thought of as hidden or concealed. The reading is differentiated from the reading of photographs, appearances and visual resemblances: Walter says, in a significant passage, when he is acting out the position of the reader of the important Marriage Registry, '[s]moothly and fairly as appearances looked in the vestry, there was something wrong beneath them— there was something in the register-book, for aught I knew, that I had not discovered yet'.[51] It is Walter's ability to go beyond mere 'appearances' as a reader and his status as the bearer of the idealised gaze that means he is successful at finding out the truth. And, indeed, Walter's success in finding 'the truth' is in being able to read that which seems invisible, a blank, white space which defies representation, a blankness which the insensitive patron of photographic copies, Frederick Fairlie, was unable to read in his own case to protect his women when he was sent a blank letter in the post:[52]

> The last entry on one page recorded the marriage of the man with my Christian name. Below it, there was a blank space—a space evidently left because it was too narrow to contain the entry of the marriages of the two brothers, which in the copy, as in the original, occupied the top of the next page. That space told the whole story! There it must have remained, in the church register, from eighteen hundred and three (when the marriages had been solemnised and the copy had been made) to eighteen hundred and twenty-seven, when Sir Percival appeared at Old Welmingham. Here, at Knowlesbury, was the chance of committing the forgery, shown to me in the

51 Ibid., 452–453.
52 Ibid., 310.

> copy—and there, at Old Welmingham, was the forgery committed, in the register of the church.[53]

The letter allows Walter to see that Percival Glyde is an imposter. That is, Glyde's parents were never married. Thus, Walter finds that Percival's identity and individual character or individuality is illegitimate. Walter is the type of reader who goes beyond the mere letter to 'the spirit' of the text, the master of the invisible and the reader who is able to understand what absence signifies and how to discern identity and individuality in writing. He stands opposed to the literalist reader who is tied to the letter of the writing, and promotes photographic copying of artwork, such as Mr Fairlie with whom he is implicitly contrasted. Thus, the idea that both identity and legal truth have to be hidden or 'invisible' determines the type of reading and reader that stands opposed to photography and literalism in the novel.

Walter's reading draws on ideas of resemblances and copies and demonstrates how his non-literalist reading is conditioned by the threat of likeness. Firstly, Glyde's attempt to alter the marriage register is seen as a forgery. I have discussed the relationship between forgery, resemblance and photography in Collins' work above and it can be seen to inform *The Woman in White* as well as *Armadale*. Walter can discern the illegitimate attempt to visually resemble writing and identity in order to exploit it which characterises forgery and the forger. Secondly, what allows Walter to decipher the marriage register in order to determine identity and individuality is that the legal copy has its other in the form of a false and misleading resemblance. Walter's non-literalist reading of the marriage register relies on the idea that he is able to tell which one is merely a resemblance of the truth and which one is the authentic and original article. This is despite the fact that it is the legal 'copy' which contains the blank space and the real truth: Walter is still able to realise which is the original and the copy in the case: Glyde's forgery is the photographic copy, while it purports to be the original document, while the lawyer's 'copy', despite being a copy, is actually a true representation of what is the original document and is hence the original.

It is important to note the glaring paradox in Collins' novel in which resemblance is seen as fatal. It is the legal copy, the resemblance to the original, which is seen as authoritative and truthful. There is a 'mirroring' in the positions of the crucial marriage registers which reveals 'the truth' of the imposter and their 'inversion' of the story where the copy threatens to replace the original. What explains the difference? On the one hand, the copy of the marriage register, which is not just the writing, but also the reading of the law, since the lawyer has to have read the original register in order to copy it, is certified by the lawyer as being faithful to 'the truth' and authoritative and locked away in his office, in the legal domain. On the other hand, the original marriage register contains the forgery and is not securely kept, is kept away from the legal domain and is thus open to the public and their erroneous reading, including a photographic reading which aims to

53 Ibid., 458.

imitate and corrupt, as in forgery. The original is thus corrupted. The legal copy inaccessible to the general public and the lawyer's writing and reading is therefore privileged as bearing 'the truth' and thought of as being incorruptible. However, paradoxically, for evidence, Walter needs the two opposing copies, the fraudulent, and the legally certified, the corrupted original and the pristine copy. In this, there is a mirroring of his determination of the identities between Anne and Laura. Anne is the corrupted original in Count Fosco's scheme of resemblances since she is an illegitimate child. Laura is the pristine copy since she is legitimate. The concept of the law and how it is conditioned by the idea of resemblance is important because it points to a larger shared idea across the fiction I have studied and not just Collins' work. Structurally, the law, individuality and a reading which is the finding of individuality must always have its resembling other in order to bolster its claims to 'truth' and objectivity. The law is always threatened by its usurping double, the bad twin of the law. The identity and character of accepted or 'good' law is thus revealed. The true law must contain blank spaces. Its writing has to capture the invisible. Therefore, writing which contains blank spaces is a true resemblance of the truth. On the other hand, that which fraudulently resembles the law as its usurping double has the blank space filled with writing. There is no space for invisibility and therefore no space for legal interpretation. The usurping double is tied to the letter, to the visible. It is the product of a literalist conception of law where everything is to be spelled out and nothing is to be left to the imagination, or laboriously deciphered and 'read in'.

Collins thus established reading as the finding of invisible individuality and its legitimacy through an inventive interpretation of literalist and non-literalist reading and accepted or conventional ideas of an idealised law. It can be seen how his construction of reading was related to ideas of authorship. As an individual, the author was seen as original, unique and inimitable. However, at the same time, this is how the political elite saw themselves and I will now consider how Collins' construction of reading as a reading of the invisible relates to power and the maintenance of the status quo.

Group identity vs. individual identity: the political dimensions of reading as an exclusion of finding and exploiting resemblances

I have attempted to show how fatal resemblances develop in Collins' fiction through their failure to recognise and represent individuality, and how they introduce chaos into conceptions of the truth and English law. I have argued that the construction of reading is to be seen in relation to these ideas. Because reading is represented as the finding of identity and its legitimacy, it can be seen to be constructed along lines which exclude copies and forgeries which aim to resemble original pieces of writing. I now wish to concentrate further on the political implications of photographic resemblances to show why they are seen as dangerous alternatives to individualising practices such as the finding of identity through reading. This is so that I can show the larger aim of Collins' fiction, as it exists as part of a larger grouping of culture and the law within society. I will do so by showing how resemblances are associated with the formation of alternative group identities to those of the political elite, while the 'reading of the invisible', that is the reading which finds individuality and its legitimacy, is associated with the 'solitary individual', who is considered capable of original and thus 'true' thought.

The Moonstone (1868) can be read as an attempt to marginalise the finding of photographic resemblances so as to prevent the political grouping and identity politics of women and Indians. I contend that in the novel finding resemblances is seen as characteristic of a group vision and as a growing threat to Empire and the law from the political grouping of women and foreigners. Here, again, misogyny operates to eliminate this form of truth-telling, as a woman's truth is again cast as false by the shared truth of a group of men. Collins explores the idea of what would happen if the vision of an amateur (photographic) female copyist was able to determine more public, legal questions of guilt and innocence and the ordering of legal identities. At the same time, Collins also endorses and casts as normative the reading and the science of the invisible, which aims to find individuality and its legitimacy. This reading is associated with 'the solitary individual' who stands against the vision and perspective of the group.

Some commentators have seen the novel as reflective of the mutually supporting Victorian structures of law and science. Ronald R. Thomas writes that the novel's 'significance is due to the methodical way in which it reconstructs the past through deploying techniques of the emerging nineteenth-century science of forensic criminology and the practices of criminal investigation it inspired'.[54] The argument rests on the fact that 'the master detective is not even primarily responsible for solving the mystery. That privilege falls to an obscure scientist working at the forefront of Victorian forensic medicine'.[55] However, I aim to show that science and the eye of science is only accepted in the novel as 'the truth' so long as it matches the order of 'individuality', invisibility and misogyny within which the legal operates. It is this complex which I see as politically important to describe and analyse because it has been the means of consolidating the political elite's power and eliminating difference and the formation of counter-politics. Furthermore, as I have shown, Collins frequently turned to negative characterisations of science in his novels. Even though novels such as *The Moonstone* have been seen to support ideas of Victorian science, Collins relied on ideas of 'scientist-villains' continually throughout his fiction rather than scientist heroes and I suggest an explanation for this.[56] I will show that the eye of science as associated with the idea of finding and exploiting visual resemblances, and, with them, the perspective of groups that stand opposed to the grouping of the political elite are contained and rendered powerless in the novel. The novel and the larger aim of fiction such as Collins' can therefore be newly understood as relying on an asymmetry of power and as a deliberate

54 Ronald R. Thomas, 'The Moonstone, Detective Fiction and Forensic Science', in *The Cambridge Companion to Wilkie Collins*, ed. Jenny Bourne Taylor (Cambridge: Cambridge University Press, 2006), 66.

55 Ibid., 66.

56 Melissa Frazier, 'The Science of Sensation: Dostoevsky, Wilkie Collins and the Detective Novel', *Dostoevsky Studies*, XIX (2015), 21.

pre-emption of political resistance and difference, as well as an outline of the strategies and methods used in its operations, a diagram of power, as it were.

The act around which the novel turns is that Franklin Blake unconsciously tries to hide the Moonstone, which is the eye of an Indian idol, the moon god. The association between moonlight and the daguerreotype was in evidence in Collins' earlier work, since Walter sees the woman in white as the photographic image in the monochromatic light of the moon in *The Woman in White*. At the beginning of *The Moonstone*, Rachel, whose inability to separate law and sense from the visual realm causes such confusion regarding the legal order of things, has a great affinity with the photographic image. She keeps a photograph of Godfrey Ablewhite, a barrister and a rival suitor to the hero of the novel, in her room in a prominent position. Godfrey Ablewhite is not only a representative of the law in general, but also one that peculiarly represents women as a group. Indeed, he supports women's rights as they oust 'poor men' from their 'rightful' position. As Gabriel Betteridge, the butler, and one of the narrators of the tale writes (the novel is a collection of 'eyewitness accounts'):

> If you ever subscribed to a Ladies' Charity in London, you know Mr. Godfrey Ablewhite as well as I do. He was a barrister by profession; a ladies' man by temperament; and a good Samaritan by choice. Female benevolence and female destitution could do nothing without him. Maternal societies for confining poor women; Magdalen societies for rescuing poor women; strong-minded societies for putting poor women into poor men's places, and leaving the men to shift for themselves—he was vice-president, manager, referee to them all. Wherever there was a table with a committee of ladies sitting round it in council, there was Mr. Godfrey at the bottom of the board, keeping the temper of the committee and leading the dear creatures along the thorny ways of business, hat in hand.[57]

In a precursor of seeing Franklin as a moving image, Rachel also sees him in the same way or at the same moment as a photograph. Gabriel Betteridge's daughter, Penelope, tells her father, that '[s]he had detected Miss Rachel, apparently engaged in appeasing Mrs. Threadgall by showing her some photographs, and really occupied in stealing looks at Mr. Franklin, which no intelligent lady's-maid could misinterpret for a single instant'.[58] When Franklin Blake arrives in Yorkshire, he encourages Rachel Verinder to take up painting, through which she begins to impose her own 'photographic' vision on the world, the vision of an unoriginal and derivative copyist who cannot organise material correctly. As Gabriel Betteridge writes:

> Miss Rachel then covered the surface, under his directions and with his help, with patterns and devices—griffins, birds, flowers, cupids, and such like—copied from designs made by a famous Italian painter, whose name escapes me:

57 Wilkie Collins, *The Moonstone* (New York: The Century Co. [1868] 1906), 63.
58 Ibid., 86.

> the one, I mean, who stocked the world with Virgin Maries, and had a sweetheart at the baker's.[59]

Betteridge describes the activity of copying designs in the same terms as the pursuit of natural history and photography which are representative of the idleness of gentlefolks and he says too that the design has a terrible smell, like the smell of chemical vapors.[60] The final design, completed on the morning of Rachel's birthday, is described later by Betteridge as disorganised and inharmonious and as disturbing the consciousness:

> [t]he griffins, cupids, and so on, were, I must own, most beautiful to behold; though so many in number, so entangled in flowers and devices, and so topsy-turvy in their actions and attitudes, that you felt them unpleasantly in your head for hours after you had done with the pleasure of looking at them.[61]

The entanglement with flowers points to the association of the design with nature and with the subsequent distraction of nature and botany for Sergeant Cuff, the detective. Bettridge alludes to how the legal identity of the Sergeant conflicts with his knowledge of botany and horticulture, for instance:

> To the gardener's astonishment, and to my disgust, this celebrated policeman proved to be quite a mine of learning on the trumpery subject of rose-gardens.[62]

The science of botany is seen to intrude upon the legal determination of truth and make its own claims for attention, although it is seen as irrelevant. In fact, Cuff can't initially find out who the criminal is.

It is in the context of this copying of art, or the validation of finding and exploiting resemblances, associated by Betteridge with natural history, photography, and illegitimacy, that the Moonstone enters Rachel's life.[63] As Thomas observes, the Moonstone is associated with science, particularly chemistry, much as photography was in the period.[64] When the diamond had come into his keeping, Colonel Herncastle became known for 'trying strange things in chemistry'.[65] The will in which he bequeaths the Moonstone to his niece also establishes a professorship of experimental chemistry at a northern university. Thus, according to Thomas, '[t]he diamond and experimental science are from the beginning presented as the two principal aspects of the 'legacy of trouble' that Herncastle gains for himself in his imperial plundering and leaves behind him in his will for his heirs'.[66] Rachel's new turn as an amateur copyist is quickly followed by her seeing Franklin taking her

59 Ibid., 58–59.
60 Ibid.
61 Ibid., 69.
62 Ibid., 110.
63 Ibid., 69.
64 Thomas (n 54) 72.
65 Collins (n 57) 37.
66 Thomas (n 54) 72.

birthday present the Moonstone *in a mirror* through the very same door frame which she had just decorated, that is in the frame of resemblances. Crucially, Rachel sees him take the Moonstone on her way to the sitting room to get a book – the interruption between the woman and the book and the assumption of the position of reader. Although, he is innocent, motivated only to safeguard the Moonstone, and only acts under the involuntary taking of opium, Rachel judges him solely on the evidence of her own eyes as a thief and criminal, confounding the ability of the police to retrieve the stone. She decides a man's legal identity. This is again a case of resemblance which subverts racial identities: Franklin becomes like the Indian 'thieves' who are attempting to steal the stone. As Rachel mistakenly marks Franklin as a criminal, symbolically, the door frame with its disorganised and undiscerning copies of Raphael's designs leaves a stain on Franklin's nightgown. Later, Rachel's belief in her own vision leads her to declare Godfrey Ablewhite, the guilty party, the man who supports the political grouping of women, as the innocent one. Rachel sees Franklin through the mirror, the passive glass. In Rachel's mirror, legal identity is subverted, cast into its polar opposite. Her vision remains focused on surface appearance, which can see the commission of crime but not the criminal intention: in legal terms, she can see the apparent *actus reus*, but is so legally illiterate that she cannot consider the question of the hidden or invisible *mens rea*. Rachel becomes representative of the undiscriminating and material, chemical and 'scientific' photographic vision with which the Moonstone and the idea of finding and representing visual resemblances is associated.

The female copyist's vision and her uninformed reliance of legal judgement on that vision is exposed in Collins' novel as mistaken, non-indexical and as a false interpretation of law. This vision is that of the fatherless woman of fierce 'independence'.[67] The problematisation of Rachel's fierce independence of thought in the novel is evident, since it is associated with her vision and disrupts the exposure of 'the truth' and 'legal truth'. As a woman who does not submit to the masculine perspective, Rachel is seen as problematic for the determination of a legal truth which a masculine interpretation constructs since she is able to conceive of alternative conceptions of legal truth. She thus stands as a bearer of difference and political resistance, a different direction in thought, perspective and the understanding of legitimacy, even a different form of individuality. Significantly, Rachel's photographic vision and independence almost lead her from a potential marriage to Franklin to his rival. The rival is Godfrey Ablewhite, the lawyer who supports the political grouping of women, or 'represents' women. As we have seen, Ablewhite is in charge of numerous ladies' committees which were gaining in political power at the time. Thus, Rachel is almost led to marriage with an individual that appears to legally endorse and support the organisation of women's rights. The novel's dismissal of Rachel's independent and photographic vision and its casting out of the photographic Moonstone idol from the centre of the Empire to its colony in India is therefore a reaction against both the threat of the gaining of political importance of woman and the 'native' (and the scientist), who all occupy the same symbolic

67 Collins (n 57) 61.

space. It is telling that Godfrey Ablewhite, the villain of the piece, has to have a 'swarthy complexion' when he is reunited with the Moonstone, because he is connected with the Indian as well as with photographic appearance.[68] Ablewhite's organisation and representation of women's groups is an integral part of the story and forms a continuum with the attempt of the Indians to found a small organisation to bring the Moonstone back home, since both are constructed outside of the framework of British law and empire. Rachel's vision has to be seen as the group vision of those that stand opposed to the grouping of the political elite since I have already observed that she kept a photograph of Ablewhite, the organiser and representative of women.

'The truth', 'scientific truth' and 'the legal truth' in the novel are all conflated at the end of the novel in an act which is supposed to legitimate an act of interpretation or reading so as to cast Franklin the individual as innocent, or to find legitimacy in his character. This act of reading is a contradiction of Rachel's determination of the illegitimacy of Franklin's identity in the frame of resemblances. The contradiction to Rachel's account is found in mastering the unspoken and invisible evidence of the doctor, Mr Candy, a task which is accomplished by Ezra Jennings' reading of the blank space. Mr Candy is sick, so he can only articulate the truth that he administered opium to Franklin in a series of fragmentary sentences. The opium is itself seen as having affected Franklin's state of mind and causing him to act unconsciously so that he took the Moonstone for safekeeping without realising what he was doing. The doctor's fragmentary testimony is interpreted or read by Ezra and reconstituted into a whole so that his reading can legitimate Franklin's character or individuality.

Collins presents this reading as that of the individual and it is set against the group worship of the Moonstone at the end of the novel by the Indians who characterise the worship of the moon (or nature), photography and science. Ezra Jennings conspicuously stands as 'a solitary individual', rather than as a member of a group. For instance, he is a bachelor who has been rejected in love and something of a social outcast. He is said to be 'unpopular everywhere'.[69] If Ezra Jennings is a solitary and individualised man of science, he is divided from the other men of science who are negatively associated with the photograph. This is because Ezra can also read the blank spaces of whiteness and is not associated with literalism, or reading to the letter. Ezra reads between the lines of Mr Candy's spoken account which he has written down and puts the blank spaces together like 'a child's puzzle' to bring them into 'order and shape' and rehabilitate the spoken words into a narrative. He thoroughly outlines this method of reading the invisible blank spaces of writing and the invisible thoughts of the individual which will ultimately support the finding of Franklin's character and individuality to be without blemish:

> 'At odds and ends of time,' Ezra Jennings went on, 'I reproduced my short-hand notes, in the ordinary form of writing – leaving large spaces between the

68 Ibid., 492.
69 Ibid., 404.

> broken phrases, and even the single words, as they had fallen disconnected from Mr. Candy's lips. I then treated the result thus obtained on something like the principle which one adopts in putting together a child's "puzzle". It is all confusion to begin with; but it may be all brought into order and shape, if you can only find the right way. Acting on this plan, I filled in the blank spaces on the paper with what the words or phrases on either side of it suggested to me as the speaker's meaning; altering over and over again, until my additions followed naturally on the spoken words which came before them and fitted naturally into the spoken words which came after them. The result was that I not only occupied in this way many vacant and anxious hours, but that I arrived at something which was, as it seemed to me, a confirmation of the theory that I held. In plainer words, after putting the broken sentences together, I found the superior faculty of thinking going on, more or less connectedly, in my patient's mind, while the inferior faculty of expression was in a state of almost complete incapacity and confusion.'[70]

Thus, once again, even in the field of science, it is the masculine mastery of the invisible which is contrasted to the woman's and the idolater's photographic bondage to the visual realm, resemblances and nature in the mastery of the truth. An acceptable and true reading is tied to the idea of an invisible and hidden truth, that of identity and its legitimacy. Thus, the man of science and reader who is integrated into the law and the knowledge of 'the truth' is one who is 'truly individual' and can witness the invisible and the space of whiteness. Ezra Jennings' 'truth' destroys the resemblance between Franklin and the Indian 'thieves'. It also leads to a 'good' grouping of 'witnesses, or the company' in the experiment that proves that it is true, with the legal connotation that this word carries, a group bound in similar legal vision and with a shared idea of legal truth.[71] The grouping is 'invisible' since the characters are thought of as 'individuals' as they have been characterised as having voices and separate accounts of the same events, as in their eyewitness narration: it is only foreigners and women who can be seen as indistinguishable from each other in the 'bad' group. Bad science, based on things visible, is now replaced by a good, new, individualistic paradigm of science based on invisible entities which stand opposed to the 'bad' group vision and perspective, precisely because of their difference from the political elite in terms of gender and race. It can thus be seen how Collins manufactured a model of reading individuality and the truth as a reading of the invisible against the threat of literalism and of photographic resemblances. The association between literalism and photography provided the foil against which the normative model of reading defined itself and the conditions on which that form of reading depended.

In summary, as I have aimed to show, in the novel, the finding of 'photographic' resemblances and likenesses between individuals is thought to be dangerous because it is tied with political groups which are seen as subversive of the power of the political elite, such as women fighting for equality. The exclusion of finding

70 Ibid., 410.
71 Ibid., 453.

resemblances is part of a strategy of dividing and conquering. False individualisation of members of what could be groups is instilled because individualisation destroys the finding of connections and support between members of a society and groups. Thus, Rachel, whose vision is systematically destroyed and depicted as false, is unable to unite with other women and the lawyer who could promote woman's rights. False individualisation of the political elite also conceals the shared ways in which they act to treat and exclude others. When Franklin unites with the other men in order to exclude the vision of Rachel and of women, this is depicted as being in support of his own individuality rather than being shown to be a grouping of the powerful against the powerless on shared and familiar patterns that resemble one another.

Conclusion

Collins constructs reading as the finding of a unique and individual, invisible identity such as in Walter's reading of the blank spaces in the marriage registers. Like Walter, the reader must access this truth by excluding the literalist finding of visual resemblances and identities through photographs and discerning the difference between originals and copies. As I have aimed to show by addressing its connection with forgery, the literalist reading is associated with finding what merely resembles and exploits individuality and, furthermore, threatens to usurp its position. The finding of individuality is presented as the finding of the legal truth in Collins' novels: when Walter proves that Laura is who she is, he also proves how a fraudulent crime was committed against her. I have also discussed how Rachel's perspective of law is excluded because she saw Franklin as resembling the Indians, who were seen as thieves in *The Moonstone*. Her conception of the law, as I have aimed to show, is countered by an idea of the legal truth as discrete and individualistic. I have aimed to show how this treatment of the law is calculated to destroy a conception of the truth as politically derived and politically motivated to exclude group perspectives and the formation of group identities that could challenge the political elite, particularly where the legal representation of women is concerned. In the next chapter, I will again concentrate on what was understood as a fundamental attribute of photography, the detail, and how both constructions of reading and the reader emerged in a reaction to this characterisation. Through a discussion of the work of Henry James, I will outline how conceptions of the legal truth as universal, timeless and abstract determine a proper and non-literalist reading as one that abhors context and ignores the historical and material conditions of being. Thus, I will again show what the conditions of reading in the period are and how they operate to eliminate political difference and resistance: how unrecognised guides to thought have limited political and legal conceptions of reading and individuality.

3 Representation and reading against photographic details in the work of Henry James

In each of the previous chapters of this monograph, I have shown how opposition to understandings of photography determines the shape of reading and the identity of readers supported by works of fiction. In this chapter, I will again explore how a reading which characterises the law and legal truth as timeless, or ahistorical, and apolitical determines the nature of an ideal reading and reader. This reading preserves its power and politics by stealth, setting them as unquestionable and unassailable because they are unrecognised and supposedly objective and universal guides to thought. I aim to show how such a reading of the law emerges from a conception that photography's key contribution is the attention to detail in the work of Henry James. As I noted in the introduction to this monograph, photography was commonly associated with details. John Leighton stated that 'minute detail is the attribute of the sun-picture'.[1] Similarly, in the text accompanying Plate X, 'The Haystack' in *The Pencil of Nature* (1844), Henry Fox Talbot wrote that:

> One advantage of the discovery of the Photographic Art will be, that it will enable us to introduce into our pictures a multitude of minute details which add to the truth and reality of the representation, but which no artist would take the trouble to copy faithfully from nature.

In my chapter on Wilkie Collins I have tried to show how a legal reading grounded in identity politics, particularly the identity politics of women, is rigorously denounced in works of fiction. My study of Henry James' work aims to show how such a reading is characterised as untruthful and too literal, and to reveal how it is seen as associated with the representation of women, because of their association with detail. Furthermore, Henry James is a very different writer to Collins, and his writing had pretensions to fine art. A study of his work therefore shows how the constructive opposition to photography by writers of fiction was shared across both popular culture and high culture and was central to authorship. Furthermore, precisely because James' work presents itself as a high art form, it is an exceptionally rich source of material which can reveal how art and fiction were implicated in a larger game of politics. Here I will argue that, as with Collins, Henry James'

1 John Leighton, 'On Photography as a Means or an End', *The Photographic Journal* (21 June 1853), 74.

DOI: 10.4324/9781003173854-4

painterly background and legal education determined key aspects of his work and his understanding of reading and the law. In my analysis of James' writings, I will concentrate on underlying currents of misogyny in fiction again, this time in relation to the economic status of women. I will argue that Henry James criticises the detail within photography which he sees as the main attribute of this form of representation, its ability to represent 'particulars'. James saw both details and particulars as the same thing, as non-idealised remnants of existing reality in representations which attempted verisimilitude. Such particulars are seen to portray femininity and historical conditions in society, including relationships of power and asymmetries in power, those conditions which groups such as women and the lower class denounced. I believe that James was attempting to convince the reader that seeing in terms of photographic particulars which reflect real historical conditions leads to particularism and selfishness in political representation and the formation of laws. This is because in James' work the context and real conditions are opposed to the ideal reading, as the latter relies on ideas of universality and abstraction, rather than being in the world. James consistently explores the theme of representation in relation to reading, photographic particulars and law by concentrating on the meaning of the representation of women in terms of identity and politics. Photographic particulars are seen as linked to a woman's materialistic and literalist reading of reality and history. James countered a form of representation that realistically assesses the political conditions of society in order to support a form of legal representation that affects to ignore them, even while it supports asymmetries of power and consolidates the dominance of the political elite. He does this by supporting an ideal form of blindness which does not see photographic particulars which are associated with literalism. While a number of studies have analysed the role of photography in James' fiction, my analysis will differ in its concentration on law and photographic detail in relation to women, reading photography and representation.[2] Such a concentration will demonstrate one of the larger aims of James' fiction, which was to oppose the representation and subjectivity of women in order to consolidate the power of the political elite. James' work, then, can be seen as an elimination of political difference just like the other writings I have studied and reveals in detail some of the major historical strategies used to marginalise alternative sources of reading and formulating laws.

I am aware that this reading is set against opposing conceptions of James' work in both feminist research and queer studies research. For instance, Sarah B. Daugherty's essay 'James and the Representation of Women: Some Lessons of the Master (')s' (2000) suggested that James 'sided with female characters against male writers who belatedly defended the status quo' and did not politically criticise

2 For example: Owen Clayton, 'Flirting with Photography: Henry James and Photographic Exchange', *History of Photography*, 41:4 (2017), 329–342; Julie Grossman, '"It's the Real Thing": Henry James, Photography, and *The Golden Bowl*', *The Henry James Review*, 15:3 (Fall 1994), 309–328; Edward L. Schwarzschild, "Revising Vulnerability: Henry James's Confrontation with Photography', *Texas Studies in Literature and Language*, 38:1 (Spring 1996), 51–78; Adam Sonstegard, 'Painting, Photography and Fidelity in *The Tragic Muse*' (English Faculty Publications, 2003) 27 http://engagedscholarship. csuohio.edu/cleng_facpub/27 (last accessed 18 September 2018).

women.[3] Queer studies scholars have also characterised James' work as feminist and resistant to the status quo. For instance, Kathryn Wichelns writes that:

> What I suggest is that James's complex identification with (normative) femininity reflects the distinctive forms of resistance available to him, as a male author who was both 'queer' and, just as significantly, formed in a nineteenth-century, upper middle-class, and Anglo-American cultural context.[4]

Whilst it may the case that James identified with women and was sympathetic towards them, he joined in the larger formative movement of structural misogyny which I have argued characterised idealist art in the first chapter of this monograph. This was precisely because of James' intention to create novels which presented themselves as high art. James used painterly tropes to describe his composition in his prefaces to his novels. Because art was important to James, he could not help but repeat what was important to building that discourse and in aesthetising the novel. If James was sympathetic to women, this sympathy competed with his sympathy for idealist art which marginalised women and there is a productive tension between the two sympathies as they struggle against each other. My own research illuminates this structuring of misogyny derived from the legal and art discourses and allows James' work and larger aims to be newly reappraised, as well as the terms in which his political resistance could be couched.

In the beginning of this chapter, I will concentrate on how photographic details are associated with the representation of women, the representation of political conditions and identity politics. I will first introduce James' ideas about photography and detail in his early review of Anthony Trollope's novel, *Miss Mckenzie* (1865). This is because in this review James explicitly associates details with literalism, the representation of women and material conditions in fiction. I will then explore how novels such as *Roderick Hudson* (1875) and the *Princess Casamassima* (1886) portray the way in which photographic particulars and the representation of women are seen to threaten ideal legal reading and political conditions through ideas of particularism. In doing so, I aim to show how political difference was framed and outlined in relationship to detail so as to characterise how it was seen and understood. The next section of the chapter will aim to show how opposition to ideas of photographic particulars produce a specific type of political and artistic representation and reading based in conceptions of universality, abstraction and timelessness, which James supports. I will outline the form of this representation in *The Tragic Muse* (1890). This is to characterise the type of legal truth which James and other writers of fiction supported in their writings and to make evident the implicit standards by which they judged alternative forms of truth such as photography. Lastly, I will show how James links together ideas of blindness, reading and

3 Sarah B. Daugherty, 'James and the Representation of Women: Some Lessons of the Master(')s', in Peggy McCormack (ed), *Questioning the Master: Gender and Sexuality in Henry James's Writings* (London: Associated University Presses, 2000), 179.

4 Kathryn Wichelns, *Henry James's Feminist Afterlives: Annie Fields, Emily Dickinson, Marguerite Duras* (Cham, Switzerland: Palgrave Macmillan, 2018), 6.

truth in order to valorise a specific type of reader who does not look to the photographic details and material things which portray the relationships of power within society and their asymmetries. Blindness is a crucial shared aspect of ideal identity in the works I have studied and it is therefore important to outline precisely why it was seen as key to individuality and discernment.

Photography and its particularity: details and women

I first wish to contextualise my study of James in relation to existing scholarship which has noted that Henry James repeatedly denounced photography as a form of representation and also scholarship which has explored the historical association between particulars and femininity. My intention in doing so is to show that James represents positions which supported idealist art because of the perception that it was broad and general rather than concerned with details, and that he translated such concepts of idealist art in constructing the law in his fiction. That is, I see the construction of the law in James' fiction, as well as in the works of the other authors discussed in this study, as modelled upon idealist art, and I wish to make it clear why I believe that this modelling and cross-pollination occurred.

Even after his approval of the photographic frontispieces for his monumental New York edition, in 1912, James was able to write to the photographer he collaborated with, that 'photography insists for me, in remaining at best *but* photography'.[5] It has been noted that James' denunciation of photography relied on the idea that it was associated with details. Although he does not explore the matter, Stanley Tick has previously noted that James' inability to regard photography as an art form derived:

> from his conviction, widely held in the last century and still occasionally heard today, that its achievements could not partake of the 'general' and the 'comprehensive'. He saw its expressive possibilities as being confined to that superficial reality which it inevitably captured, to the particular and the specific.[6]

I will expand this idea with the intention of showing how photographic details in James' work are associated with femininity and how they are seen to corrupt reading and the law. As I will show, in terms of James' fiction, denouncements of photography turn around ideas of the representation of women and the photographic detail, or the particular. Such ideas in James' work can be seen to exploit a larger aesthetic tradition. Naomi Schor, in *Reading in Detail: Aesthetics and the Feminine* (1987) argued that detail is historically gendered as feminine and is also associated with decadence. Schor argues that 'the censure of the particular is one of the enabling gestures of neo-classicism, which recycled into the modern age the

5 Quoted in Ralph F. Bogardus, *Pictures and Texts: Henry James, A. L. Coburn, and New Ways of Seeing in Literary Culture* (Ann Arbor: UMI-Research Press, 1984), 201.

6 Stanley Tick, 'Positives and Negatives: Henry James vs. Photography', in Stanley Tick, *Essays on Charles Dickens, Henry James, and George Eliot* (Philadelphia, PA: Xlibris Corporation, 2005), 203.

classical equation of the Ideal with the absence of all particularity'.[7] It is particularity that is particularly problematic for James since particularity destroys pretensions to abstraction, universality and timelessness. It could be argued that James' fiction, and his theories of fiction, do espouse a particular kind of particularity, that of the subject; that is, that the determining shaper of his fiction is the view of the particular individual. However, it is interesting to note how James himself praised a piece of artwork and 'individuality' in terms of 'largeness' and 'universality'. He did so in the same article in which he first criticised Tissot, mentioned below, for his 'vulgar and *banal*' art. Tissot's art was seen as a form of 'realism', and led James to denounce art that looked like it was 'based upon photographs'. Having launched these criticisms, James then wrote:

> Next this work hangs the portrait of an admirable model, Mrs. Percy Wyndham. 'It is what they call a "sumptuous" picture,' said my companion. 'That is, the lady looks as if she had thirty thousand a year.' It is true that she does; and yet the picture has a style which is distinctly removed from the 'stylishness' of M. Tissot's yellow-ribboned heroine. The very handsome person whom the painter has depicted is dressed in a fashion which will never be wearisome; a simple yet splendid robe, in the taste of no particular period—of all periods. There is something admirably large and generous in the whole design of the work, of which the coloring is proportionately rich and sober. For the art of combining the imagination and ideal element in portraiture with an extreme solidity, and separating great elegance from small elegance, Mr. Watts is highly remarkable.[8]

The universality of the individual figure, clothed in a seemingly 'timeless' fashion is associated with 'largeness' and 'greatness', something bigger. Even though it is a very particular portrait, it is still seen as somehow signifying something transcendental. There is a deliberate contrast to art seemingly modelled on photography since James contrasts the piece to M. Tissot's realistic productions which he again mentions. If James modelled his fiction on a type of artwork, then, it would appear to be one that showed 'universality' and 'timelessness' through the particular and the individual. James, who associated particularity with poverty, saw this painting as rising above particularity because of its exhibition of wealth.

The theories of ideal art upon which Schor makes her case about the association of details with femininity and which appear to have strongly influenced James are those most clearly enunciated in the work of Joshua Reynolds, an influential eighteenth-century painter. Reynolds wrote in *Discourses on Art* that 'the whole of beauty consists, in my opinion, in being able to get above singular forms, local customs, particularities, and details of every kind'.[9] Schor writes that Reynolds' argument is that because of their material contingency, details are incompatible

7 Naomi Schor, *Reading in Detail: Aesthetics and the Feminine* (New York and London: Routledge, 2007), xlii.

8 Henry James, 'The Picture Season in London', *The Galaxy*, 24:2 (August 1877), 156.

9 Quoted in Schor, *Reading in Detail* (n 7) 3.

with the ideal and that because of their tendency to proliferation, details subvert the sublime.[10] Schor goes on to write:

> For though Reynolds never explicitly links details and femininity, by taking over a metaphorics grounded in metaphysics—and Reynolds' debt to both Plato and Aristotle is well-documented—he implicitly reinscribes the sexual stereotypes of Western philosophy which has, since its origins, mapped gender onto the form matter paradigm, forging a durable link between maleness and form (*eidos*), femaleness and formless matter.[11]

In James, the perceived formlessness in the representation of woman is apparent, as it is women who are seen as photographic models and are not 'refined' by the male artistic gaze who consistently trouble law. Reynolds may have called for sacrificing the detail to the higher ends of the ideal and the sublime, however Schor notes that his strictures were far from absolute. For Reynolds, the complete absence of detail or ornament is 'no more desirable than their excessive presence'.[12] Reynolds was very ready to allow that some circumstances of minuteness and particularity frequently tend to give an air of truth to a piece, and to interest the spectator. However, it is important to emphasise that the detail was widely seen as the mark of an inferior art. Schor suggests that there is an historical association of detail with artistic decadence which is transnational and spans two centuries.[13] Schor writes that the 'equation of an excess of details and decadence is an essential tenet of neo-classical doxa'.[14]

In this chapter so far I have tried to introduce an idea of the larger aesthetic context in which James was situated and from which his ideas about photography and its details, and their association with women, emerged. Through a reading of his 1865 review of Anthony Trollope's novel *Miss Mackenzie* (1865), I now wish to demonstrate how he himself constructed a reading against photography and particulars which he explicitly associated with women in his literary criticism. James remarks that the novel represents 'the experience of unmarried English ladies', that is, that it is a representation of women, but also criticises the novel because 'it is impossible to overstate the habitual monotony of such lives'.[15] Trollope is able to represent the 'literal' truth of women, but, despite this, is not seen as being wholly truthful. Thus, James writes that:

> Literally, then, Mr. Trollope accomplishes his purpose of being true to common life. But in reading his pages, we were constantly induced to ask ourselves whether he is equally true to nature; that is, whether in the midst of this

10 Ibid., 8.
11 Ibid., 9–10.
12 Ibid., 17.
13 Ibid., 45.
14 Ibid., 47.
15 Henry James, *Nation* (New York, 13 July 1865), i., 51–52, reprinted in Donald Smalley (ed), *Anthony Trollope: The Critical Heritage* (London: Routledge, 2013), 233.

> multitude of real things, of uncompromisingly real circumstances, the persons put before us are equally real. Mr. Trollope has proposed to himself to describe those facts which are so close under every one's nose that no one notices them. Life is vulgar, but we know not how vulgar it is till we see it set down in his pages. It may be said therefore that the emotions which depend upon such facts as these cannot be too prosaic; that as prison discipline makes men idiots, an approach, however slight, to this kind of influence perceptibly weakens the mind.

What is particularly troubling for James is that Miss Mckenzie is concerned with money matters. That is, James sees her as a poor woman who has to think about sordid details such as money. As he writes, 'The work may be qualified, therefore, in strictness, as the history of the pecuniary embarrassments of a middle-aged spinster'.[16] James did not explicitly state why he saw the poor woman as particularly troubling, he merely criticised her for the 'stupidity' in which she took life.[17] However, it is evident that a figure such as Miss Mckenzie is the converse of the political elite, therefore she represented a difference, or a different perspective which, however inadvertently, because of his belief in the novel as a high art form modelled on idealist art, James was unable to bear and set out to eliminate.

For James, the subjectivity and experience of poor women, their troubles over money and their representation in fiction weakens the mind, even if women are seen as more alert to the 'truth' of life, since they are knowledgeable about money matters. This is a key idea in James' first novel, *Roderick Hudson*, where Christina Light has to make a material marriage and she corrupts the artist. In James' view, then, Trollope's fiction thus corrupts the mind by conveying 'literal' truth, as he says. Even if women are depicted as more receptive to reality, then this is a weakness, not a strength. They are seen as literalists, not idealists: the 'literal' representation of Trollope is reflective of women's 'literalism'.

James sees the representation of women and individuals in *Miss McKenzie* as intimately associated with details and particulars. He writes that:

> The figures are the generals in the argument; the facts are the particulars. The persons should accordingly reflect life upon the details, and not borrow it from them. To do so is only to borrow the contagion of death. This latter part is the part they play, and with this result, as it seems to us, in 'Miss Mackenzie'.[18]

For James, the details and particulars which make up historical conditions impose a form of 'death' upon the subject if they assume dominance. Although James does not state why this is so, it appears to be because individuals are understood as somewhat divorced from context and material conditions, as having some sort of

16 Ibid., 233.
17 Ibid., 235.
18 Ibid., 234.

trans-historical essence. This is why he saw photography as a means of extinguishing the individual since he saw detail as its key attribute.[19]

James' suggestion, never explicit, is that by understanding the experience of women through his writing, Trollope has become emasculated, a woman himself. Thus he has become married to the detail and the particulars, to literalism. It is in this context that we have to read James' ironic praise of the novel in terms of its relationship to photography and photographic details. Like a camera, the novel does reflect a limited version of 'reality', but not greater 'truth'. He writes that:

> His matter is literally freckled with virtues. We use the term advisedly, because its virtues are all virtues of detail: the virtues of the photograph. The photograph lacks the supreme virtue of possessing a character. It is the detail alone that distinguishes one photograph from another. What but the detail distinguishes one of Mr. Trollope's novels from another, and, if we may use the expression, consigns it to itself? Of course the details are charming, some of them ineffably charming. The ingenuous loves, the innocent flirtations, of Young England, have been described by Mr. Trollope in such a way as to secure him the universal public good-will; described minutely, sympathetically, accurately; if it were not that an indefinable instinct bade us to keep the word in reserve, we should say truthfully.[20]

The truthful representation of women in fiction, alongside the depiction of real conditions, is therefore seen as an unpromising avenue for James. The photographic form of representation, with its detail, is itself presented as work which cannot possibly be that of a 'man of imagination'.[21] This is because James sees it as tied to reality and the event and sees it as lacking distinctive, unified form, since all Trollope's novels are fundamentally 'the same', save for the difference in details. The novel, because of its details, is therefore represented as the work of a writer without

19 Critics such as Laura Saltz have noted that James saw the photographic vision as unable to convey real meaning and as a form of death imposed on the subject. As Saltz writes, in his autobiography, *A Small Boy and Others* (1913), James mentions sorting through a collection of photographic and lithographic theatrical portraits to find out why he loved drama as a child. The images, however, fail to represent the personalities portrayed to James. They are, instead, 'rather dismal' and show 'the histrionic image with the artificial lights turned off—the fatigued and disconnected face reduced to its mere self and resembling some closed and darkened inn with the sign still swung but the place blighted for want of custom'. Henry James, *Autobiography*, ed. Frederick W. Dupee (New Jersey: Princeton University Publishing, 1956), 60. As Saltz notes, these images: 'extinguish the light—the very life—of their subjects. Each "disconnected face" is an empty, darkened shell, a death mask. "Reduced to its mere self," it gives no hint of the inward life of its subject, nor does it strike a responsive chord in James'. Laura Saltz, 'Henry James's Overexposures', *The Henry James Review*, 25:3 (Fall 2004), 254. James reiterates the sentiment in writing to thank a friend for a photograph of 'the admirable little niece', where he asserts that 'no photograph does much more than extinguish the life and bloom (so exquisite a thing) in a happy child's face'. Henry James, *The Letters of Henry James, vol 1* (Percy Lubbock (ed), New York: Scribner's, 1920), 424.

20 Ibid., 236–237.

21 Ibid., 235–236.

faculty and real creativity or originality. Details appear to dominate the individual's works. They are seen as a powerful, alternative form of representation which seems to obliterate art, voice and personhood while substituting a chimera of fiction for truly original work. This is why they are so problematised in the writings of James.

For James, Trollope is 'an excellent, an admirable observer' but he does not 'observe great things as well as little ones'.[22] The idea is that Trollope misses larger truths by paying attention to lesser ones. In the consistent manner of such criticisms, ideas of judgement, with their legal connotations, are involved. For James, Trollope does not have strong 'judgment' which should have compensated for his lack of imagination.[23] James' own status as a reader is consolidated in his review because he himself denigrates fiction which is based upon details. James reads against the detail in order to present himself as a just reader.

Particulars and particularism as an alternative to conventionally reading the law

James thus associated the photographic with denigrated detail, poor women and preoccupation with money matters. He was part of a larger aesthetic tradition which coupled details with women and which has been described and analysed in Schor's *Reading in Detail*. He saw details as a threat to art and a broader and more general scope or vision. As I will show, such associations will play an important and consistent role in the work of James, and will be associated with particularism in reading the law and politics, as James himself referred to details as 'particulars' in his review of *Miss Mckenzie*. I now aim to show how legitimate reading as represented by the reading of the law in James' fiction is corrupted by details. I wish to do so, first, in order to show how strongly the accepted reading of the law was characterised by a writer with a legal and artistic education in its exclusion of attention to the details. That is, I argue, the implicit condition of a law and writing accepted as legitimate was that it was modelled on idealistic art that aimed to represent the broader and the general, and this significantly affected the way the law was read, conceptualised and legitimated.

Detail is presented as a corrupting alternative to the conventional reading of the law in James' first novel *Roderick Hudson* (1875). The novel investigates the education, development and subsequent failure of the eponymous sculptor Roderick Hudson who is taken up by Rowland Mallet, the wealthy art connoisseur at the very beginning of the novel. James links the decline of the artist and his reading with the corruption of his moral and spiritual nature, since the artist has once been a law student, or reader of the law. In the novel, Roderick not only fails as a sculptor, with the eventual loss of all inspiration, but he also becomes an unscrupulous, unfeeling and self-serving monster. Towards the end of the novel, before Roderick's fall in the mountains, which literalises his descent, we see him attempting to forsake his fiancée (and the legal institution of marriage) for a married woman and even going so far as to take money from his fiancée to do so. It is my argument that

22 Ibid., 234.
23 Ibid.

photographic details and particulars play an important role in this moral decline, especially since they are contrasted against an idealised vision of blindness, the blindness of the artist and reader of the law. This blindness is one that does not see particulars or details, and through details, the historical and material conditions of being. The blindness treats individuals as discrete and removed from the actual conditions of being or abstracts them from context to present them as universal and timeless subjects. I will return to an analysis of this form of blindness in the last section of this chapter.

The novel begins with Roderick's introduction to Rowland Mallet, the altruistic connoisseur. Rowland will become Roderick's patron and tutor but also the foil to his degeneracy. Significantly, the person who makes the introduction between the two men is Cecilia, Roderick's beautiful, intelligent and motherly cousin. Amongst other things, the name Cecilia represents blindness and has been translated from Latin as 'the way of the blind'. At this stage of the novel, both men are friends of this charming intermediary. However, the friendships of the two men with Cecilia also differ in an important way which reflects their status, respective characters and constancy in relation to art. Rowland respects Cecilia, who acts as a counsellor to him, and he holds a special, chaste place for her in his heart. She is of equal standing to him in terms of wealth and birth. James writes that Rowland was so impressed with the woman that he gladly took up bachelorhood rather than find someone inferior to her, although he has abandoned any plan to marry her in her widowhood.[24] On the other hand, Roderick is of lower social standing than Cecilia and unequal to her. He often visits Cecilia and Rowland and sees their relationship as 'a flirtation without the benefits of a flirtation' and he does not approve of it.[25] A votive offering of Roderick's friendship with Cecilia, a tribute to blindness, is a beautiful statue of his, an idealised figure of a thirsty youth drinking from a bowl. Rowland's eye is caught by the beauty of the thing in Cecilia's house and he subsequently decides to sponsor Roderick, otherwise a law student and amateur sculptor, to leave his native America for Europe in order to study the antique and thus become part of the Western artistic tradition. In the break with Cecilia and America, the first conflict arises between Mallet and the sculptor in their competition for a particular 'prize': Roderick proposes to the ironically named Mary Garland, a woman who Rowland has secretly fallen in love with.

In the beginning of the novel, Roderick is in the position of idealised blindness since he is united with Cecilia and makes art for her, the woman that represents blindness. Significantly, this idealised blindness is associated with an ideal or conventional reading of the law since Roderick is also a student, or a *reader* of the law. Roderick has a regular 'routine' at the office of Messrs. Striker and Spooner, counsellors at law. As a student, Roderick has not attained a perfect, complete legal reading, but an incomplete one. There is perhaps a photographic pun since he is unable to maintain the proper 'focus' in his studies, although he is able to 'focus' on the photographic model Christina to his eventual destruction (Rowland refers to this idea by referring to Roderick's ability to 'concentrate' rather than using the

24 Henry James, *Roderick Hudson, vol 1* (New York edn, London: Macmillan and Co, 1908), 1.
25 Ibid., 48.

word 'focus').[26] I believe that this connection between the order of art and the order of law is crucial. This connection is implied in Rowland's seemingly facetious comment about Roderick's artistic ability stemming from his reading of the law; that Roderick 'has found something in Blackstone that I never did'.[27]

In Europe, at first, away from Cecilia and the reading of the law, Roderick seems to surpass Rowland's expectations. He rapidly learns how to interpret and situate himself amongst the masterpieces of Italy. He also produces universally acclaimed sculptures of Adam and Eve, the latter of which is tellingly done very much in the manner of the 'blind' with eyes closed shut, the imaginatively idealistic over the gross material, which significantly takes the form of the poor, lower-class woman:

> Roderick lost his temper, time and again, with his models, who offered but a gross, degenerate image of his splendid ideal; but his ideal, as he assured Rowland, became gradually such a fixed, vivid presence, that he had only to shut his eyes to behold a creature far more to his purpose than the poor girl who stood posturing at forty sous an hour.[28]

Roderick assumes an idealised state of blindness against the lower-class woman's body. This body reflects the asymmetry of power in society since the model has to pose because she is poor and without any power herself. In addition, the model is almost the total reverse of the identity of the political elite: she is a woman, is poor and is also a foreigner. In this state, Roderick becomes an artistic 'reader'. He composes idealised *scriptural* figures. The reading of law has prepared him well for situating himself in the visual order based upon the text and textual authority, but which is not tied to a literalist reading, since the Bible does not include physical descriptions of Adam and Eve. There are a number of connections between the law and the bible which James implicitly invokes. What seems significant is that both the Bible and the law are conceived as 'eternally true' and conceptualised as written by an invisible, or concealed, and transcendent, removed male author. Indeed, the Bible is regarded as the source of eternal law, since it contains the Christian God's Ten Commandments.

However, Roderick quickly becomes distracted from his artistic reader's vocation as he lacks proper 'focus'. It becomes evident that his reading of law is incomplete and unfinished. A dissolute stay in Germany corrupts his idealistic art and he creates a very worldly statue of a woman. Rowland was not sure that he liked it and it is described thus: 'It differed singularly from anything his friend had yet done'.[29] Gloriani, a worldly sculptor, remarks that through it, Roderick has stopped his 'flapping of his wings in the blue, and he has already come down to earth'.[30] That is, idealism and abstraction has been replaced by a representation of real life. Gloriani is very pleased with the sculpture in fact, and it thus represents his idea of

26 Henry James, 'Roderick Hudson', *The Atlantic Monthly*, 35 (1875), 68.
27 James, *Roderick Hudson* (n 24), 18.
28 Ibid., 104.
29 Ibid., 143.
30 Ibid., 146.

art. Gloriani is later described as a materialist and merely 'clever' at art, James' constant euphemism for a lack of morals when it came to questions of art, without any deference to the 'spirit' of art:

> Gloriani, with his head on one side, pulling his long moustache and looking keenly from half-closed eyes at the lighted marble, represented art with a worldly motive, skill unleavened by faith, the mere base maximum of cleverness.[31]

By raising issues of faith, James suggests that the sculpture lacks deference to the supreme patriarchal figure, the Christian God. Rowland, the connoisseur, does not approve of this representation of a woman. Rowland suspects it is of a woman he has encountered during his dissolute holiday. Roderick himself in fact comments that it is 'curiously, almost interestingly bad' and that it 'was false from the first; it has fundamental vices'.[32] From artistic 'truth' and 'the truth' of the word and letter, the form of a woman, as a representation of earthly life, has brought the artist down to the level of falsity.

It is at this critical juncture, when Roderick seems to have abandoned the reading of the law, 'the truth', idealistic art and his glorious imagination for the 'gross' materiality of a mere woman's body that an even worse distraction enters: Christina Light. Christina represents the 'type' that Roderick has a susceptibility to. Earlier, at a picnic suggested by Cecilia a photogenic model had distracted Roderick: 'Miss Striker had her father's pale blue eye; she was dressed as if she were going to sit for her photograph, and remained for a long time with Roderick on a little promontory overhanging the lake'.[33] Mary Garland is one of the party, but Roderick pays no attention to her, so his spending of time with Miss Striker is emphatically an abandonment and an act of infidelity, since we later find that Roderick was involved in a relationship with Mary Garland that led to an engagement at the time. The attention to the photogenic model is also an abandonment of the party's organiser, Cecilia - and the blindness that she represents - for vision. Christina Light is also aligned with the photographic image, by her surname which alludes to photographic light. At her first introduction to Roderick, she significantly remarks that 'I have spent half my life sitting for my photograph, in every conceivable attitude and with every conceivable coiffure'.[34] Christina is a femme fatale and her mother also remarks that '[w]hen she goes into a studio, she's fatal to the pictures'.[35] Christina's worse offence, however, is that she represents material conditions in society, like the artistic model who Roderick had previously shut his eyes to. She is poor enough to have to think of money, and is advised by her mother to only think of money when it comes to marriage. Eventually, she does marry Prince Casamassima for his wealth. She is a materialist.

31 James, 'Roderick Hudson' (n 26), 311.
32 James, *Roderick Hudson* (n 24), 149.
33 Ibid., 73.
34 Ibid., 157.
35 Ibid., 155.

Roderick decides to sculpt a bust of Christina. Christina begins her relationship with Roderick by reducing him from the idealistic sculptor who literally closed his eyes to his models to the level of a portrait artist who reproduces 'an extreme fidelity of detail' from his sitter.[36] Roderick is a man with an attention to detail. Earlier, Rowland remarks that 'when he turned sculptor a capital novelist was spoiled, and that to match his eye for social detail one would have to go to Honoré de Balzac'.[37] The point is that, like Balzac the Realist, Roderick represents detail and through detail, social conditions. Balzac actually wrote, 'the author firmly believes that details alone will henceforth determine the merit of works improperly called *Novels* [*Romans*]'.[38]Balzac therefore has an excessive fidelity to details as well. However, Roderick does not have the 'sense of detail', like Rowland.[39] His adherence to details, one infers, is 'senseless'. The 'senselessness' is apparent in the loss of idealisation in the portrait. Christina causes Roderick to circumvent idealisation since it is said of the bust that, 'without idealization, it was a representation of ideal beauty'.[40] That is, the bust problematically takes on the qualities of 'representation' without a reliance on ideal art. The implicit political dimensions of this form of representation will be further explored in the sequel to the novel, when the image of Christina leads to political anarchy. From then on Roderick's art – and his moral sense – is slowly corrupted. He is unable to rise above the level of portraiture and a 'photographic' fidelity of detail, or particulars, a contrast to his earlier imaginative idealism and reading of the text (one should perhaps say the Text, the Bible). He is tied to the event, the opportunity, and pulled away from the abstract, the removed and the transcendent, the ideal. Now Roderick's photographic gaze is associated with incompleteness, illiteracy, ignorance and unknowing, in contrast to his previous high ability as artist-reader and reader of law. Notably, he fails to complete Mr Leavenworth's statue of culture which is to adorn his library, the commission he receives after he models Christina's bust. He can no longer place his art in the general grounds of reading represented by the library. The suggestion is that Roderick is trapped in a realm of formlessness since he can no longer create. More seriously, Roderick also becomes fascinated by Christina, the photogenic model. He forgets his engagement to Mary Garland and the sanctity of the legal contract of marriage and his filial responsibilities to his mother and he begins a reckless pursuit of her. His fidelity to photographic details causes him to lose all other fidelities. In stark contrast, Rowland the connoisseur, the 'mallet' that is able to bear the burden of the artist (and the art tradition), the constant admirer of Cecilia and thus 'blindness' who keeps up his correspondence with her in Europe *via the letter*, a man who is able to remain immune to the beauty and attentions of Christina, recognises and counters her threat to Roderick's art. Notably, Rowland calls Christina 'dangerous' and 'unsafe' on first seeing her.[41] He also writes disparagingly of her to Cecilia to affirm that he does not love her and sometimes even hates her:

36 Henry James, *Roderick Hudson*, ed. Geoffrey Moore (New York: Penguin, 1986), 165.

37 James, 'Roderick Hudson' (n 26), 299.

38 Honoré de Balzac, *La Comédie Humaine*, I:1175, quoted in Ruth Bernard Yeazell, *Art of the Everyday: Dutch Painting and the Realist Novel* (Princeton, Princeton University Press, 2008), 61.

39 Henry James, *Roderick Hudson* (Boston: James R. Osgood and Company, 1876), 399–400.

40 James, 'Roderick Hudson' (n 26), 519.

41 Henry James, 'Roderick Hudson' in Percy Lubbock (ed), *The Novels and Tales of Henry James, vol 1* (New York: C. Scribner's Sons, 1907), 159.

> And you may take this for truth, because I'm not in love with her. On the contrary I sometimes quite detest her. Her education has been simply infernal. She is corrupt, perverse, as proud as a potentate, and a coquette of the first magnitude.[42]

In the middle of the novel, Rowland meets Christina – where else? – in the Church of St Cecilia, the patron saint of blindness, and effectively warns her away from the sculptor, assessing her as nothing more than a coquette who will not marry him but who has the capacity to drive him to distraction and ruin his 'concentration' and his art.[43]

Rowland's attempt to rescue Roderick from his destructive fascination with Christina Light is unsuccessful and in the closing scenes of the novel he is ultimately to return to Cecilia by himself, while Roderick dies in a symbolic fall in the mountains in his aim to subvert the legal institution of marriage on a number of levels. While photographic vision destroys this artistic subject on the one hand, Christina Light, the materialist, remains a vague threat to order.

Roderick's degeneration is illustrated by the contrast in his subject matter as his career progresses. The subject matter also reveals the qualities of legal representation as compared with a form of representation considered illegitimate. When Roderick is in the phase of being the blind reader of the law, a favourite of Cecilia, he composes a bust of the lawyer who has kindly and paternally given him a place as a legal student. It is a representation of the law. The lawyer is a substitute father figure and reflects patriarchal authority. When his art has been completely corrupted, however, Roderick composes a bust of his mother, his final production. Notably, the bust, the representation of a woman, is 'photographic'. It is incredibly 'minute' and 'detailed', and, again, without 'character', a crucial textual metaphor. It is described thus:

> [t]he poor lady's small, neat, timorous face had certainly no great character, but Roderick had reproduced its sweetness, its mildness, its minuteness, its still maternal passion, with the most unerring art. It was perfectly unflattered, and yet admirably tender; it was the poetry of fidelity.[44]

From the representational order of the law, the patriarchal figure, the reader of the law, a public figure, Roderick moves to the representational order of the maternal figure who is almost characterless, a domestic figure, in keeping with the descent into photographic illiteracy and the position of unknowing and ignorance associated with this vision. The woman is a widow without a husband, an independent woman. She also represents poverty and material conditions. However, Roderick is never entirely within the representational order of the patriarchal figure since his reading of law is incomplete: he demolishes his own bust of the patriarchal figure of the law on learning that he is to be released from the legal reading in a foreshadowing of his total fall.

42 Ibid., 296.
43 James, 'Roderick Hudson' (n 26), 68.
44 Henry James, 'Roderick Hudson', *The Atlantic Monthly*, 36 (1875), 388.

James resurrects Christina Light as an image that threatens writing, reading and law in 1885 with the publication of *The Princess Casamassima*. This novel develops the idea of the type of illegitimate reading which is seen as contrary to the conventional reading of the law and relates it to photography and capitulation to material conditions that Christina represents. This illegitimate reading is seen by James to lead to anarchy if it remains unchecked by art. James associates the reading associated with Christina and details with particularism in politics since she influences a class-based activist, Hyacinth Robinson. Photography is associated with the identity-first politics of the lower classes, or politics which rely on affirming the identity of a group and the oppression that it faces, a form of politics that threatens to subvert and overtake the rule of the dominant economic class. The particularity of details therefore extends to particularism in politics which opposes politics predicated on notions of transcendence and pretended universality in favour of the group identity of the political elite. The novel is written in the context of the aesthetic movement. The main character is Hyacinth Robinson, a bookbinder who considers his profession of turning a book into an image through the embellishment of artisanal craft 'a fine art'.[45] That is, Hyacinth's reading is associated with turning the book into a picture. In order to develop this point, James characterises Hyacinth as representative of a reader seduced by images. This is illustrated not only by his occupation of bookbinding, which interprets the word as an image without any reference to its meaning, but also by the way in which Hyacinth's chosen reading material places the image above the word. Hyacinth's reading habits as a child when he used to stand in front of shop windows consisted of:

> spelling out the first page of the romances in the *Family Herald* and the *London Journal* and admiring the obligatory illustration in which the noble characters (they were always of the highest birth) were presented to the carnal eye. When he had a penny he spent only a fraction of it on stale sugar-candy; with the remaining halfpenny he always bought a ballad, with a vivid woodcut at the top.[46]

Hyacinth's reading shares in the lower class or 'carnal' vision which is directed at those of the highest birth and which therefore removes from them the aura of invincibility and power.

Up until the time he meets Christina Light, now known as the Princess Casamassima, Hyacinth is not very actively political. Yet he is, again, hungry and starved of resources and dwells in a lower-class world of want. He is defined by material conditions, the particulars. The result of his meeting with the Princess leaves Hyacinth 'transformed into willing submission'[47] to the Princess' professed anarchism, earlier 'fascinated submission'.[48] The emphasis is on the idea that

45 Henry James, *The Princess Casamassima, The Novels and Tales of Henry James, vol 5* (New York: Charles Scribner's Sons, 1908), 1: 67.

46 Ibid., 1: 4–5.

47 Ibid., 1: 293.

48 Henry James, *The Princess Casamassima* (London, New York: Macmillan and Co., 1889), 219.

Hyacinth is visually overwhelmed by the Princess. Hyacinth becomes 'fascinated' by Christina Light, an oppressed woman, and what she represents, adaptation to material and economic conditions. Significantly, Christina demands details from Hyacinth, as she appeared to demand of Roderick. When they ride in a coach together, Christina called his attention 'to some prospect, some picturesque detail'.[49] Again, Christina forces the particular details of being from Hyacinth in writing when they correspond as 'she didn't wish vague phrases, protestations or compliments; she wanted the realities of his life, the smallest, most personal details'.[50] The Princess' demand for particulars leads to Hyacinth's acceptance of particularistic politics. Hyacinth becomes immersed in the anarchist movement and Christina Light subsequently invites him to visit her at her London town house. Here, Hyacinth's head is turned. He recklessly pledges his allegiance to the movement at a meeting, and says that he will follow whatever order Hoffendahl, the main foreign plotter and planner, gives him. Christina Light then invites Hyacinth to stay at a country home she has leased which is significantly named 'Medley House' (a 'medley' being a mixture or assortment of various things, such as an image and a word, for example) and where Hyacinth awakes to a view which looked 'everywhere infinitely like a picture'.[51]

Here, like Roderick Hudson who made her his muse over 'the excellent Cecilia', Hyacinth makes Christina Light the votary 'offering' of a bound copy of Tennyson's poems that he has made, a task he completes 'with religion'.[52] The book implicitly represents the merging of writing and the photographic image, and above all, Hyacinth's own form of reading which is primarily visual. This is because, while James may have chosen Tennyson's poems for any number of reasons, it is notable that, in 1874, Tennyson's *Idylls of the King* had been illustrated by the photographer Julia Margaret Cameron. Photography had appeared in poetry before that time, notably in the form of landscape photography, but the collaboration between the poet and photographer seems to be among the first in which the photographs of persons were present enacting scenes. The fact that the collaboration involved the vision and reading of a woman and the text of a man appears significant in the work of gendering in which the allusion is placed. The suggestion is that Hyacinth threatens to begin to read like a woman and to impose that reading onto the book. Such an anxiety is present in a newspaper article of 1892, where the collaboration is described as an imposition on the part of the photographer.[53] The writer depicts the poet as 'pursued by Mrs. Cameron's mania for photography'.[54] The photographer is also presented as corrupting the idealism of the poet and her reading and interpretations are depicted as fallacious and a tying of the imaginative text to gross reality and matter. It is indicative that the journalist refers to the

49 Henry James, *The Princess Casamassima, vol II* (London, New York: Macmillan and Co., 1886), 118.

50 Ibid., 213.

51 James, *The Princess Casamassima* (n 48) 275.

52 Ibid., 1: 299.

53 Anonymous, 'The Lady Photographer and Lord Tennyson', *The Newcastle Courant* (Saturday, 22 October 1892), 5.

54 Ibid.

construction of women, rather than remarking on the depiction of male figures in the collaboration – he ties photography to the presentation of the female form. The writer states of Tennyson that:

> [p]ossibly he had his own ideas of the various female characters of his poems, but it is extremely doubtful whether his ideals correspond to Mrs Cameron's realities. Indeed, I fancy from his manner that he was not always convinced of the suitability of the sitters for the purpose.[55]

Hyacinth's placing as the type of reader that sees poetry in terms of photographs seems to define him, like the woman photographer, as the corrupter of the ideal and the text and poetry, the materialist, he who gives the people of the mind a 'gross' form in the real.

Hyacinth is not able to give Christina the book. To do so would be to accomplish an act of revolution in 'representation' since photography and its details, alongside the vision of a woman, would be united with the highest form of ideal poetry and art. His failure to make the gift is a foreshadowing of Hyacinth's move away from Christina and what she represents. However, the book represents a connection between Hyacinth and Christina, between 'life' and 'death'. It is a tribute to the appearance of Christina and takes on the connotations of a 'ghostly' photographic image materialised, almost a form of representation which she has herself composed:

> it seemed to create a sort of material link between the Princess and himself, and at the end of three months it almost appeared to him, not that the exquisite book was an intended present from his own hand, but that it had been placed in that hand by the most remarkable woman in Europe … the superior piece of work he had done after seeing her last, in the immediate heat of his emotion, turned into a kind of proof and gage, as if a ghost, in vanishing from sight, had left a palpable relic.[56]

There seems to be a further photographic connotation, a reference to spirit photography which indeed appeared to capture ghosts. Indeed, there is perhaps a reference to the photographic image itself, which remains after the event as a kind of ghostly trace.

Hyacinth's seduction by Christina Light, and the illegitimate reading of the female photographer, is however thwarted by his immersion in the artistic tradition. When he returns from his visit to the Princess in the country and his foster mother dies, leaving him a small inheritance, Hyacinth spends several months in Paris and Venice, absorbing European art and culture. He concludes that nothing the 'great rectification', the anarchist solution to injustice, can do for society will sufficiently replace the best that European culture has already produced. The conflict in allegiance between art and anarchy, culture and Christina Light is evident in his last letter to the Princess in this period where he feels 'capable of fighting' for

55 Ibid.
56 James, *The Princess Casamassima* (n 48) 1: 300.

Western art objects. He forgives 'all the despotisms, the cruelties, the exclusions, the monopolies and the rapacities of the past' which were the conditions of manufacture of pieces of fine art. Hyacinth sees his class-based activism 'to hold them too cheap and to wish to substitute for them something in which I can't somehow believe as I do in things with which the aspirations and the tears of generations have been mixed'.[57] As James writes in his preface to the novel from 1908, this conflict of consciousness between the art tradition on one hand and anarchism on the other is the pivotal moment of the novel and Hyacinth's characterisation:

> The complication most interesting then would be that he should fall in love with the beauty of the world, actual; order and all, at the moment of his most feeling and most hating the famous 'iniquity of its social arrangements' so that his position as an irreconcileable pledged enemy to it, thus rendered false by something more personal than his opinions and his vows, becomes the sharpest of his torments.[58]

On returning to England, with this enlarged consciousness of 'order and all', and the 'rendering' of his political desire for revolution as 'false', Hyacinth also realises that the Princess is a 'false idol' since she has fallen into a union with Paul Muniment, the chemist that supersedes Hyacinth (Muniment's brown-stained fingers indeed recall the hands of Victorian photographers). Indeed, there is a strong suggestion that the two are conducting an illicit affair. Hyacinth thus realises that the image of Christina Light, or her form of 'representation', which may be aligned with photography, is on the side or order of *science* and not *art*. This drives Hyacinth into a despair from which he never recovers. It is in the context of his disillusionment with the Princess and his increased 'taste' that he suddenly receives an order from Hoffendahl: he is to attend a ball and assassinate a duke. Hyacinth's response is to turn the pistol he's given for the assassination on himself rather than serve the Princess' cause of anarchism and reproduce the earlier murder of his father by his lower-class mother.

Hyacinth's suicide represents a distancing from Christina Light and the photographic and materialistic, and her position of anarchism, as well as an embracing of the western art tradition and an insistence upon its continuation. It represents a turning away from what James saw as the realistic and literalist assessment of material conditions. Hyacinth fails to move away from the representation of women and their protest against patriarchal power, since women like Christina Light denounced the conditions that made them captives to men's wealth. Through death, Hyacinth is able to 'transcend' the 'particulars' of historical conditions.

In the narrative of these two novels, the body of a woman forced into a materialistic marriage and which appears to demand an attention to details imposes death upon the grand imaginative, artistic conceptions of the artist. It also impacts

57 Henry James, *The Princess Casamassima, The Novels and Tales of Henry James, vol VI* (New York: Charles Scribner's Sons, 1908), 2: 145–146.

58 Henry James, *The Princess Casamassima, The Novels and Tales of Henry James, vol V* (New York: Charles Scribner's Sons, 1908), 1: Preface, xvii.

on his ability to read in an acceptable and conventional manner, particularly in his reading of the law. Christina Light, who is associated with sitting and modelling for the photographs, is a poor woman who represents the almost complete opposite of the political elite. The woman is forced by circumstances that defeat her will, by a larger oppression of women. Thus, her legal identity as wife seems determined by context and material conditions rather than being the product of her own choice and will. James appeared to see this situation as reflective of compromise, submission, passivity and weakness, even if he was sympathetic to the plight of women. I have already indicated above that Hyacinth was first seen to 'submit' to Christina before he changed his intentions: James thus implies that he has adopted passivity, powerlessness and weakness. It seems that James could not grant activity, power and strength to those who he felt had submitted to conditions and been compromised, and could not allow them to change existing conditions through politics. Thus, Christina and Hyacinth, as anarchists, seem to be politically defeated. Through the figure of Hyacinth, James fleshed out his own position: like James, Hyacinth is highly sympathetic to Christina and her 'revenge' on the society that oppressed and wronged her. After all, Hyacinth first joins with her as an anarchist. However, he chooses art over the oppressed woman's social reform, as I suggest James does. Through the lens of the idealist art that both Hyacinth and James adopt, detail and particularity are themselves translated into a political particularism which is seen as selfish and in Hyacinth's case it also puts paid to his ambitions to become a writer.

James elaborated how an illegitimate and photographic reading of the law led to particularism over an implicit idea of universality in both reading and writing the law in *The Tragic Muse* (1899). As I will show, this novel significantly illuminates how a reading of the law dissociated from literalism and particulars was presented as transcending the individuality of the reader and bringing him or her to what was considered to be a greater truth and power. Such a reading was also tied to the power of forming laws and thus ruling, so it was implicitly fashioned in the same terms as the reading of the political elite and could be seen as an outlining of that reading. *The Tragic Muse* is a story about how the photographic gaze takes over a man's life and begins to threaten all of the major legal relations that govern his life. In the novel, Nick Dormer takes up the profession of portrait painting as against the political life he has been brought up to follow in the footsteps of his father, and James explores the repercussions that follow from this choice. As Adam Sonstegard observes, the portrait painting is associated with the photographic gaze in the novel, as Nick Dormer himself thinks of his profession as photographic.[59] Representation relates to a way of seeing rather than a medium in this work: it is not about photography itself, but a kind of vision that is fostered by photography, but can also occur in painting. Sonstegard points out, for example, that when Nick Dormer asks Gabriel Nash for a 'sitting', he likens his art to the art of the photograph, for he says:

59 Adam Sonstegard, 'Painting, Photography, and Fidelity in *The Tragic Muse*', *The Henry James Review*, 24:1 (Winter 2003), 27–44.

> Let me at any rate have some sort of sketch of you as a kind of feather from the angel's wing or a photograph of the ghost—to prove to me in the future that you were once a solid sociable fact, that I didn't invent you, didn't launch you as a deadly hoax.[60]

The association between the photographic and portrait painting does not stop there. It can also be observed that Miriam Rooth, the aspiring actress who is the subject of Nick Dormer's first works in the field, is somehow only 'fit' subject matter for the photographer. For example, when Nick asks Miriam if some of the RAs haven't expressed the wish to have her as a model, she replies, 'Oh dear no, only the tiresome photographers; and fancy them in the future. If mamma could only do that for me!' And she adds, with the charming fellowship for which she was conspicuous at these hours: 'You know I don't think any one yet has been quite so much struck with me as you.'[61] Later on, Miriam is still very much a peculiarly 'photographic' subject: 'She made almost an income out of the photographers—their appreciation of her as a subject knew no bounds …'[62] Nick's portraits of Miriam are also themselves seen as 'photographic'. Their final resting place seems to be among other photographs, rather than in an art gallery, since Basil Dashwood, the man who eventually marries the actress, Miriam, has the conception of 'the eventual right place for the two portraits', which is 'the vestibule of the theatre, where every one going in and out would see them suspended face to face and surrounded by photographs, artistically disposed, of the young actress in a variety of characters'.[63] That is, the portraits are not quite seen as an artistic representation since they are not shown in an art gallery and signify a different form of public representation. There is also an implication that the portrait is not 'true' as it is associated with the photographs of Miriam in character.

The choice of taking up a form of photographic portraiture costs Nick Dormer his seat in Parliament and his ability to carry out the political mission of his father. Nick also departs from his father's readings, or textual organisation of the world through the 'blue-book', or, to put it another way, the parliamentary report. He goes on to say to the character Gabriel Nash that his father 'went through life without a suspicion that there's anything in it that can't be boiled into blue-books, and became in that conviction a very distinguished person. He brought me up in the same simplicity and in the hope of the same eminence'.[64]

Nick's choice of 'representation', artistic and political, is then linked to an idea of the way in which he reads, an unconventional form of political reading. Nick sees the world without the filter of the blue-book. He can see actual, historical and social conditions and is attracted to the reality represented by Miriam, the poor, Jewish woman, rather than seeing through the book, which simplifies and reduces.

60 Henry James, *The Tragic Muse, The Novels and Tales of Henry James, vol VIII* (New York: Charles Scribner's Sons, 1908), 408.

61 Ibid., 2: 43.

62 Ibid., 2: 385.

63 Ibid., 2: 387.

64 James, *The Tragic Muse* (n 60) 1: 181–182.

Indeed, Nick and Miriam make their perverse choice of photographic 'representation', both artistic and political, as they are both a particular kind of reader. Miriam, who 'represents' in the theatre, 'was on almost irreconcilable terms with the printed page save for spouting it'.[65] In her performances, Miriam subordinates the text of the literary dramas she is 'spouting' to her fascinating image which is a delight of the photographers and the theatre-going crowd. Madame Carré declares on first meeting her that Miriam is handsome but that she herself is not a photographer and cannot translate her mere handsomeness into talent.[66] Nick's position as an illegitimate and literal, 'photographic' reader of the law is illustrated when he forsakes a work of legal literature, a monthly 'review' that contains an essay by one 'Mr Hoppus' entitled 'The Revision of the British Constitution'. He leaves it in a round temple which is a copy of one dedicated to the goddess Vesta in the middle of a lake which is described as a passive 'open eye in a dull face', which 'reflected candidly various things that were probably finer than itself—the sky, the great trees, the flight of birds'.[67] The eye is associated with the photographic because it is like a mirror which reflects nature and because Vesta as the goddess of the hearth can be linked to photography through the etymology of the word 'focus'.

Nick leaves behind the important work of legal literature about the *invisible and unwritten laws* which form the constitution of the country and thus its identity. Miriam also presents literature to the eye as 'an image', or is the very image 'in focus and in her frame'.[68] As Miriam sacrifices literature to the focus (this word also has a theatrical connotation, being the most illuminated part of the stage), Nick sacrifices the legal text to focus on the temple in the middle of the passive eye of the lake, itself associated with women through the figure of the goddess.

It is in this context of an illegitimate reading of the law that one can understand Nick's photographic representation as limited and particularistic because the photographic representation is implicitly contrasted to a form of 'universal' political representation. The novel explicitly explores the relationship between portraiture, politics and representation with an emphasis on a politics that 'transcend' the individual. William Goetz writes that *The Tragic Muse* is a complex allegory of representation itself and that the theme of representation is its 'primary subject-matter'.[69] Goetz argues that this theme is pursued through puns and word-play. For example, the term 'representation' links Miriam's acting and Nick's photographic portrait painting. However, for Goetz, the full pun emerges a few pages later, where the conflict between Nick's political and artistic interests is discussed. A rumour has sprung up that the Member of Parliament keeps an artist's studio in South Kensington: 'It was an absurd place to see his constituents, unless he wanted to paint their portraits, a kind of representation with which they scarcely would have

65 Ibid., 1: 225.

66 Ibid., 1: 115.

67 Ibid., 1: 268–269.

68 Ibid., 2: 54, 248.

69 William R. Goetz, 'The Allegory of Representation in *The Tragic Muse*', *The Journal of Narrative Technique*, 8:3 (Fall 1978), 152.

been satisfied'.[70] Goetz notes that the pun is no accident, for after he has won the election, Nick reflects on his aptly named borough, Harsh: 'What a droll thing to 'represent,' when one thinks of it! And what does *it* represent, poor torpid little borough, with its smell of meal and its curiously fat-faced inhabitants?'[71] The perversity of Nick is that he chooses to 'represent' portraiture 'photographically' rather than politically, favouring the degraded and inferior form of representation. As political representative for Harsh, Nick would become something more than a mere man. He would become an entity which contains within itself the community and therefore become 'universal' and above the 'particular'. He would become a politician that makes laws, or become the law-giver and take on the mantle of the patriarchal figure just as he becomes one with the patriarchal 'spirit' of the law with its pretended 'universality'. The implicit comparison with the power of a Christian God, the supreme patriarchal figure, is evident. However, Nick steadfastly refuses to do this, fastening on to the photographic gaze which is anti-social or solitary, outside of the community of norms, a gaze which furthermore insists on showing economic and sexual oppression by focusing on the poor woman. The woman is Jewish and is thus associated with racist stereotypes of materialism, misers and penny-pinching, although this is never explicitly alluded to. Therefore, Nick 'represents', but only in a limited fashion rather than in a broader and more powerful way. The novel's title alludes to his limited choice of representation and how it is associated with the woman's body and particularism. Sir Joshua Reynolds' portrait of the famous English tragic actress Sarah Siddons was entitled *The Tragic Muse* (1784). The painter put his name 'the story says, to go down to posterity on the hem of her skirt'.[72] Reynolds put down his identity and name as a *detail* upon the body of a woman just as Nick decides to paint Miriam and link himself with her form. He chooses the detail and the particular, ephemeral and limited form of the representation of a woman and portraiture over the field of politics, law and legal writing which is seen as broader and universal. Similarly, Miriam makes a perverse choice in representation in the novel as well. She chooses to represent on the stage (whose lowness in status as a form of representation is in evidence throughout the novel) rather than marry Peter Sherringham and become the wife of an ambassador, a representative of his country.[73] As an ambassador's wife, she would also have represented the country. This is implicit when Peter Sherringham's view of marriage and of his wife are described:

> he held that a man in his position was, above all as the position improved, essentially a representative of the greatness of his country, he considered that

70 James, *The Tragic Muse* (n 60) 1: 83.

71 Ibid., 1: 243.

72 George R. Kernodle, *The Theatre in History* (Fayetteville, AR: University of Arkansas Press, 1989), 509.

73 My speculation is that James' attempt to write plays is like his use of photographic frontispieces in the New York edition. That is, he wishes to subvert the representations of photography and theatre from within through writing.

> the wife of such a personage would exercise in her degree—for instance at a foreign court—a function no less symbolic.[74]

The Tragic Muse then reiterates the relationships between reading the law, particulars and the photographic gaze and shows how ideas of transcendence and universality determine the concept of the law and its writing. The photographic reading of the law is portrayed as not being able to represent: it cannot lead to the writing of a law. The photographic reading and representation is contrasted to the true patriarchal, political representation and true law in which the individual becomes the symbol of the collective, 'the universal voice of the people'. The photographic gaze is associated with a form of 'illiteracy' and unknowing which presents literature or legal literature to the passive, the photographic eye, itself feminised.

In the work of James, 'particularism' is continually being pitted against an idea of political 'universality', although this universality mainly supports the economically dominant. In *The Bostonians* (1886), feminism is also implicated in the photographic vision as a particularised form of 'truth' and 'knowing' and this particularism is again defeated to support the powerful. The fascinating Verena who is the voice of the feminist position is the daughter of a mesmerist who poses like a photographic model ('his hands were now always in the air, as if he were being photographed in postures'), or accommodates himself to the photograph and the photographic vision. [75] The final scene sees her abducted from the scene of her public address and her political speechifying, covered over and thus hidden by the law in the form of the lawyer Basil Ransom and thus made invisible (in a subtle contrast to her father's photographic visibility). The name Verena means 'the truth'. The form of the 'universal truth' that a conventional or accepted reading of the law supports in James' work, as representative of the fiction I have studied, and in the covering over of Verena is thus clear: the truth must be divorced from the construction and statement of identity even as it produces persons; it must be dissociated from being and the body and situation in reality just as it is disassociated from politics while it politically orders persons and things. The fiction supports a concealed form of truth which presents itself as apolitical, even though it reinforces the political status quo. The apolitical stance of the fiction of idealism affects not only the representation of reading in writing, but also problematises political struggle against injustice in the name of false generalisations. This apolitical stance has to be seen as a deliberate, pre-emptive strategy of power to protect itself and reveals the larger manoeuvres that representation and ideas of reading are involved in: ideals are recruited in the service of the elimination of resistance and difference, the elimination of justice for the oppressed.

Blindness, reading and truth

In this chapter, I have tried to show that James saw photography and the reading associated with it to be a corruption of the conventional reading of the law. I have

74 James, *The Tragic Muse* (n 60) 1: 316.
75 Henry James, *The Bostonians* (London: Heron Books, 1976), 100.

suggested that he did so because he conceptualised the law as universal and modelled on the terms of an ideal art which was believed to portray the broader and the more general. James saw the literal, 'photographic' reading of the law as unable to move past a vision of the details and a politics associated with particularism, as I have indicated in my reading of *The Tragic Muse*. I now wish to explore blindness more thoroughly in James' work since he associated this vision with the conventional reading of the law, as I have already indicated in my reading of *Roderick Hudson*. Blindness is important to study since the works of fiction I have studied cast blindness as normative and see it to be the crucial determiner of an identity of a legitimate reader. It is blindness that is seen to separate the reader from the literalist reading, as I aim to show below. In the writings of James, this is done through the associations made around the term 'tears' in his writings. Here, I follow the insight of Jacques Derrida, who calls tears the 'veil of the eyes', in order to suggest that tears in James symbolise the idealised 'blindness' that is evident in novels such as *Roderick Hudson*. Derrida writes of 'the wisdom of tears' that:

> For at the very moment they veil sight, tears would unveil what is proper to the eye. And what they cause to surge up out of forgetfulness, there where the gaze or look looks after it, keeps it in reserve, would be nothing less than *alēthea*, the *truth* of the eyes, whose ultimate destination they would thereby reveal: to have imploration rather than vision in sight, to address prayer, love, joy, or sadness rather than a look or gaze. Even before it illuminates, revelation is the moment of the 'tears of joy'.[76]

If for Derrida, then, tears are the 'veils of the eye' and carry 'blindness' and a 'truth' which is 'wise', this is also the case in the work of James. Tears and their blurry vision, their blindness and veiling of the eye, are consistently associated with legality, community, art and order in James' works.

Above, I have already discussed a quote from *The Princess Casamassima*, when Hyacinth writes to the Princess that 'the monuments and treasures of art, the great palaces and properties, the conquests of learning and taste, the general fabric of civilisation as we know it', are 'things with which the aspirations and the tears of generations have been mixed'.[77] This quote reflects Hyacinth's indoctrination by art's order and his alienation from the desire for revolution as I have indicated above but I did not investigate why the tears that were mentioned were significant. 'The tears of generations' carry the weight of authority: Hyacinth 'believes' in these things. The mythic resonance of Hyacinth's name carries a further association with tears and art and order. In the myth, the god's tears play a crucial role in the denouement. When Hyacinth died, Apollo did not allow Hyacinth to be claimed by Hades. Instead, he made a flower, the hyacinth, from his spilled blood. According to Ovid's *Metamorphoses*, Apollo's tears stained the newly formed flower's petals as a testament to his grief. Thus, when Hyacinth sacrifices himself to art and the

76 Jacques Derrida, *Memoirs of the Blind: The Self-Portrait and Other Ruins*, (Pascale-Anne Brault and Michael Naas (trs), Chicago and London: The University of Chicago Press, 1993), 126.

77 James, *The Princess Casamassima* (n 48), 2: 145–146.

preservation of order and Apollo, there is a symbolic place in the afterlife where he is going to merge his subjectivity with the tears of the god. Hyacinth is going to be initiated into the vision of the god and the blindness within it – he is going to achieve the idealised vision which James appears to rate so highly and to merge with the spirit of the patriarchal figure. The god and his tears stand for transcendence, universality, eternity and omniscience.

Tears and their veiled vision are also a part of the crucial recognition scene in *The Wings of the Dove* (1902) and tied more explicitly to reading and law. Here, Lord Mark invites the dying Milly Theale into the house at Matcham to show her a portrait by Bronzino of a woman who he believes resembles her. As they contemplate the artwork, Milly's eyes fill with tears and she identifies with the portrait in an act of self-representation: 'Milly recognised her exactly in words that had nothing to do with her. 'I shall never be better than this.'[78] It can be observed that Milly's 'recognition' is of her own impending death, as the woman in the painting is described as 'dead'. However, this does not do justice to the complexity of self-representation and identification in this scene of recognition. I agree that on the one hand, the painting represents extinction, but that of femininity since it is reflective of the impending death of a woman and also because the tears veil a woman's vision. However, tears and their veiling of vision are also crucial to the recognition and identification that Milly finds in the painting. Mark Fenster and Kevin Ohi write that:

> The self-recognition is blurred from the outset, leaving open the possibility that the recognition is possible because her vision is blurry. More important, though, is the assertion of causality: 'the reason it came was that she found herself, for the first moment, looking at the mysterious portrait through tears.' On one level, the moment seems to assert that recognition has outpaced cognition, that Milly has seen the resemblance which her tears then allow her to cognize. But a more unsettling possibility also emerges of a groundless relation: her tears make possible the recognition that they are also generated by.[79]

Fenster and Ohi also note that Milly's self-recognition is part and parcel of the way everyone else sees her: it is an entry into the gaze of the community. Some of what Milly can recognise 'in' the painting is her own gaze at it as a redoubling of everyone else's gaze at her. For example, 'Lady Aldershaw meanwhile looked at Milly quite as if Milly had been the Bronzino and the Bronzino only Milly'. Lady Aldershaw's gaze has been prepared by Kate, who has brought her to see the resemblance: '[s]he had brought a lady and a gentleman to whom she wished to show what Lord Mark was showing Milly'.[80] Tears are associated with community (that of the wealthy), but not just this, with identity, the recognition of the self and self-representation. Significantly, Fenster and Ohi also note the implicit comparison and contrast of the

78 Henry James, *The Wings of the Dove, The Novels and Tales of Henry James, vols XIX and XX* (New York: Charles Scribner's Sons, 1909), 1: 220–221.

79 Mark Fenster and Kevin Ohi (eds), *Henry James and the Queerness of Style* (Minneapolis: University of Minnesota Press, 2008), 77–78.

80 Ibid., 80.

scene of recognition and self-representation with the opening of the novel, where Milly's nemesis, love-rival and foil, the dishonourable, false and deceptive materialist and opportunist, Kate Croy sees herself in a mirror (or 'literally'). They write that, 'like the novel's opening, this instance of mirroring raises the question of interiority'.[81] Kate Croy represents materialism and particularism since she schemes to take away money and love from Milly in her own self-interest. As a poor women who has to make the best of the system of economic and sexual oppression, Kate attempts to trap and exploit Milly. However, James invites us to see Kate as a villain, even though it is material conditions which compel her to think and act in the way that she does. Kate is 'clever' and monstrous, open to 'reality' and 'real conditions', 'the real thing', like the photographers and 'photographic' novelists that Henry James denounced.[82] In fact, if William J. Maseychik is right, it is in fact Milly, who identifies with the reader as represented by art, that is seen as 'the real thing': the name 'Theale' may come from 'Thing' and 'Real'.[83]

The painting in which Milly recognises herself is of *The Portrait of Lucrezia Panciatichi* (1545), where the subject holds an open book, according to Miriam Allott.[84] A. R. Tintner wrote more recently that the view is also supported by the likelihood that James had read a description of the painting by Vernon Lee in *Hauntings: Fantastic Stories* (1897).[85] Thus, the Bronzino portrait with which Milly identifies is that of the reader. Through her tears, through her assumption of the conventional, idealised, 'blindness', Milly is able to identify with the figure of the reader, just as she identifies with the death and extinction of woman. However, one cannot ignore the representation of wealth in the image presented through the sumptuous clothing and high social status of Lucrezia. This stands opposed to the poor woman like Christina Light (and Kate Croy) that threatens art, the law and representation in the works of James through her being and 'literalist' assessment and exploitation of material conditions. In fact, the name 'Lucrezia' actually means 'wealth'. James sees the wealthy and wealth itself as the legitimate foundations of the reader: Roderick Hudson's legal reading and art is supported by wealthy patrons like Rowland, Nick Dormer sacrifices a wealthy marriage for his

81 Ibid., 82.

82 James wrote, 'M. Heilbuth is very real … but his Roman skies are strangely gray and cold, and his pictures have to an inordinate degree that deplorable look of being based upon photographs, which is the bane of so much of the clever painting of our day. The painters have used photographs so much in their work that the result is tainted by that hideous inexpressiveness of the mechanical document. You see that the picture has been painted by a short cut.' James, 'The Picture Season in London' (n 8) 155.

83 William J. Maseychik, 'Points of Departure from *The American*', in Tony Tanner (ed), *Henry James: A Selection of Critical Essays* (London: Macmillan International Higher Education, 1968), 126.

84 Miriam Allott, 'The Bronzino Portrait in Henry James's the Wings of the Dove', *Modern Language Notes*, 68:1 (1953), 23–25.

85 Sarah Wootton, 'Henry James's Venice and the Visual Arts', in Michael O'Neill, Mark Sandy and Sarah Wootton (eds), *Venice and the Cultural Imagination: 'This Strange Dream upon the Water'* (New York: Routledge, 2015), 130. Wootton quotes A. R. Tintner, *Henry James and the Lust of the Eyes: Thirteen Artists in His Work* (Baton Rouge, LA: Louisiana State University Press, 1993), 95–104.

photographic portraiture and the incorrect literalist reading. The material conditions of property and economy which preserve the power of the political elite are lauded as the basis of subjectivity, being, reading and the reader. It is such conditions that give leisure to the leisured classes and protect them from constantly thinking about money and material conditions. It is rich men that are implicitly invoked, since the painting represents the death and extinction of women (the death of the real woman for the woman presented in art by a man). In my view, James does not actually support the absence of particularity in reading, or in the identity of the reader. The rich are only seen as being above particularity because they are rich. It is a rich person's reading and a rich reader that James supports. In *The Wings of the Dove*, Milly's moment of identification with wealth is an awful insight into the way in which ideas of economic status alienate individuals in society and create asymmetries of power which are evident in the way in which reading and the reader are understood. Law is enmeshed in such ideas, since James relates the death of Milly to her status as a testator with a 'will', or a writer of laws and a law-giver. Milly is associated with 'good' law and legal power because in dying, the death that she sees in the portrait, she gives money to Merton in her will for the sole reason that she loves him. This is despite knowing that he and Kate had set out to trap her with fraudulent love for mercenary reasons. Milly thus controls law and legal relations through her death and her wealth, or 'writes the law', and can be understood as a cipher for wealth itself, as well as for a discriminating law which allows the economically dominant to hold the reins of legal power, all under the implicit idea of benignity and philanthropy. However, the condition of Milly's law is that Kate's planning and strategies are defeated. It is only in her defeat that Milly can do what appears to be beautiful, 'large' and generous. Milly's law and love are associated with eternity, since the Bronzino portrait bears the motto 'AMOUR DURE SANS FIN' ('love lasts eternally') on the links of the necklace. The idea in *The Wings of the Dove* is that Milly is a legally minded or 'legitimate' individual because she is contrasted to the 'illegitimate' Kate Croy who is out to 'defraud' her from her money through trickery. It is notable that Kate Croy has 'illegitimate' sexual relationships outside of the legal contract of marriage with Merton Densher, another example of her status as an outlaw.

The association of Milly's identification with the reader as represented by art and with ideas of a 'larger truth' is developed later in the novel. James writes of Milly's moments of seeing the portrait:

> the moments that had exactly made the highwater-mark of her security, the moments during which her tears themselves, those she had been ashamed of, were the sign of her consciously rounding her protective promontory, quitting the blue gulf of comparative ignorance and reaching her view of the troubled sea.[86]

The moments when Milly recognises herself through the veil of tears and blindness as the reader are associated with 'her view of the troubled sea' and with the loss of

86 James, *The Wings of the Dove* (n 78) XX: 144.

ignorance and the movement into the 'larger' sphere of 'the truth' and 'knowing'. James seems to invoke a passage from Immanuel Kant. The vision of the sea, with its associations with power and the boundless, was for Kant a pre-eminent inducement to feelings of sublimity. This was if it were not seen *literally* as an entity in nature with physical existence. As he wrote:

> when we judge the sight of the ocean we must not do so on the basis of how we *think* it, enriched with all sorts of knowledge which we possess (but which is not contained in the direct intuition), e.g., as a vast realm of aquatic creatures, or as the great reservoir supplying the water for the vapors that impregnate the air with clouds for the benefit of the land, or again as an element that, while separating continents from one another, yet makes possible the greatest communication among them; for all such judgments will be teleological. Instead we must be able to view the ocean as poets do, merely in terms of what manifests itself to the eye, e.g. if we observe it while it is calm, as a clear mirror of water bounded only by the sky; or, if it is turbulent, as being like an abyss threatening to engulf everything and yet find it sublime.[87]

It is possible that James was using Kant's ideas, as Milly moves from a state of the sea's mirror-like passivity in her 'protective promontory', or 'ignorance', to a vision of the sea at the height of its power, an entity which threatens to engulf and thus contain everything within itself. The troubled sea might refer to the ambition of power, conventional knowledge and its totalitarian drive to contain and thus control everything by eschewing literality and mimesis, or 'mirroring', a vision which compares with the mirror in which Kate Croy sees herself in an act of self-representation at the beginning of the novel.[88]

Conclusion

If the representation of detail was seen as a key strength of photography, James attempted to transform it into a fatal weakness. As I have attempted to show in this chapter, he associated the detail with women of lower economic status, political particularism and an incorrect reading of the law. His fiction and his construction of ideal reading is therefore heavily implicated in a marginalisation of women and the elimination of political difference to the political elite, no matter how sympathetic he was to the plight of women.

A study of James' work reveals the version of legal truth and the ideal gaze which the supporters of the status quo held and how these were structurally reinforced by fiction. The implication of his association between details and identity politics is that the legal truth in his writings is considered general, abstract, timeless and universal, removed from particulars and particularism. The correct and ideal vision was to see the law in this way and this was figured as

87 Immanuel Kant, *Critique of Judgment* (Werner Pluhar (ed), Indianapolis: Hackett, 1987), 130.
88 James, *The Wings of the Dove* (n 78) XIX, 4–5.

intentional blindness to the body of the poor woman, as in Roderick Hudson's closing of his eyes against the vision of the poor model that posed for him in his manufacture of idealist art. Importantly, in James' work, as in the other fiction I have studied, the form of the 'universal truth' which is valued and accepted is made apparent. It is to be disassociated from the explicit assertion of identity and from explicit questions of power and political representation. This is why the anarchists in *The Princess Casamassima* are defeated, because they rely on their lower-class identities and participate in class activism. Photographic vision, the type of reading associated with it and the representation of details are all associated with the explicit statement of identity, and the formations of political identity and representations that surround it, hence the portrayals of anarchists in the work of James are tied to ideas of photography. Thus, photographic vision is associated with the voices of the subjugated and powerless who are concerned to enter into the field of power and politics on the basis of their subjugation. In the fiction I have studied, the photographic vision is consistently that of a particularistic and situated politics which challenges the political elite. It is when the powerless speak of the iniquity of the social arrangement and their placing within this system that they are seen to adopt a 'photographic' vision. This photographic vision is associated with those who aim to overturn the existing order of dominance and, also, with those who realise that representation and 'the truth' are nothing more than a contest of dominance in which the spoils go to the victor. In the fiction the photographic is associated with those groups excluded from representation in all of its dimensions, political and artistic, because it seems to be conceptualised as a form of representation which represents 'reality' and social conditions rather than gives the illusion of a removed stance, universality and abstraction.

Thus, in his support of universal truth and idealist art, James, like Hyacinth, supported the political status quo over his own sympathy to women. The writings of James reveal how individuals were forced to go against their own identities and identifications with others to the political elite in the aesthetic regime and why fiction was so focused on presenting a correct reading of the law in its strategy of control. Blindness to the oppressed and submission to the conditions of oppression was imposed upon them in the name of art and the law.

In the writings of James, and in my research so far, I have focused on how an understanding of the individual photograph and its key attributes determined ideas of reading and the power of reading. In the next chapter of the monograph, I will change my focus to a study of how the photograph album as a collection of photographs determined the reading of the law. The photograph album was seen as holding narrative power which, I will argue, was understood directly to challenge fiction and its construction of reading. As a result, I see the conditions and determinants of the reading that fiction promoted to again be made evident and to define themselves again in relation to literalism and the literalist reader. I will argue that the narrative power of photograph albums was associated with the power and plots of outsiders to the political elite and their intended readers. As a result, legitimate narratives and their intended readers can be seen to be shaped in response to outsiders so as to consolidate the power and plots of the political elite. The larger plot that fiction was engaged in against perceived difference, to create its own unique readers, I contend, is thus made visible, revealing the larger structuring of fiction and reading as well as the general strategy of power.

4 Photograph albums in fiction

The illegitimate plots and counter-narratives of the photograph-book

In her chapter on the relationship between the photograph album and fiction, Jennifer Green-Lewis has suggested that the practice of keeping scrapbooks and photograph albums was 'one obvious model for David's form of memorializing' in Charles Dickens' novel *David Copperfield* (1850)[1] Significantly, she describes the photograph album as a narrative form, much like the novel itself. As she states, 'the photograph album rendered the passage of time both as object and narrative, giving shape and solidity to the mysterious and life-conferring act of recollection'.[2] In this chapter, I share Green-Lewis' idea that photograph albums were associated with narrative function and this was why they were of importance to fiction and exploited by it. However, by concentrating on the representation of the photograph album within fiction itself and its relationship to the law within that fiction, including in writing by Charles Dickens himself, I wish to show that the narrative function of the photographic album was problematised in the fiction I have studied and to explain why this was so. I see the narrative function of the photograph album to have been perceived as competition and a significant threat to the writing of fiction. The photograph album was seen to usurp the narrative function of fiction. I suggest that it is important to study this area because it reveals exactly what the larger aims of fiction as narrative were supposed to be and in what sense they were perceived as being legitimate. That is, I argue, a study of why the narrative function of the photograph album was perceived as being illegitimate is necessarily tied to ideas of legitimate narrative function to which it is compared, either explicitly or implicitly. The analysis in this chapter builds on my previous descriptions of the denunciation of the individual photograph in fiction to show exactly how collections of photographs in books were seen as an uncanny double to fiction itself and to delineate the terms of that uncanniness: how exactly writers of fiction were afraid of their own narrative devices and resources being used by alternative authors with alternative forms of representation to produce readers. I will concentrate on aiming to show how and why photographic albums were associated with the illegitimate plots of characters in novels which aimed to produce readers. These, I argue, were seen as the photographic counter-forms of legitimate fiction. I want to show why and how ideas of law were invoked to denounce the photographic

1 Jennifer Green-Lewis, 'Victorian Photography and the Novel', in Lisa Rodensky (ed), *The Oxford Handbook of the Victorian Novel* (Oxford: Oxford University Press, 2013), 327–330.
2 Ibid., 327.

DOI: 10.4324/9781003173854-5

album as an alternative source of narrative and to legitimise conventional and accepted plots of characters. At the same time, I also want to show how ideas of reading and readers were constructed through the opposition between legitimate plots and the plots associated with the photograph album. I aim to build my analysis towards the ending of the chapter where the construction of the reading of the law in fiction can be seen against a background of the photographic album's perceived usurpation of fiction in Charles Dickens' novel *Our Mutual Friend* (1865).

The context to the relationship between the photograph album, art and fiction

I first wish to contextualise the fiction within a well-established tradition in writing which criticises the photograph album either explicitly or implicitly. I do this without in any way suggesting that the photograph album was always seen in this way by commentators across society or aiming to reductively present the photographic album, with its various forms, as always the same thing. However, I do emphasise that there were widely shared currents in writing which writers of fiction were alert to and which relied on a unitary idea of the photograph album as a collection of portraits. I will contextualise the fiction in this way, first, in order to outline directly the explicit connections made between the photographic album, art and fiction in non-fiction. I also wish to go on to demonstrate that the fiction exploits the connections made in order to go on to relate the photograph album to ideas of narrative function and the law in the same way that it did with the individual photograph and art criticism regarding photography. This survey of writings indicates that the photographic album was consistently seen as inartistic and also indicates how the photograph album was thought of as incapable of being seen as legitimate fiction and being seen as a published book.

I will first aim to show how photographic albums were seen as inartistic with a concentration on prose writing. I have concentrated on brief digressions in periodicals of the time because these seem to assume, or even state, that the audience unquestionably shared the same view and do not argue the case or aim to persuade anyone that this is the case, but outline the album's lack of artistic status as something of an accepted and conventional fact. I believe that this position indicates how well established the ideas of such authors were. One such example is a note by an anonymous author in *Chambers' Journal of Popular Literature, Science and Arts* in 1888, which discusses 'The Fading of Photographs'. The author writes:

> The family album upon the drawing-room table is a never-failing subject of interest to visitors, and among individuals who lack original ideas, forms an agreeable subject of conversation in place of that of the weather. Of late years, however, there is more diffidence in placing it in prominent positions for the ready examination of waiting friends, the sad-coloured pictures of 'the hue of a November fog in Cheapside, or a bad piece of gingerbread spoilt in the baking', being at variance with average ideas of artistic elegance.[3]

3 Anonymous, 'The Fading of Photographs', *Chambers' Journal of Popular Literature, Science and Arts*, 5: 215 (11 February 1888), 94.

Given the subjects of the photographs that he or she describes, the writer clearly views the photograph album as the repository of what is inelegant, or rather, trivial, banal and of insufficient importance or interest to be elevated into a respectable art-form. The seemingly incongruous elements which the author mentions, intended to be humorous, also seem to present the photographic album as incoherent. This idea is taken up by others. Where the photographic album is described as a species of art in the same journal earlier in 1878, in a story about the characters within it entitled 'Pictures from an Old Album', the anonymous author describes it in terms that have a very strong negative connotation. The anonymous writer states that 'To the stranger my collection must seem a curious hodge-podge of art, suggestive of past times and fashions'.[4] The noun 'hodge-podge' suggests 'a clumsy mixture of ingredients', a meaning that was often used contemptuously.[5]

As the above examples indicate, the art status and even the coherence of the photograph album was contested by writers over a number of years and this idea was presented as widely held by the authors. I now wish to show how this idea was directly related to ideas of fiction in a piece of prose writing in which the application of photography to book illustration was discussed in order to stress the connections made and because I aim to show how fiction related itself to the photograph album in a similar fashion below. The article 'Photography Applied to Book Illustration' in *The Gentleman's Magazine and Historical Review* by an anonymous author in 1867 discussed both whether photographs could illustrate fiction and whether an album of photographs could be seen as a finished book. Before discussing the album, the article clearly set out the idea that photographs could not illustrate fiction because they were inartistic even though attempts had been made to do so. As the author stated:

> The class of illustration to which photography can be applied is obviously limited. It cannot create, it can only copy; its results are descriptive rather than suggestive. Its subjects must be real, and we cannot therefore illustrate poetry or fiction by it. It is true, many attempts have been made to produce and multiply artistic compositions by its aid; but successful as those have been in their way, they have only been regarded as curiosities—seldom, if ever, as works of art. The use of photography as an illustrative art thus becomes restricted to the representation of natural scenes and objects, and artistic or architectural works. Hence the books which can be successfully illustrated by it are mostly of the topographical or descriptive class.[6]

For the author, photographs were to be separated from fiction as well as most other kinds of writing and artistic composition. They were seen to have a limited use.

4 Anonymous, 'Pictures from an Old Album', *Chambers' Journal of Popular Literature, Science and Arts* (23 December 1878), 783, 826.

5 *Oxford Dictionaries, s.v.* 'hodge-podge' (last accessed 12 December 2018) http://www.oed.com/view/Entry/87541?rskey=24mpwV&result=1&isAdvanced=false#eid.

6 Anonymous, 'Photography Applied to Book Illustration', *The Gentleman's Magazine and Historical Review*, 3 (February 1867), 174.

It is in this context that we can situate the article's ideas of the photograph album as an unfinished article. The same article set out the idea that some collections of photographs in books, along with writing, only counted as albums, not as a finished book, despite the fact that they had been published. The article therefore also implicitly excluded photographic albums as proper books. As the author wrote:

> In the volume of 'Memorials of the Rev. J. Keble' we have some thirty photographs of places with which the author of the 'Christian Year' was associated. The volume is rather an album of scraps, pictorial and literary, than a complete work; indeed, the writer of the notes, which seem to be secondary to the photographs, regards the book in the light of a help to the reader of any life of the poet, inasmuch as the *disjecta membra* he has brought together constitute such material as might, and possibly would, be neglected in any but an exhaustive biography.[7]

What is important to emphasise is that the book discussed combined photographs with writings in the same way that much of the fiction I have studied did and it was perceived as mistakenly presenting writing as inferior to photography. As such, it was seen as not forming a coherent whole with an organised narrative function, but as a series of fragments, contemptuously referred to as scraps, as though they were also something left over or unimportant in their own right and recycled. This is an echo of the photograph album as a hodge-podge of art and, indeed, at the same time the author echoed and stressed the point I have indicated above, that the photographic book described as an album was not sufficiently important to figure as a book in its own right. It can be seen from this example then, that where the photographic album incorporated writing and impinged on its carefully guarded terrain, it was seen as a usurper and its narrative function was rejected. The photograph album was also regarded as unfinished and without much value. I stress these points because the fiction I have studied, as I aim to show, exploited these ideas in order to stress the illegitimacy of the photographic album as an alternative to fiction in the traditional medium of writing. Thus, the plots associated with the photograph book were deliberately thwarted in fiction so that they remained forever 'unfinished'.

A last example shows that the photograph album was seen as deficient in narrative power and also suggests why this was said to be so. I suggest that it is an important source, although it is, again, a brief digression. In this piece of writing, the author divested the photograph album of narrative function and this strategy, I will aim to show, was exploited by the fiction that I have studied and allows it to be understood as a response to competition from other forms of representation. I will aim to show that fiction similarly attempted to take away the photograph album's claims to be a narrative by foiling the plots of the characters that were associated with it, plots which, most importantly, aimed to produce readers. In this crucial source, in the conclusion of a critique of photography, penned by an anonymous author in *The London Review and Weekly Journal of Politics, Literature, Art, and Society* in 1862, the author stated that:

7 Ibid., 178.

> Still, just as something may be learned or guessed from the back of a book about its contents, so photographs give some hint of the profession and promise of men. But the amount which they reveal is very small, and a photographic album which should contain all the actors on the stage of history would be of little more value than the table of *dramatis personae* prefixed to a play.[8]

The author thus saw a photograph album as severely limited because of its association with photographic portraiture, as a list of the characters or actors in a drama rather than the drama itself. In his or her view, the photograph album was not able to support narrative function, whether of telling the story of the unfolding of history, or the drama in a play. The photograph album was again separated from the writing of fiction in a way that was energetically taken up by the writers I study in this chapter, who could not allow the plot associated with photograph albums to establish relationships between characters as in a drama, or to characterise individuals.

A fictional representation of the photographic album as a narrative powerhouse

Having shown how the photographic album was separated from art and fiction in prose writing, I now wish to outline why precisely its narrative function was seen as such a threat to the writing of fiction. This is because the fiction I will discuss in this chapter implicitly relied on and suggested ideas of the photograph album's narrative function and I wish to make explicit what these ideas actually were. It can be noted that photograph albums could be seen to compete directly with works of fiction in terms of the books market and that they had a considerable influence, so the fears of fiction writers were not wholly irrational. Most prominently, Mayall's *Royal Album* of portraits of the royal family in 1860 was a sensational success which led to a second published album and has been described as both the beginning of the 'carte-de-visite craze' (the craze for having and collecting visiting cards, including photographs) and providing the impetus for people to have their own family album.[9] Around this time, photograph albums were explicitly recognised as having a narrative function. The poem, 'The Photograph Album', semi-anonymously authored by H.C. in 1873 stated of the photographs in the photograph album that 'such tales are told beneath the sun'.[10] However, rather than looking to earlier accounts of the photograph album's narrative function, I will discuss Vernon Lee's short story 'Ghosts in a Roman Photograph Album' (1920) in terms of the photograph album's perceived power, influence and narrative function. This is because this piece of writing explicitly invokes a

8 Anonymous, 'Photographs', *The London Review and Weekly Journal of Politics, Literature, Art, and Society*, 5 (9 August 1862), 110, 119.

9 Patrizia di Bello, +*Women's Albums and Photography in Victorian England: Ladies, Mothers and Flirts* (Aldershot, Hampshire and Burlington, VT: Ashgate, 2007), 70.

10 H.C. 'The Photograph Album', *The Gentleman's Magazine* 11 (August 1873), 193.

number of connections between fictional writing, narrative and the photograph album from the 1860s and also because it presents the photograph album of this period as a peculiarly 'overwhelming' narrative powerhouse. In short, Lee presents an account of the photograph album as a narrative that seems to realise all of the fears of its power that the authors I have studied responded to and shows why the photograph book was seen as such a source of competition. Lee may have been writing at a time when writers were no longer threatened by photography because modernist fiction no longer tried to be mimetic in the same way.[11] Furthermore, Lee, who frequently wrote about travel, can be seen to have been strongly influenced in this short story by travel photography towards the end of nineteenth century and the commercial marketing and drives of the tourism industry behind it. Prior to the short story, Lee had written in the essay 'On Modern Travelling' (1897) that:

> All I can ask is, do you know what it is to meet, say, in some college room, or on the staircase of an English country house, or even close behind the front door in Bloomsbury, the photograph of some Florentine relief or French cathedral, the black, gaunt Piranesi print of some Roman ruin; and to feel suddenly Florence, Rouen, Reims, or Rome, the whole of their presence distilled, as it were, into one essence of emotion?[12]

The tourist photograph therefore had a strong effect of the immediacy of place on Lee and she ranked it alongside the art of Piranesi. Her reaction to the travel photograph, about which she writes above and in the narrator's account in 'Ghosts in a Roman Photograph Album' seems to have been conditioned by the commercial imperatives and marketing of the tourism industry, which relied on photographs which are specified, as Sara Dominici writes in her doctoral thesis, as 'tourists' photographs as first-hand experience images'.[13] Dominici, in her focus on photography, elaborates that such photographs provided a form of 'indoor travel':

> [t]he idea that knowledge of the world could be acquired by means of travelling both physically and visually facilitated the perception and use of visual media as a form of indoors travel. The world was appropriable inasmuch as its representations could convey the same information one would acquire by travelling in first person.[14]

11 The story was published in the *English Review*, edited by Ford Madox Ford, and one of the primary little magazines to disseminate new forms of writing such as modernism in the period.
12 Vernon Lee, 'On Modern Travelling', in Vernon Lee, *Limbo and Other Essays* (London: Grant Richards, 1897), 105.
13 Sara Dominici, 'The democratisation of photography and the promotion of tourism: the Polytechnic Touring Association (1888-1939)' (Doctoral Dissertation), University of Westminster, 2014, https://westminsterresearch.westminster.ac.uk/download/a45da-892b67af59ca717b6c1e11760cd99265b03d09db370873dd79caad654db/5855387/Sara_DOMINICI_2014.pdf (last accessed 9 January 2019).
14 Vernon Lee, 'Ghosts in a Roman Photograph Album', *The English Review* (May 1920), 54.

'Ghosts in a Roman Photograph Album' is, quite exclusively, the recounting of an unnamed narrator's attempt to recapture an experience of the photograph album of the 1860s which she saw during the First World War (as a form of 'indoor travel'). The narrator writes about finding a photograph album about a holiday in Rome in a rented house which seemed to characterise the photographs of a family that decorated the walls of that rented house. What is emphasised in the short story, which is important for my analysis, is that the photographic album is repetitively conceived of as a collection of stories, as a rich source of narrative. This is clear from the concluding paragraph of the story, where the narrator writes of the ghosts of the title:

> Ghosts, who kept me company quite unperceived of all others, making bearable a few days of that last but one war-year with their peaceful stories of the Rome of my childhood.

The characterisation of the photograph album as a collection of stories builds on previous hints in the short story that the photograph album is an alternative source of fiction and of art. On the opening page, for example, the narrator writes of the Rome of the photograph album:

> The Rome, I might almost have said, of Clive Newcome; certainly that of Roderick Hudson, so much do those immortal sketches sum up, bring to a focus, my own childish recollections, lending them the clearness and point of the third person instead of the first, as in a perspectived and framed picture. For it was in the third person, not the first, that, during that particular week in 1916, I lived back in the Rome of Pius the Ninth.[15]

That is, first, that to the narrator, the Rome of the photograph album is that of a number of mid-century fictional characters that are artists: the eponymous hero in Henry James' novel *Roderick Hudson* (1875) and Clive Newcome in William Makepeace Thackeray's *The Newcomes: Memoirs of a Most Respectable Family* (1855). The photograph album presents an artistic vision which derives from fiction, fiction's idea of art. Secondly, there is also the important assertion by the narrator that the album itself organises his or her own childish recollections into a coherent narrative, or a pictorial and thus artistic form in the third person. Thus, it can be seen that the narrator conceives of the photograph album as simultaneously narrative and art, as fiction's idea of art or the art of narrative. This allows the narrator to organise his or her own experiences of the real Rome. The photograph album is thus put on equal terms with works of fiction and with art itself in the story or given equal status. This is one of the key threats which writers of fictions feared, as I will aim to show below.

In fact, not only is the photograph album given equal status with fiction and art, but in some sections of the story it is suggested that it actually overtakes art, another

15 Ibid., 432.

perceived threat which the writers of fiction I have studied responded to. As the narrator writes:

> Only I knew what to expect from that slab of shining black marble bound into its leather cover, and on which spread (far lovelier such works of art had been in my childish eyes than all the statues and pictures my priggishness pretended to love!) the sharp white petals and emerald-green leaves of a magnolia-blossom made of variegated marbles.[16]

The narrator thus conveys the idea that the photograph album is a superior work of art to all traditional art. It is thus seen to usurp and overtake the position of traditional artistic media as a form of modern representation and to do away with the whole Western artistic tradition and civilisation. The writers that I have studied thought of themselves as custodians of this larger Western civilisation and thus, for them, the threat of the photograph album as a pretender to the throne had to be carefully countered.[17]

The narratives of the photograph album are seen as especially powerful by the narrator in a way that threatened the power of fiction. First, the photograph album immersed the narrator in the way in which an engaging fictional work could do. As the narrator writes, 'And I can still see and hear what those, probably long demised, unknown owners of the album must have seen and heard'.[18] The photographic album had the sense of immediacy that comes from immersion in a form of representation. Secondly, the photograph album had the power to shape not only memory, but also consciousness and lived and experienced reality, also like fiction. As the narrator states:

> All these impressions of Papal Rome were duly received, more or less, by that West Sussex family, fifty and more years ago. And through them, by myself, fifty years later, their images getting framed and interlaced (like patterns on an old chintz or lacquer screen) in my own mind with the orange-tiled South-country cottages, the reedy ponds, the jagged pines profiled against the pale escarpments and chalk-gashes of the South Downs, and the last phloxes and dahlias in the war-neglected garden.[19]

In a number of ways, then, the photograph album could be seen as infringing on the territory of traditional writing and even Western civilisation itself. It could be seen as a powerful contender to fiction because it was seen as a narrative powerhouse which immersed the viewer in art and fiction and changed their consciousness and perception of reality.

16 Ibid.

17 Vernon Lee herself was important as an aesthetician and often wrote about what it meant to look at visual art. The story remains ambiguous as to whether the narrator's position on the photograph album as art has matured since childhood or not.

18 Ibid., 434.

19 Ibid., 435.

Lastly, one can remark on the comforting escapism that the photograph album offered to the narrator in wartime in the concluding lines which I have given above. The narrator says that the photograph album enabled him or her to live once more in Rome 'vividly, overwhelmingly'.[20] The photograph album was perceived to be able to offer immersion in another time and place, despite its depiction of scenes from real life.

In particular, the photograph album, like the individual photograph, was thought to threaten the identities of those that it portrayed, as well as those that viewed it. The narrator in the short story sees the English father of the family transformed into a Roman paterfamilias while the English mother is transformed into a Roman materfamilias.[21] It is further indicative that the photograph album represents a foreign country and evokes memories of living in that foreign country for the English narrator. The photograph album's perceived threat to the idea of identity, and particularly the identity of the reader, I suggest, considerably shaped the fiction that I have studied, as I will show below.

Although Leigh was writing later, and reflecting at a distance of some years on the photograph album of the 1860s, I argue that it can be seen in Vernon Lee's short story why the authors I have studied were concerned to neutralise the threat the photograph album posed to their craft and livelihood. It was seen as a troublesome and gifted competitor, an influential, world-changing, 'overwhelming' narrative powerhouse. As I will show, the earlier fiction responded to this precise, and perhaps prophetic, characterisation of the photograph album, no matter the fact that Lee was writing after such fiction.

Fiction's response to the threat of the photograph album's writing through the lens of the law: the construction of the failed and illegitimate plot of characters

I have thus far aimed to establish precisely why the photograph album was seen as direct competition to fiction and why it was perceived as threatening to overtake it. I have stressed the perceived political dimensions of the threat too – how the photograph album was seen to change the world and identities. I now wish to introduce the way in which the fiction responded to the threat of the photograph album, including, in particular, its political threats. I argue that an understanding of this dimension of fiction makes clear the way in which it used ideas of the law to counter the narrative function of the photograph album and to legitimise the claims of writing as the dominant mode of representation and the bearer of identity. I see the photograph album as associated with the failed and illegitimate plots of characters in works of fiction. The plots of such characters either rely on photographic albums, usually combined with a form of writing, to create readers, or revolve around photograph albums in some crucial and meaningful way and are thus more indirectly associated with them. The plots may variously be intended to corrupt character, exploit or defraud and divert. Photographs were also strongly

20 Ibid., 434.
21 Ibid., 436.

associated with illegitimate plots and therefore with narrative functions in fiction – the fiction which portrayed photographic albums built on these ideas more explicitly. In Wilkie Collin's *The Woman in White*, the villainous plot to substitute one likeness for another forms a parallel to the photographic substitution of art. The association is also evident in the work of Thomas Hardy. In Hardy's first published novel, *Desperate Remedies* (1871), Aeneas Manston has murdered his wife, Eunice Manston, and attempts to evade the law and discovery by recruiting a wife that is an imposter. A photograph where the imposter masquerades as the original is part of the deception. Those who take the photograph 'literally' at face value are deceived. However, Cytherea Graye rejects the photographic evidence because she bases her ideas on reading, not seeing, and on written evidence. Cytherea does not accept that which is given in the photograph. Instead, Cytherea reads a love-poem from Manston to Eunice and notices that he describes her eyes as 'azure' when she has read that they are black in a letter.[22] Cytherea's non-photographic and non-literalist reading ultimately leads to the recognition of the murder and to the legal truth. Hardy again frustrated the photographic plot in *A Laodicean* (1881), where the villain photographer William Dare puts his own candidate forward as Paula Power's husband, his father Captain de Stancy. The plot threatens the interests of the hero, George Somerset, the architect that loves Paula. Dare uses a fabricated photograph of the hero represented as drunk to try and further his legal scheme of marriage. The contest is clearly for 'power', in the guise of Paula Power, as the contest for legitimate and illegitimate photograph album plots is in the fiction I will interpret here. In such novels, while illegitimate photographic plots are represented and thoroughly denounced and defeated, it is more difficult to see the authors' rules of construction of legitimate legal plots, which are much more implicit. However, in the fictions in which photographic albums are represented, such constructions of legitimate legal plots are much more visible and contrasted much more strongly with the printed book and the rules of legitimate narrative, hence my concentration upon them.

I wish to introduce and discuss the ideas of the plots associated with the photograph album through a reading of the short story 'My New Idea', published in *All the Year Round* in 1871 in which a combination of the photograph album and writing can be seen to threaten the sphere of politics and ideas of identity, since the writing is in the form of signatures.

In the story, the unnamed narrator tells of his unsuccessful and illegitimate plot to use the writing in a photograph album to obtain money from his unsuspecting victims. He contrives to collect autographs in his photograph album from his rich friends underneath their photographic portraits, but has concealed cheques within the pages, which his duped victims are in effect signing off. The narrator thus makes an audience of the rich write in the photograph album. He then writes up the cheques at his writing desk and attempts to cash them in, but is caught, and his plot is foiled. The narrator says that his plot arose 'through the immediate agency of a photograph book', since he got the idea for it when he was examining a young

22 Thomas Hardy, *Desperate Remedies, Vol. 3* (London: Tinsley Brothers, 1871), 102–103.

lady's photograph album, which contained autographs of the individuals in the photographs.[23] The suggestion is that the photograph album itself produced the illegitimate writing of identities. The quote also emphasises how his plot arose from a simultaneous viewing and reading of a woman's photograph book and is therefore the production of a reader and viewer of the photograph album. Thus, the experience of the photograph album culminates in a form of writing which claims to be authoritative, but is depicted as illegal and has to be curbed and prosecuted by the agency of the law.

What I wish to emphasise about the story, first, is that the photograph-book plot, which is intended to create trusting readers of the cheques and the support of the illegitimate writing of identity, is explicitly intended to give the narrator sufficient resources to pursue a political career.[24] This invocation of ideas of political representation, I argue below, enable us to see the ways in which ideas of constitutional law are invoked and the photograph album is seen as a sort of elementary constitutional document or social contract. The story can thus be seen to play on the fears that the photographic album could change society through its readers and viewers and recognises its perceived power. The emphasis on politics is introduced towards the beginning of the story, when the narrator actually describes himself as an ideal social reformer, although this is to be seen as a comic symptom of his delusions of grandeur:

> I could have advised mankind upon all sorts of subjects. I should have been in a position to inform all those who might have consulted me exactly what course to pursue in every difficulty, great or small, besides furnishing, without hesitation, satisfactory solutions to all those social problems by which society is so continually puzzled.[25]

In fact, I suggest that the photograph album is implicitly associated with the work of not just social, but also legal reformers. After all, the rich, who form the typical representatives of the political elite, all agree to write their signatures within it to imbue it with their identities and consent to share their resources through the album to advance the narrator in a political career, or a form of political representation, although they are duped into doing so. The photograph album then takes on the connotation of a work of constitutional law introduced by the reformers of society through the law, although it is an illegitimate form.

The story suggests what sort of a writer the author of this photograph-book and false constitution is by making hints as to the form of the writing within. On the one hand, the narrator appears to privilege writing in the photographic book, and has little use for the photographs above the writing themselves. The crucial things are the signatures and the affirmation of the identities of capitalists which he can use to obtain money. However, the narrator is also consistently seen to be unable to separate an idea of writing from an idea of identity and the body. One of

23 Anonymous, 'My New Idea', *All the Year Round*, 5:121 (25 March 1871), 407.
24 Ibid., 406.
25 Ibid., 404.

his numerous failed schemes before the failed photograph-book plot was to suggest to the world at large a 'system of tattooing every human being at birth with his or her name, rendering identification, under any circumstances which could possibly occur, a thing of certainty'.[26] This system compares with writing names underneath portraits in the photograph album, or writing names which reference the body depicted in the photographs. The point is that the narrator seems to see names as bodies and bodies as names and suggests to the reader that they do the same. He conflates identity with bodily existence and this is precisely why his plot to create duped readers is seen as so nefarious. That is, he aims to make a signature in a photograph album next to a body into a signature in the real world of commerce and to exploit it for the purpose of political representation.

I now wish to further elaborate how the plot associated with the photograph book seems to be related to ideas of the law in the story. It is clear that the plot is considered to be criminal. However, the writer is not finally convicted of forgery, although this is the argument made in court which fails due to the strict, technical reading of the law. Rather, he is convicted of obtaining money under false pretences.[27] The inclusion of the argument that the narrator is a forger seems intended to suggest the idea to the reader of the short story: that he is a copyist and a literalist without real original ideas. In fact, the law in the fiction does not explicitly address how the narrator encroaches on the identity of others. These connections are suggested outside of the courtroom. When the narrator sits at his writing desk, writing the cheques off, next to the photograph album where they came from, there is a very strong suggestion that he is impersonating the typical representatives of the political elite, or that he is masquerading as those in power. For example, he hesitates and imagines what writing off a cheque of a thousand means to Jingle's finances (Jingle is one of the intended victims of his scheme) rather than how colossal the sum seems in his own eyes, stating that: 'It was large to me, no doubt, but not large to Jingle—not large to Jingle's bankers.'[28] The point is that he rejects his own perception for the perception of the rich. His plot therefore implicitly involves a usurpation of the identities of those typically in power, the identities of those that the short story is in fact dedicated to. The narrator is heavily suggested to be an imposter and a forger that models his behaviour on the powerful. He is, in all senses of the word, a copyist or an imitator.

The plot of a character which involves the photograph album is therefore denounced through an invocation of ideas of the law in this short story, as in the other fiction I have studied. The power of the writing which emanates from the photograph album to shape and reform reality is depicted as illegitimate and obtained through false pretences, and portrayed alongside ideas of impersonation and copying. By denouncing the plot and the writing associated with the photograph album, the short story rejects the claim of the photograph album to perform a narrative function which can be seen as an equal to writing considered to be legitimate. At the same time, a reading which gives legitimacy to the writing in the

26 Ibid., 404.
27 Anonymous, 'My New Idea", *All the Year Round*, 5:122 (1 April 1871), 432.
28 Ibid., 430.

photograph album, and sees it as the bearer of identity, while literally correct, since the signatures are authentic, is problematised as supporting crime and such readers are seen as dupes. Thus, the story can be seen to amplify and exaggerate the threat of the narrative function of the photograph album by casting it as criminal and a threat to society and order. It does so to exploit the photograph album to bolster its own status as the dominant form of narrative and to destroy competition and difference.

Fiction's inventive literary criticism of the plot associated with the photograph album

'My New Idea' presents the plot associated with the photograph album and intended to create readers in a comical vein as a farcical failure, since the narrator is associated with various other failed and ludicrous schemes such as his intended tattooing of babies, despite his delusions of grandeur. The terms of the comedy work through subtle nuance and implication which it is difficult to convey to the reader, however I believe that this strategy is fiction's criticism of the plot associated with the photograph album, or its criticism of the photograph album's narrative function. I wish to analyse exactly how such fiction denounces the narrative function of the photograph album by considering the plots associated with it in the work of Sir Arthur Conan Doyle. Such an analysis will elaborate precisely how and why such plots were thought of as illegitimate, using ideas of the law, and will also, I suggest, disclose some of the implicit rules governing the construction of narratives and plots. I introduce Conan Doyle into my argument for a number of reasons. First, I want to demonstrate how fiction exploited ideas of the law in the Holmes stories to criticise the photograph album in the 1920s when photography was in fact banned in the courtroom and writers like Vernon Lee were writing of the strength of the photograph album. Secondly, I want to extend and complicate existing scholarship. Conan Doyle has been historically associated with the *reductio ad absurdum* of 'photographic truth', as a photographer himself and also the entirely gullible believer in spiritual photography and the photographs of the Cottingley Fairies, the photographic plots intended to dupe the viewer. Such ideas seem to have implicitly informed responses to how photography and its relationship with the law have been portrayed in his work. For instance, Ronald Thomas sees Sherlock Holmes as peculiarly representative of both the law and the photographic vision.[29] However, I aim to show that the work of Conan Doyle criticises the reading and viewing of the plot of the photograph album and how it does so.

I have discussed Conan Doyle's short story 'The Adventure of the Illustrious Client' (1924) at length in the introduction to this monograph. I now wish to analyse the relationships that the story constructs between the photographic album and the Baron's plot to produce a reader and viewer of his photograph book

29 Ronald R. Thomas, 'Making Darkness Visible: Capturing the Criminal and Observing the Law in Victorian Photography and Detective Fiction', in Carol. T. Christ and John O. Jordan (eds), *Victorian Literature and the Victorian Visual Imagination* (Berkeley, Los Angeles, Oxford: University of California Press, 1995), 134–168.

(himself) by mesmerising and marrying Violet and adding her photograph to that of other women he has conquered and collected. This is the first step to understanding how exactly the story criticises the plot of the photograph album. The photographic album and book in the story is the Baron's collection of photographic snapshots. The Baron is a rapacious collector, not only of pictures and books,[30] but he also 'collects women' and chronicles his conquests in a book in which there are photographic snapshots of his victims. In the introduction, I have explained why the book can be seen as a form of literalism too which threatened to turn Violet into a living image. I have also explained how literalism is seen as corrupting the legal truth in the story since the Baron uses it to subvert law and justice, both in a criminal trial and in the form of the legal contract of marriage. The Baron himself is associated with deception and lies as he is seen to trick Violet into loving him. Kitty says that he has a 'lying tongue'.[31] The photographic album is therefore the product of untruth which attacks the law. Kitty Winter, the Baron's jilted partner, describes the book to Holmes. As she explains, the book is an archive combining photography and writing:

> I tell you, Mr. Holmes, this man collects women, and takes a pride in his collection, as some men collect moths or butterflies. He had it all in that book. Snapshot photographs, names, details, everything about them. It was a beastly book–a book no man, even if he had come from the gutter, could have put together. But it was Adelbert Gruner's book all the same. 'Souls I have ruined.' He could have put that on the outside if he had been so minded.[32]

Holmes immediately realises that this photograph book is suspect and will show Violet that the Baron is a monster. He says,

> Here is the book the woman talked of. If this will not break off the marriage, nothing ever could. But it will, Watson. It must. No self-respecting woman could stand it.[33]

The book itself is not illegal, but it is presented as illegitimate. What is particularly monstrous about the book, we assume, is that English women can't bear to be seen as photographic snapshots in a photographic album and to be understood, seen and represented in that way and to be associated with literalism. That is, the photographic archive and its form as a representation of women provides 'evidence' of a monstrous vision outside of the traditional domain of the legal contract of marriage. That is how the book is perceived as extra-legal or illegitimate. Eventually the book is retrieved and the marriage between the Baron and Violet is broken off. It can be seen that the Baron's marriage plot intersects with the 'plot' of his

30 Arthur Conan Doyle, 'The Adventure of the Illustrious Client', in Arthur Conan Doyle, *The Complete Sherlock Holmes* (London: Magpie Books Ltd, 1993), 987.

31 Ibid. 990.

32 Ibid., 991.

33 Ibid., 998.

photograph album, which represents the body rather than the soul, on several levels: it depends on his marriage plot being successful and is also the crucial motivation for the marriage plot since it represents his conquests.

Having described the Baron's plot and how it is associated with the photograph book, I now wish to suggest how exactly Doyle's fiction characterises the plot through its denouncement of it. The Baron's plot, as I have noted in the introduction, in which photography poses a threat to identity, suggests an act of fictional *reductio ad absurdum*. As I wrote previously, the Baron threatens to turn Violet not just into another photographic snapshot in his book, but also into a living and breathing photograph, an entity in which the image has usurped life. This appears to be the case since when Holmes meets Violet, he sees her as transformed by the Baron's love into 'a snow image on a mountain'.[34] The inference is that the Baron is able fantastically, whether literally or metaphorically, to substitute English womanhood with a monochromatic image and thus represents a unique threat to English identity. The Baron uses his powerful 'photographic vision' to take away Violet's identity and replace it with a photograph. Thus, the Baron's plot and the narrative function of the photograph album are together characterised as fantastical and bizarre, unbelievable because they threaten to turn what is real into a photograph, a form of two-dimensional representation. Furthermore, the plot threatens to change existing reality and the identity of individuals through severe reduction. The further inference is that the Baron's plot illegitimately confuses differing categories with each other in a 'hodge-podge' of construction, since I have shown in the introduction that Violet, who seems transformed into a photograph, is likened by Holmes, the champion of the law, to a work of idealist art. These sorts of criticisms of plot were *de rigueur* in literary criticism of the time. For instance, an anonymous reviewer of the main plot of Charles Dickens' novel, *Our Mutual Friend* (1865), which I will discuss myself below in terms of ideas of plots and plotting, used the exact same terms to criticise it. He wrote, 'the whole plot in which the deceased Harmon, Boffin, Wegg, and John Rokesmith, are concerned, is wild and fantastic, wanting in reality, and leading to a degree of confusion which is not compensated by any additional interest in the story'.[35]

The criticism of the plot of the photograph book is developed through a criticism of the reader of the plot, that is, the reader of the photograph book that accepts it. I have explored what type of reading the Baron, who is the reader of his own diary, is associated with at length in the introduction and have thus shown what the outcome of his plot through the photograph book is in terms of conceptions of the law. However, I will remind the reader of its key dimensions by focusing on one of the Baron's key reader-dupes. Kitty Winter is one of the duped victims of the Baron's photograph book and the culmination of his plot or the writing and photography conducted within it. Kitty is initially seduced by the Baron's justification of the photographic book. As I wrote in the introduction, Kitty Winter has been one of the

34 Ibid., 991.

35 Anonymous, 'Reviews of Books – Our Mutual Friend', *London Review* (October 28, 1865) in Sean Grass, *Charles Dickens's Our Mutual Friend: A Publishing History* (London and New York: Routledge, 2017), 215.

photographic subjects of the Baron and her photographic snapshot is in the Baron's book. Kitty is persuaded by the Baron to accept the photographic book when she discovers it by accident and to forgive the Baron for possessing it and to continue her relationship with him, irrespective of his deviance. As she says:

> Whatever he did went with me, same as with this poor fool! There was just one thing that shook me. Yes, by cripes! If it had not been for his poisonous, lying tongue that explains and soothes, I'd have left him that very night. It's a book he has–a brown leather book with a lock, and his arms in gold on the outside.[36]

Despite being shaken by the photograph book, Kitty acquiesces in untruth, supporting the literalist reading in the diary and being treated like a body and being reduced to a photograph. This submission to literalism and being treated like a body ultimately leads Kitty to occupy the status of a fallen woman and, it is suggested, prostitute, a mere body and nothing else. She becomes an illegitimate woman outside of the law. The plot of the Baron via the photograph book is thus revealed: To corrupt English womanhood through reading and viewing and the production of readers and viewers and thus to corrupt the identities, particularly the legal identities, of the English, as he again threatens to do so through marriage to Violet and making her his legal wife.

My argument is supported by Conan Doyle's characterisation of a plot associated with the viewing of the photographic archive which could be seen as a sort of institutionalised photograph album. In *The Hound of the Baskervilles* (1902), the criticism of the plot associated with the photographic archive again takes the form of a criticism of the reader of the plot that accepts it. The duped Doctor James Mortimer values Alphonse Bertillon, the late nineteenth century French officer, above the English detective Sherlock Holmes.[37] Bertillon shaped how 'the mug shot', or the photographic portrait, was used in police detection. Bertillon thus represented the establishment of the photograph album-like photographic archive within law. Mortimer, who favours photographic portraits as the superior medium of crime detection, and researches physiognomy, or the appearance of the body – and classifies head shapes in types of Celts, Gaelic and Ivernian, and sees individual character to correspond to racial type as a result – is a literalist reader who is duped by an outré plot.[38] He reads and sees plausibility in a bizarre and supernatural fictional work of terror which describes the fictional Hound of the Baskervilles as a literal truth, unaware that it is a bizarre deception and misdirection from the villain which exploits his credulity.[39] The work of fiction is a hackneyed gothic superstition which relies on ideas of the devil buying souls, family curses, includes gratuitous violence and is, in short, extreme and presented as not conveying any sort of

36 Doyle, 'The Adventure of the Illustrious Client' (n 30) 990.

37 Arthur Conan Doyle, *The Hound of the Baskervilles* in Arthur Conan Doyle, *The Complete Sherlock Holmes* (London: Magpie Books, 1993), 672.

38 Ibid., 700.

39 Ibid. 680–681.

truth or relation to reality, although it masquerades as being truthful and an authentic representation of reality. Predictably Holmes, the champion of the law, scoffs at it. Ironically, given that Conan Doyle was to be criticised as such for giving credence to photographs of fairies, Holmes says that the piece of fiction was 'interesting' only to 'a collector of fairy tales', and that it was not relevant to the case.[40] Significantly, this piece of fiction that is a crucial part of the villain's plot is introduced and subsequently referred to as a 'legend' which is an indication of how it is related to photography and the writing in a photograph album.[41] According to an electronic search of an electronic text of the story, the word 'legend' is repeated an ominous thirteen times in the story. The word is obviously defined as a sort of popular and unliterary narrative, however, another connotation of the word is 'a caption to an illustration, photograph, etc'.[42] That is, the legend is only to be understood with reference to pictures and cannot be disassociated from it and could easily have come from something like a photograph album. Mortimer, who values the photographic archive, thinks that this legend explains murder. The gullible, literalist reader cannot discriminate between legal truth and fiction, reality and deception, falsity and fact. He cannot determine what true writing divested of images is. However, in contrast to the use of photographs, and giving credence to the bizarre 'plot' on the part of the villain,[43] Holmes actually solves the case by noticing the resemblance between the villain and a portrait painting, calling himself a 'connoisseur' and affirming his artistic knowledge in the statement that 'Watson won't allow that I know anything of art, but that is mere jealousy because our views upon the subject differ'.[44] That is, Holmes turns to the knowledge of art and not photography and the photographic archive to determine questions of legal truth and guilt. Holmes relies on ideas of artistic truth in order to determine questions of legal truth and to exclude and conclusively prove the legend associated with the photograph archive and the photograph book as a failure. Holmes proves that the true reader must not read writing such as that which comes out of the photograph album.

In summary, the plot associated with the photograph album is severely criticised in the fiction of Conan Doyle and particularly with reference to the readers of this plot. Thus his fiction can be seen as taking on the role of a literary critic and, indeed, used the same terms as conventional literary criticism. That is, his fiction became the means of conveying reading and literary criticism and its inventions derived from that criticism. It was thoroughly rooted in accepted positions of reading. In the reading of Conan Doyle's fiction and the inventions that proceeded from it, the plot associated with the photograph album was criticised as absurd, contrived and fanciful. At the same time it was seen as incoherent, as confused and confusing. Most importantly the plot was seen as a threat to identity and society.

40 Ibid. 676.
41 Ibid., 673.
42 Oxford Dictionaries, s.v., 'Legend' (last accessed 4 December 2018) http://www.oed.com/view/Entry/107040?rskey=mmLmLO&result=1#eid.
43 Ibid., 747, 762.
44 Ibid., 749.

Readers of such plots were presented as gullible dupes like Kitty Winter who sacrifices her character by accepting such a reading. Such inventions of reading are reinforced by referring to art and the law in order to legitimise the terms of the criticism and render it more authoritative. Thus, when fiction reads, or adopts the amalgamated position of literary critic, lawyer and art connoisseur, the plot associated with the photograph album is shown as illegitimate not only in terms of literary quality and art status, but also as legally illegitimate. Readers like Kitty Winter are seen as illegitimate. Fiction thus secures its criticisms of the narrative function of the photograph book in a foundation of the law and art by exaggerating and amplifying the threat of the photograph album which threatens accepted reading and writing practices, the idea of art and that of the law. Fiction can be seen to have exploited the authority of the law and of art and their ideas of reading to combat the narrative function of the photograph album and entrenched itself in the means of representation which were considered to be the most powerful, recognised and valuable. Fiction presented itself as at one with these means of representation and their readings to derive status from the affiliation and to consolidate its own claims to power. The idea of reading and the idea of power were inseparable, as I have shown throughout this monograph.

Fiction's 'legitimate' counter plot as it emerges through contrast to the photograph book plot

As I have stated beforehand, delineating the illegitimate plot associated with the photograph book illuminates exactly why legitimate plots in fiction are seen as being legitimate. Such an analysis allows us to understand the precise terms and conditions of the idea of a legitimate narrative and, I argue, further elaborates how such terms and conditions relate to the power of the political elite. This is because these supposedly legitimate plots are explicitly shown to be counterplots and are heavily contrasted with the plot associated with the photograph book. Such an analysis of the legitimate plot reveals a startling truth: the terms of 'legitimacy' rely on untruth and the deception of readers and there seems to be little difference from the illegitimate plot associated with the photograph album.

Such ideas can be seen in 'The Adventure of the Illustrious Client', where Sherlock Holmes is explicitly described as a 'plotter', that is 'He pushed to an extreme the axiom that the only safe plotter was he who plotted alone'.[45] Like the plot associated with the photograph book, his plot also creates readers. In fact, it defeats the Baron's plot in the story through its manipulation and duping of readers, the same strategy the Baron used against Kitty Winter. Holmes' plot is the deception or fiction of his death in the newspapers. Holmes' fiction manipulates figures of authority in the form of doctors and journalists. For instance, he tells Watson to 'exaggerate [his] injuries'.[46] Holmes' plot relies on deference and through manipulating this, Holmes effectively lies to the mass readership of the newspapers in the register of truth and the reading public to suggest that he is dying. Thus, 'For

45 Doyle, 'The Adventure of the Illustrious Client' (n 30) 994.
46 Ibid.

six days the public were under the impression that Holmes was at the door of death'.[47] Holmes uses this device against the Baron to introduce the element of surprise in his attack against him. Holmes' plotting and deceptive strategy also intends to distract the Baron through a reading, although this is unsuccessful. Watson's reading of Chinese art is deceptive since he wishes to masquerade before the Baron as an interested expert in order to distract him. The reading supported by those in the law, and their legal and artistic reading, is coupled with the abuse of authority, deception and fiction, not with photography, truth and literalism. It is antagonistic to the actual. What is false in reading and art and in the role of reader is considered to serve truth and law even while what is 'too true' in reading and photography in the form of the Baron's photograph book is considered to go against them. Such is the instability and illegitimacy of narrative function and reading in the fiction studied in this monograph, since the rule of those with power is unjust, illegitimate and self-serving and cannot be grounded in any truth or law, reason or rationality. What Holmes is fighting for is actually the monopoly on untruth, not truth. What precisely are the conditions and terms of legitimate narrative function? The 'legitimate' plot to produce a deceptive reading and duped readers protects the self-interest of Violet's would-be protector who is a rich and privileged member of society and who wishes to control the 'English rose' and her matrimonial prospects. The plot to produce readings and readers therefore functions to control the subjectivity of others and force them to conform to the subjectivity and desire of the powerful in society, the political elite. It also controls legal identities: the identities of wife and husband which come from the legal institution of marriage.

In fact, Holmes' overall method is telling legal stories. He is not just a plotter in 'The Adventure of the Illustrious Client' whose plots lead to a form of writing, as in the stories in the newspapers, but is always a writer. This fact is emphasised in 'The Red-Headed League' (1891), again in connection with a photographic plot and the reading it inspires. The photographic scheme aims to create a dupe and literalist reader and copyist in the typical fashion of Conan Doyle. Jabez Wilson, a struggling pawnbroker, is induced by a criminal masquerading under the guise of photographer to vacate his shop for short periods in the afternoon, to copy the *Encyclopædia Britannica*, the archive. The activity is to be performed for purely 'nominal' compliance with a fictitious will, an empty legal form masquerading as reality. The photographic deception, which masquerades as an authorised and legally determined form, transforms a man into a dupe: a merely passive reader and copyist of an archive, stuck on entries under the letter 'A' which are given in 'minute'[48] detail, like the minute detail of the photograph itself. The literalist reading is constraining and it fixes the pawnbroker in physical space away from the pursuit of his proper business. The reading supports crime: the purpose behind the constructed scene of reading is a bank robbery and the invented reading is part and parcel of the imagination, not only of a figure masquerading as a photographer, but

47 Ibid.

48 Arthur Conan Doyle, 'The Red-Headed League', in Arthur Conan Doyle, *The Complete Sherlock Holmes* (New York: Doubleday & Co Inc, 1927), 204.

also of a convicted forger,[49] or a copyist, who himself has an 'almost womanly hand'.[50] 'A womanly hand', besides referring to the appendage, could also be womanly writing. Sherlock Holmes thwarts the plot and ends the story by (misquoting) a literary quotation which emphasises not only his status as an educated reader of letters, but also his affiliation with an author of fiction, not an author of factual prose as in the encyclopaedia. He says, "*L'homme c'est rien – l'oeuvre c'est tout*,' as Gustave Flaubert wrote to George Sand'.[51] It can be seen throughout his individual adventures that Holmes adopts the posture of a constructive of narratives. Holmes describes the motivations of characters and the story behind their crimes. He puts disconnected details and events into a coherent and organised whole to tell legal stories. However, even though he plots like a liar, as in 'The Adventure of the Illustrious Client', Holmes' stories are accepted as legitimate, valid and authoritative stories about law.

It is important to emphasise that Holmes also functions as a literary critic as well as a story teller. He combines both roles. Thus, he describes the plots of criminals in detail and thwarts them or renders them as failures. It can be seen in 'The Adventure of the Illustrious Client' that he aims to present the Baron's photographic book as the mark of a flawed mind and character to Violet. His scheme is successful: Violet, the good woman who has fallen into a misapprehension of the Baron's character, immediately realises that the book is evidence of a monstrous vision and that it can have no justification. She sees the book as evidence of wrong and legal transgression and accepts Holmes as the literary critic.

The characterisation of the counterplot to the plot associated with the photographic book thus reveals that literary criticism and the legitimate plotter and plotting are wedded together to create inventive readings. The reader of a Sherlock Holmes story waits in suspense for Holmes' inventive reading to emerge and accepts it as legitimate, authoritative and unquestionable. He is, after all, the champion of the law. However, the terms of legitimacy and of upholding the law are themselves revealed to be based in deception, untruth, the abuse of authority and deference. Legitimacy is anything but based on legitimate practices. Holmes reveals that in fighting over the terms and purposes of narrative, the photograph book and fictional writing fight over the grounds of untruth, not truth.

The mirroring of legitimate plots and illegitimate plots and how a reading of the law emerges out of the mirror relationship

What exactly is the artistic viewer's and legal mind's plot as it is opposed to the plot of the photographic album? How exactly are the conditions and terms of the legitimate plot and therefore the terms and conditions of what was understood as legitimacy to be delineated? I have already shown how the supposedly legitimate plot was associated with deception and fiction in the newspapers which appears to be truthful. I now want to develop it particularly in terms of the legitimate plot's

49 Ibid., 207.
50 Ibid., 210.
51 Ibid., 212.

power and concealment. In 'The Adventure of the Illustrious Client', Holmes is in the service of an anonymous and thus concealed client. This is the source of patriarchal power in the story and the anonymous client is the man for whom Holmes plots to stop the marriage. Holmes specifically has to guard the incognito of the illustrious client. Similarly, Holmes' plot against the Baron relies on an idea of concealed identity: Watson has to change his name to present the Baron with the Chinese work of art. I want to show why the champion of the law had to protect and use concealed identities against the plot associated with the photograph book in order to describe the terms of legitimacy. I aim to show that the larger plot which the fiction is involved in is the concealment of identity of the powerful, men. Thus, it can be shown exactly how constructions of reading depend upon asymmetries of power in society.

Charles Dickens' novel *Our Mutual Friend* (1865) connects the photograph book with marriage plots and plots to read the law by the villain by marshalling it as a significant detail which resonates throughout the whole work. The novel was written in the wake of the success of the *Royal Album* in 1861 and I argue that it can be seen to respond to it. In the novel, all the marriage plots are related to the concealment of identity since not only one of the central characters, John Harmon, fakes his own death in order to deceive his intended wife, but a minor character, Fascination Fledgeby, who is involved with the marriage plot associated with the photograph album, also conceals his identity for the purposes of exploitation through hiding behind the figure of a Jew, Mr. Riah. As Stanley Friedman has noted, the novel is particularly concerned with the representation of reading,[52] therefore ideas of concealment and the photograph book can also be related to reading as I aim to show. In particular, there is a reading of a will in the novel, so it can be seen how a reading of the law emerges in relation to the photograph book and ideas of plots, both legitimate and illegitimate.

I will first describe how marriage plots are explicitly linked to the photograph album in a significant detail. The disruption of a marriage plot over a photographic 'book of portraits', an album of 'Public Characters', between Mrs. Sophronia Lammle and Twemlow occurs half-way through the novel.[53] Mrs. Lammle disrupts an intended marital plot of materialistic entrapment that she has concocted with her husband after having had second thoughts. She moves away from the materialistic vision of photography and away from the photographic album to safeguard the 'purity' of Victorian marriage which should be based on love. The book of portraits is not explicitly described as a collection of photographs, but has been assumed to be such.[54] Daniel A. Novak has argued that the number of different portraits and the observation that several are too 'dark', suggest photographs rather than other forms of image.[55] As

52 Stanley Friedman, 'The Motif of Reading in Our Mutual Friend', *Nineteenth-Century Fiction*, 28:1 (June 1973), 38–61.

53 Charles Dickens, *Our Mutual Friend* (London: Chapman and Hall, 1865), 345.

54 Norman Kelvin, 'The Painting as Physical Object in a Verbal Portrait: Pater's "A Prince of Court Painters" and Wilde's "The Portrait of Mr W. H."', in Elicia Clements and Lesley Higgins (eds), *Victorian Aesthetic Conditions: Pater Across the Arts* (Basingstoke: Palgrave Macmillan, 2010), 123–124.

55 Daniel A. Novak, *Realism, Photography and Nineteenth-Century Fiction*, (Cambridge: Cambridge University Press, 2008), 164.

Norman Kelvin observes, in addition to destroying the meretricious, manipulated marriage between Georgiana Podsnap and the significantly named Fascination Fledgeby, whose very name suggests the mesmeric captivation of the eyes, the photographic disruption of marriage also encompasses Mrs. Lammle's betrayal of her own husband's desire and is thus a double blow to marriage in the form of her own meretricious marriage:

> When Mrs. Lammle wishes to convey to Twemlow the danger Georgiana Podsnap is in, and to do so without being overheard by her husband, she persuades Twemlow to examine with her the Lammles' 'book of portraits'. Meant to be a typical Victorian household fixture, signifying domestic sentiments and memories, it becomes a cover for secrecy and a device to register the total lack of sympathy between husband and wife.[56]

The communion between the man and the woman over the photographic album excludes the bad, meretricious marriage, and the bad, meretricious husband who aims to prostitute Georgiana, and, of course, 'Fascination' in the form of Fledgeby. The vision shared by Mrs. Lammle and Twemlow over the photographic album is 'anti-photographic'. Thus, Twemlow, in the web of words and gentlemanly duty, is not only troubled by looking at the portraits, but also described as blind:

> Aghast at the light manner of her throwing her head back to look at it [the portrait] critically, Twemlow still dimly perceives the expediency of throwing his own head back, and does so. Though he no more sees the portrait than if it were in China.[57]

Significantly, the closing of the photographic album is the sealing of the promise between the man and the woman that the meretricious intended marriage will be destroyed through Twemlow's words since Mrs. Lammle says 'close that book before you return it to me, and I shall know what you mean, and deeply thank you in my heart'.[58] This blindness set against the scene of photographic copying and woman's vision is invoked again later, when sketching a design on the pattern of the damask cloth on a side table with her parasol and photographic copying of it leads to Mrs. Lammle's tears which reveal her sentiment for Georgiana, as Mr. Lammle observes. She then becomes non-mercenary and non-selfish, an echo of her closing of the photographic book and her frustration of her husband's meretricious scheme.[59] The anti-photographic support of non-materialist marriage and the upholding of the stature of the legal contract of marriage is based on Mrs. Lammle's recognition of Georgiana as a person, rather than a body to be exploited. The anti-photographic vision is based on the recognition of fellow persons, just as

56 Kelvin, 'The Painting as Physical Object in a Verbal Portrait', Ibid.
57 Dickens, *Our Mutual Friend*, 409.
58 Ibid., 347.
59 Ibid., 538.

the portraits of the public figures in the pages of the photographic album are not to be recognised in the contract between Mrs. Lammle and Twemlow.

Thus, the frustration of the bad and meretricious marriage plot is coupled with the shutting of the photographic book and with the exclusion of the photographic vision. However, it is also an exclusion of the untruth and plotting in itself. On realising that they have both deceived each other as to their respective wealth through false representations, the Lammles renewed their marriage with the aim of taking others in as they have been taken in themselves.[60] There is thus a more abstract exclusion of plotting and deception in the closing of the photograph book and Sophronia's distancing of herself from mercenary motives.

Having described the photograph plot in some detail, I now wish to note its relationship to reading. The closing of the photograph album and the frustration of the marriage plot is also the exclusion of literalist and prosaic readers. The reading of the intended husband in the plot, Fascination Fledgeby, is chained to the letter:

> Why money should be so precious to an Ass too dull and mean to exchange it for any other satisfaction, is strange; but there is no animal so sure to get laden with it, as the Ass who sees nothing written on the face of the earth and sky but the three letters L. S. D.—not Luxury, Sensuality, Dissoluteness, which they often stand for, but the three dry letters.[61]

The closing of the photograph book therefore also signifies an exclusion of the literalist. I have described the plot associated with the photograph book in some detail, but will now show how it can be contrasted point by point with the legitimate plot in the novel in a revealing manner. What distinguishes the illegitimate plot is how it almost exactly mirrors the supposedly 'legitimate' plot in the story through ideas of photography and concealment. It is the idea of acceptable concealment that is crucial to understanding why some plots were accepted and seen as legitimate and others were not in this novel as in other fiction. Indeed, ideas of concealment frame the expression of authorised identities and expressions of character in the fiction I have studied too, so it is particularly important to study. I will first establish how the legitimate plot aims to defeat photography and literalism through the investigation of details in the novel, to show how it can be seen as a working out of the plot associated with the photograph album. In the main marriage plot in the novel, the materialistic Bella is left to John Harmon as a wife in a will and thus in a constraining, double law of marital contract and will. However, Harmon, who amazingly and coincidentally just happens to fall in love with Bella, the wife intended for him and upon whom his fortune hangs, hides his identity to win her over. Bella, at first, appears to represent illegitimate plotting since she is the product of the photograph and literalist reading of the law and has to be reformed into a recognisable person and good reader through the legal contract of marriage. Her father, Mr. Wilfer, is a photographic stereotype who appears to have no specific identity of his own beyond the image. Thus Dickens writes, '[i]f the conventional

60 Ibid., 104.
61 Ibid., 224.

Cherub could ever grow up and be clothed, he might be photographed as a portrait of Wilfer'.[62] Bella's mother is associated with a constrained and literalist reading of law, by continual reference to her speaking as though she is reading an Act of Parliament which creates a new law or changes an existing law. Thus she speaks on a number of occasions 'with severe monotony, as if she were reading an Act of Parliament aloud'.[63] Bella is the outcome of photography and literalism in reading law and is therefore described as a plotter herself, 'a mercenary plotter whose thoughts and designs were always in her mean occupation'.[64] However, Bella is transformed from this union of the photograph and the constrained legal reading, and its resultant plotting, into a wife-reader of *The Complete British Family Housewife*.[65] Marriage reforms her reading and her plotting. The way that it does so is that Bella herself falls in love with John Harmon, a man that has a counterplot to her own scheming designs and 'plots' to carefully conceal his identity and maintain his incognito.[66] Harmon hides not just his identity, but also the fact that his father's will had made his inheritance conditional on an arranged marriage with Bella. He thus dupes Bella on a number of counts. Harmon's successful marriage counterplot to win over Bella without revealing his true name and the true legal situation depends on Mrs. Lammle's plotting, which emphasises that both narratives of deception are intertwined. Mrs. Lammle's successful plot to oust Harmon from his employment, when he is also insulted by his employer Boffin, is the key moment when Bella begins to take Harmon's side and falls in love with him.

Harmon's counterplot to conceal identity, his interest in affairs and the true legal situation, as I have stated above, besides being seen as a defeat of photography and literalist reading of the law, can be seen not only to mingle with, but also mirrors Mrs. Lammle's plot which she dissolved over the photograph album because both plots are distinguished by their relationship to concealment. Thus, the 'legitimate' plot actually mirrors the 'illegitimate' plot and is almost indistinguishable from it. Therefore, I argue, the terms and conditions of legitimacy cannot be distinguished from the terms and conditions of illegitimacy. In Harmon's successful marriage plot, he effectively conceals his identity, his interest and the true legal situation in regards to property. In Mrs. Lammle's plot with her husband, the pair also wanted to marry off their duped victim to a man who concealed his identity, interest and the true legal situation in regards to property. Fledgeby's business is to make a profit from extortionate loans of money and he does so by hiding behind the figure of the Jew, Mr. Riah. Significantly, this concealment of identity is referred to as a plot, or a 'story'. As Mr. Riah describes his occupation as the face of extortion:

> I always saw that the poor gentleman believed the story readily, because I was one of the Jews that you believed the story readily, my child, because I was one

62 Ibid., 26.
63 Ibid., 29.
64 Ibid., 266.
65 Ibid., 565.
66 Ibid., 305.

> of the Jews that the story itself first came into the invention of the originator thereof, because I was one of the Jews.[67]

Thus, the only real difference between the legitimate plot and the illegitimate plot is this. Fledgeby conceals his identity to make money in a supposedly mean occupation. On the other hand, Harmon conceals his identity to make money in the supposedly romantic occupation of love (the terms of the will do change, but Harmon and the readers do not know this until much later in the novel). Thus, Harmon's deceit is romanticised and idealised. Fledgeby's deceit is associated with all the negative stereotypes associated with Jews and the ethnically other. Where deceit is associated with rich, white men, who are born into wealth and privilege, like John Harmon, it is acceptable and accepted. If there is any association with perceived difference, then deceit is presented as illegitimate. Such are the grounds and terms of legitimacy and illegitimacy in the legitimate and the illegitimate plots. It can be seen, therefore, that ideas of the legitimacy and illegitimacy of the plot in fiction are conditioned by the acceptance and deference to the power of the political elite. The larger plot that fiction can be seen to convey is maintenance of the status quo.

In the novel, the reading of the law emerges out of these terms and conditions of legitimacy and illegitimacy which mirror each other, again with particular reference to photography, story-tellers and their plots. This is evident in the reading relationship and paid reading contract between Boffin and Silas Wegg which culminates in the reading of wills, or legal writings. Wegg, the literalist reader, is associated from the outset with storytelling in the form of 'halfpenny ballads'.[68] Since the ballad presents competition to fictional writing, Wegg is therefore cast as a dark plotter and his plot is contrasted with Boffin's plot to conceal the true terms of the will, itself a representation of the law, and the source of his own prosperity. Dickens explicitly alludes to this deliberate contrast in plots on the part of the two men:

> The undesigning Boffin had become so far immeshed by the wily Wegg that his mind misgave him he was a very designing man indeed in purposing to do more for Wegg. It seemed to him (so skilful was Wegg) that he was plotting darkly, when he was contriving to do the very thing that Wegg was plotting to get him to do.[69]

Of course, Boffin's plot eventually triumphs over Wegg's plot as becomes evident in the reading of the will, or the reading of the law. Boffin's triumph illuminates how the reading of the law is to be seen in relation to the mirroring of the legitimate and the illegitimate plots and, as I will show below, photography. Such readings are to be seen in terms of the concealment of the law and of self-interest. Wegg, the dark plotter and the false, literalist reader, sees the will, or the law, as purely an object which allows money to be distributed between parties and aims

67 Ibid., 603.
68 Ibid., 483.
69 Ibid., 153.

to exploit it for his own purposes. When he finds a will that appears to be written later than the one he believes is in Boffin's possession, one that gives all his property to the Crown, he attempts to blackmail Boffin by offering to conceal it for a price, like the others in the novel conceal the law and the true legal situation in regards to property. Adrian Poole elaborates the ideas behind the literalist reading of Wegg, noting that there is a distinction made in the novel:

> between two types of reading, one passive and mechanical, the other active and performative ... The difference between the two kinds of reading is marked by the change that overtakes Boffin's relations to literature. In the first volume, he is entirely at the mercy of Gibbon and Wegg, aghast and perplexed at what to believe. In the second volume, he takes control, using the tales of misers for his own purposes, directing their interpretation, playing a role.[70]

Thus, Boffin emerges as a true reader with the true and supposedly non-literalist and non-mechanical reading of the true will. He has a will that has been written even later than Wegg's which gives him all the property outright (he has himself concealed it very carefully, just like John Harmon concealed his true interest and true legal situation). Therefore, Wegg remains a legal illiterate with the constrained and 'mechanical' reading of an outdated and untrue will, a reading in which the form and the appearance is more important than the legitimacy of the document. This is where we can see how photography is again linked to literalism and to plotting. Wegg's false and legally illiterate reading of the untrue will, which he hopes to use in a plot to blackmail Boffin, aims to construct Boffin as a photographic portrait and give him the identity of a photograph. Thus, when Wegg is about to begin to read, and attempt to assume the position of master, he forces Boffin to sit in a constrained and posing manner, like a photographic model: 'Mr Boffin, as if he were about to have his portrait painted, or to be electrified, or to be made a Freemason, or to be placed at any other solitary disadvantage, ascended the rostrum prepared for him'.[71] Thus, it can be seen that Wegg, with his ballads and his alternative source of narrative is presented as a villain. Dickens does this by associating him with literalism in reading the law, photographic portraits which were included in the photograph album of Mrs. Lammle, and with dark and illegitimate plots. He is particularly presented as a villain because he aims to conceal and exploit the true legal situation as it emerges from the will and to usurp the position of those that conceal what the true law is. However, all of the negative characterisations aimed at Wegg can be seen to be justified and celebrated in Boffin and John Harmon, who each use the same strategies to conceal their own interest and the true legal situation in order to dupe readers, such as Wegg himself. How different in fact is their reading of the will and their reading of the law from Wegg's? It just happens to be luckily the case that the document in question is written later. Again, legitimate reading is very difficult to differentiate from an illegitimate reading, just as

70 Charles Dickens, *Our Mutual Friend*, ed. and introduced by Adrian Poole (London: Penguin Books, 1997), xxi.

71 Dickens, *Our Mutual Friend*, 546.

legitimacy is incredibly different to differentiate from illegitimacy. All are concerned to conceal the law in their own self-interest and all their readings emerge from this attempt, whether it is a failure or a success.

Conclusion: the success of the concealed legitimate plot

What ultimately seems to mark the illegitimate plot associated with the photograph book from the legitimate plot is that the latter is successful because it remains concealed and that it conceals the law. The photograph book plot fails because it becomes too evident and is thus successfully thwarted. The narrative function of the photograph book is therefore defeated and described as false and illegitimate. The successful and legitimate plot of fiction is, however, not completely evident. Not only does the legitimate plot involve the concealing of the identities of the powerful and the law itself, but mimics this identity and this power by aiming to conceal itself. However, Dickens framed this concealment of the plot in terms of its 'suggestion' and differentiated it from the idea of concealment. As he wrote in the postscript to the novel, about the successful plot concerning concealed identity:

> WHEN I devised this story, I foresaw the likelihood that a class of readers and commentators would suppose that I was at great pains to conceal exactly what I was at great pains to suggest: namely, that Mr. John Harmon was not slain, and that Mr. John Rokesmith was he. Pleasing myself with the idea that the supposition might in part arise out of some ingenuity in the story, and thinking it worth while, in the interests of art, to hint to an audience that an artist (of whatever denomination) may perhaps be trusted to know what he is about in his vocation, if they will concede him a little patience, I was not alarmed by the anticipation.[72]

The successful concealed plot, then, which reveals the larger aim of fiction to support and consolidate the power of the political elite, is intended by Dickens to be understood as informing a reading of the entire novel to the better class of readers. The 'suggested' plot is intended to be shared by writer and reader, although a reading of Dickens' novel suggests that it would be extremely difficult to realise Harmon's plot at the beginning of the novel. I suggest that Dickens expected the difficulty of understanding the obscurity of his story to be solved through a method of suggestion and a reliance on the legibility and widely shared recognition of the realities of power and the concealed identities of the political elite. As I have indicated throughout this monograph, the concealed identity of the powerful conditioned the function of fiction, its status, its success and its meaning here as elsewhere. Such a concealed identity was thought to be crucial to representation, as was the political elite's concealment of the true legal situation, their concealment of their self-interest and their concealment of what truth, fiction, the law and justice actually did and actually was.

72 Ibid., 681.

Conclusion

The spur to this monograph is the question of why photography was treated the way it was in the fiction I have looked at. The way that I formulated this as a research question was 'how is reading related to vision and law in the period from the mid-nineteenth century to the 1920s?' I have addressed this question through a study of photography in nineteenth- and early twentieth-century fiction, by relating fictional representations of photography to constructions of literalism, idealism and readings of law. I concentrated on photography because its portrayal in fiction raised larger questions of representation, both artistic and political. I have shown how photography has been tied to ideas of literalism and has therefore been seen as a threat to an accepted reading, which is related to idealist art. I have argued that the way in which photography has been implicitly opposed to conventional reading illuminates some historical limitations and conditions of the accepted process of reading. During the course of this research I have discovered that photography posed such a threat to reading because it was understood to capture the imagination, represent reality and influence the public in a way that only writing, including fiction, was previously deemed capable and worthy of doing. In this study, an exploration of how reading is related to vision and law is necessary not only for understanding a central and insistent complex in fiction from the mid-nineteenth century to the 1920s. The question pertains to real historical law, not only to fiction and helps us to understand why photography was prohibited in the courtroom following a legal statute of 1925. Much of the fiction studied in this monograph is informed by the writers' legal education, leading to a particular stance towards legal reading and, at the same time, towards reading more generally. One aim of this study of authors who are also legal readers has been to make a contribution to understanding how the Victorians and later writers conceptualised the law, reading and the reader, and to show how this was supported by wider reading practices. I have tried to show how the modelling of law on idealist art has determined the identity of the ideal readers as well as the identity of the ideal reading. This complex of law, art and reading can be seen to be present in the work of key Victorian authors such as Charles Dickens and Wilkie Collins, as well as in key Victorian texts such as *The Woman in White*, all of which have been studied in detail here.

In each chapter, I have aimed to demonstrate that larger ideas of legal truth, and also of gender, have determined how reading was represented in fiction in relation

DOI: 10.4324/9781003173854-6

to photography, both positively and negatively. I have, for example, explored why Henry James' poor women have been understood in fiction as the source of perceived threats to power. I have explored how different aspects of legal truth, which have been opposed to the truth of photography, have conditioned ideal forms of reading. I have shown how this has led to the denunciation of alternative forms of reading and alternative versions of legal truth which have been tied up in questions of the legal representation of women.

In the first chapter, I showed that an idea of idealist artistic truth went on to determine how legal truth was understood and portrayed in fiction. Through an analysis of John Ruskin's writings on both art and reading, I demonstrated that both artistic and legal truth were considered to be superior to the truth of photography, in much the same way. The nature of this legal and artistic truth was considered to be spiritual and reflective of the patriarchal authority and legitimacy of the Christian God. It was modelled on scripture and the Christian God's 'timeless' and 'unconditional' laws in the Bible. Conceptions of idealist truth were allied with constructions of the artistic reader who could sense the spirit of the supreme patriarch in scripture and did not take the letter for the spirit but saw a 'hidden' treasure in the writing. I argued that legal truth was seen to be inaccessible through a reading characterised as literalist and that the idealist reading was seen to be an expression and consolidation of power, ideas which informed and influenced my subsequent analyses of fiction.

In the second chapter, I further showed how ideas of legal truth in fiction aimed to distinguish themselves from the truth claims of photography so as to maintain legitimacy and status, and, in doing so, further determined and individualised ideas of acceptable reading. In this chapter, I argued that ideas of superior legal truth in fiction were differentiated from literal writing as they were modelled on invisibility. I demonstrated how, in order to maintain the uniqueness of legal truth, which was seen as the truth of individuality, Collins' fiction accordingly grouped the truth claims of photography with forms of truth considered literalist and therefore inferior. The forms of truth that were the most denounced appeared to be the natural sciences which were said to be based on 'observation' and finding visual resemblances between things. Thus, literalist and photographic reading was paired with the finding of resemblances between individuals and identity politics of the group. On the other hand, the idealist reading was paired with the finding of real individuality and with a form of politics which relied on notions of the discrete individual. Like the other writers, Collins associated the finding of resemblances with women who subverted patriarchal authority and male ideas of the legal truth. Such women were presented as mistaken because they could only see sameness and think of themselves and others as a group rather than discriminate between individuals.

The third chapter of the monograph is based on the writings of Henry James. In the previous chapters, I showed how the characterisation of ideal legal truth determined the shape of reading and the identity of readers supported by works of fiction. In each case, this characterisation was supported by misogyny and patriarchal conceptions of authority and legitimacy. In this chapter, I again explored how the characterisation of legal truth as both timeless, or ahistorical, and apolitical determined the nature of an ideal reading and reader. I concentrated on underlying currents of misogyny in fiction again, this time in relation to the economic status of women. I have attempted to show how a legal reading grounded in identity politics and the representation of women was rigorously denounced in works of fiction. This chapter further elaborates why such a reading was characterised as untruthful and too literal and how it was associated with the representation of women. Even despite James' sympathy to women elsewhere in his writing, I argue, he could be seen as part of this larger oppression of women. Hence the study of James illuminates how a commitment to idealist art forced writers against their own identification with oppressed groups in society, and against their own self-interest. Here I showed how Henry James criticised the detail of photography, or its ability to represent the 'particulars'. Such particulars were seen to portray femininity and historical conditions in society, including relationships of power and asymmetries in power, those conditions which groups such as women denounced. I saw James as attempting to convince the reader that seeing in terms of the photographic particulars and in terms of real historical conditions led to particularism and selfishness in political representation and the formation of laws. This was because seeing context and real conditions in James' work was opposed to the ideal reading, as this reading relied on ideas of universality and abstraction, rather than being in the world. I argued furthermore that James consistently explored the theme of representation in relation to reading, photographic particulars and law by concentrating on the meaning of the representation of women in terms of identity and politics. Photographic particulars were seen as linked to a woman's materialistic and literalist reading of reality and history. I have demonstrated how James counters a form of representation that realistically assessed the political conditions of society in order to support a form of legal representation that affected to ignore them, even while it supported asymmetries of power and consolidated the dominance of the political elite. He did this by supporting an ideal form of blindness which did not see the photographic particulars associated with literalism. I thus demonstrated that one of the larger aims of James' fiction was to oppose the representation and subjectivity of women in order to consolidate the power of the political elite. If James portrayed women sympathetically, he was unable to allow such women to transform reality because of the conservative political stance of the idealist representation that he had committed himself to.

In each of the previous chapters, I concentrate on how the individual photograph is represented in fiction and how it is related to the construction of reading and the reader. The final chapter of this monograph demonstrates how and why writers of fiction challenged the photographic book as a usurper of fiction's status as a narrative form and saw it as a rival for fiction's readers. In this chapter, I aimed to show how ideas of not only legitimate fiction, but also the law, legal truth and legal reading emerge out of the contest for supremacy over the reader. Ultimately, I demonstrate that the photograph book and fiction compete as narrative forms over the ability to conceal legal truth, the true legal situation. Literalism is excluded so that the legal self-interest of the political elite, who win the competition for legitimate narrative, can be disguised and presented as acceptable. It is the disguising and concealment of legal truth established through a larger, shared narrative and its production of readers that ultimately characterise the fiction I have studied, an acceptable reading of the law and the interpretation of the asymmetry of power in society.

The main findings of my research are that representations of legal reading in fiction confer acceptable and unacceptable identities through ideas of literalist reading and idealist reading. By constructing literalist and photographic readers as outsiders, the fiction I have studied regulates a community of insiders based on ideas of idealist art. This is largely done through assigning gendered identities and countering the formation of the legal representation of women.

Having summarised the key findings and arguments of this monograph, I will now suggest how my work may be situated in terms of recent scholarship and assessed as an original contribution to knowledge. While recent commentators have classed photography and reading as mutually reinforcing in the late nineteenth century, predominantly through analysing the form of the novel, I have shown that the opposite appears to be the case when I look at the depiction of the relationship between reading and photography within fiction itself. According to my analysis of fiction from the mid-nineteenth century to the 1920s, photography and reading are coupled only when they are both problematised under the idea of narrow literalism and an ideal reading is constructed as both 'anti-photographic' and 'anti-literalist'. The literalist reading is insistently and obsessively devalued. Sir Arthur Conan Doyle repetitively associated it with criminals and their criminal schemes. Conversely, the vision of the ideal, just and artistic reader opposes 'photographic' vision, reading and literalism. Walter Hartright in *The Woman in White*, for instance, stands opposed to Count Fosco and his photographic scheme because of his legal interpretation of a marriage register which he read non-literally because it contained a blank space. This reading is tied to the identity of the political elite. It is modelled upon the seeing and reading of things invisible, like the blank space in Collins' marriage register. This type of reading is seen as cultured, transcendent, universal and timeless. The readers who read in such a way are seen as artistic souls capable of the finest discriminations, like Walter Hartright who is a drawing master. Fiction therefore presents the text as invisible and the reader as 'blind' as they must not read to the visible letter. I have discussed the outlines of this shared sense of blindness in the chapter on Henry James. It is indicative that the portrait of the reader that Henry James references in *The Wings of the Dove* is only implicitly suggested and referenced, despite it being perhaps the key symbol in the entire novel. An invisible law therefore supplies the mould for the identity of the reader, who is also modelled upon invisibility, like the law, in contradiction to the photograph. Ultimately, vision and law are tied to this 'invisible' identity in the period at the cost of the exclusion of the vision and the identities of women, foreigners and those of the lower economic class, the Count Foscos of *The Woman in White*, the Kate Croys of *The Wings of the Dove* or the Christina Lights of *Roderick Hudson* and *The Princess Casamassima*.

I see my research as a niche investigation of the representation of photography in fiction that addresses the larger question of both the artistic and political dimensions of representation and reading. I have chosen to focus on an area of reading, legal truth, power and legitimacy which Nancy Armstrong and other writers mentioned in the introduction to this monograph have not treated in detail, or in terms of the work of gendering. My research has therefore complicated their position which holds that reading and photography are mutually reinforcing practices in the late nineteenth century. My research contributes an original explanation of reading and the creation of truth, order and readers via an appraisal of the model of invisibility. I have attempted to add to existing scholarship by investigating ideas of invisibility and the non-literal in relation to power, photography, law and fiction.

I will now consider the implications of my original contribution to knowledge. My monograph makes a larger claim about the historical construction of truth by focussing on how photographic truth was seen to contest idealist truth. Critics of photographic truth in the period write of the idealist 'truth' that they support quite explicitly as a form of falsity or fiction. It is conceived as a departure from firm fact-telling. The presentation of reality by idealist readings is therefore ideological in that it constructs an illusion opposed to concrete reality. The veil that the Victorians and later writers impose on things and individuals not only conceals them but also allows them to be framed as something else. The domains of law, nation, empire and private life in the home can therefore be portrayed as something more worthwhile than the crude realities that they embody, just as the realities of being a woman, a foreigner or lower class can be obscured and systematically devalued so that their real worth is never realised. The photographic vision and the literalist reading have stood as a counter to this ideology in fiction, as an alternative formation and strategy over the grounds of fiction and falsity, the domain of power which tells stories about its own legitimacy. In *Our Mutual Friend*, the lower-class Wegg competes with Harmon and Boffin's concealment of legal truth and legal interest so that he, too, can taste power and become ascendant over his economically and politically dominant rivals, worthy in his own right as ruler.

It is precisely because of photography's association with subversive truth that literalism and the photographic vision have been devalued in fiction from the mid-nineteenth century to the 1920s. In this reading, photographic vision and literalism could not form the basis for truth-telling. Counter to this, an invisible 'truth' gave scope for mystification and concealment. In terms of law, this gave political elites the flexibility and adaptability to frame their actions as though they were legitimate, however self-interested or capricious they may be, as in the case of Harmon in *Our Mutual Friend*. This invisible 'truth' created a community of insiders and knowers while denying entry to other forms of action, knowledge and knowing from the lower classes, foreigners and women. This can be seen clearly in *Our Mutual Friend*, where Wegg's knowledge and reading is excluded. The invisible was an instrument for withholding knowledge and of preventing other actions and knowledges to enter into the arena of the truth. This invisible 'truth' was modelled on 'spirit' as differentiated from the physical body, the epitome of truth and power. John Ruskin clearly saw it as the truth of the Christian God or 'the holy spirit'. It was associated with the 'souls' of the political elite, who Ruskin alluded to as earthly kings in 'Of Kings' Treasuries'. A privileged invisibility formed the centrepiece of a strategy of annihilating difference and multiplicity. It forced other identities to be moulded in its form in spite of resistance (as in the case of James).

In doing so, it secured the submission of groups to the subjectivity, self-interest and will of the political and economic elite. The striking fictional example that stands out is Kitty Winter's act of throwing vitriol in the face of the literalist, the Baron, in 'The Adventure of the Illustrious Client' in order to 'blur' his features according to the veiled aesthetic of idealist art. That act represented how poor women were forced into a position of submission through a complete abandonment of any practical means to their liberation.

I believe that my monograph provides a basis for further scholarship and investigation, which I will now discuss. My work has concentrated on the representation of photography and reading in fiction from the mid-nineteenth century to the 1920s, with a brief review of art criticism and art. It has focused on the limitations and conditions of reading caused by modelling legal truth on anti-photographic and anti-literalist invisibility rather than the scope for resistance. This is a result of my feeling that it was more urgent and politically valuable to analyse constraints and limitations in historical thought which had previously gone unrecognised. Future work needs to be done on analysing the structures of resistance. There are a number of avenues for further research that have not been covered in the present study. For example, the way in which the opposition to literalism and photography has been systematised within law and the legal education of the period deserves more detailed study. This topic could also be studied in other areas outside of this specific focus, such as in the wider conservative discourses which aimed to counter the close legal readings of the suffragettes and class activists, and also in studies relating to how early feminists and class activists formulated their readings of law. Key historical questions also remain outside the scope of my research. My monograph invites a reconsideration of the matrixes that the operations of modelling invisibility and reading against literalism are derived from. Perhaps most importantly, I have not considered an ending: I have not considered the history of the visual regime after the anti-photographic and anti-literalist regime of the period from the mid-nineteenth century to the 1920s. The history of the visual regime after the late nineteenth century could be readdressed in the light of my contribution.

Lastly, I will explore the role and topic of reading in my work and suggest how it might be approached in further scholarship, based on my own academic experience. Reading has been the subject and method, style and substance of this monograph. The reader, too, has been both subject and author, result and cause of my reading. I have given this attention to reading and the reader because of their importance in the construction of history and our present moment, historical realities in which laws are framed in writing and in which ideas of truth and knowledge are transmitted through books and newspapers. It is my firm belief that reading has shaped the identities and cultures of the human race for millennia; that it is always necessary to reflect on our readings and their constructions; that such a reflection always has the most urgent claim for attention. As I hope I have shown in this monograph, reading makes us what we are and can be. It is both our submission and our resistance. Historically, as I have argued, constructions of law and legitimacy via representations of reading in fiction can be seen as relating directly to formulations of real law.

Bibliography

Abi-Ezzi, Nathalie. *The Double in the Fiction of R. L. Stevenson, Wilkie Collins and Daphne Du Maurier*. Bern: Peter Lang, 2003.

Allott, Miriam. "The Bronzino Portrait in Henry James's the Wings of the Dove". *Modern Language Notes*. Vol. 68, No. 1, (1953): 23–25.

Anderman, Elizabeth. "No Reality Here: Sensation Novels and Photography." In *Picturing the Language of Images*, edited by Nancy Pedri and Laurence Petit, 297–312. Cambridge: Cambridge Scholars Publishing, 2014.

Anonymous. "My New Idea." *All the Year Round*, 5, 121 (Mar 25, 1871): 403–408.

Anonymous. "Photographs." *The London Review and Weekly Journal of Politics, Literature, Art, and Society*, 5, 110 (Aug 9, 1862): 118–119.

Anonymous. "Photography Applied To Book Illustration." *The Gentleman's Magazine and Historical Review*, 3 (Feb 1867): 172–183.

Anonymous. "Pictures from An Old Album." *Chambers's Journal of Popular Literature, Science and Arts*, 783 (Dec 28, 1878): 826–828.

Anonymous. "Reviews of Books – Our Mutual Friend." London Review (October 28, 1865). *In Sean Grass, Charles Dickens's Our Mutual Friend: A Publishing History*, 213–217. London and New York: Routledge, 2017.

Anonymous. "The Expression of the Emotions in Man and the Animals." *The Athenaeum*, no. 2351 (November 16, 1872): 631–632.

Anonymous. "The Fading Of Photographs." *Chambers's Journal of Popular Literature, Science and Arts*, 5, 215 (Feb 11, 1888): 94–95.

Anonymous. "The Lady Photographer and Lord Tennyson." *The Newcastle Courant* (Saturday, October 22, 1892): 5.

Anonymous. "Visits to Noteworthy Studios: Mr. Sarony's Studio at Scarborough." *Photographic News*, March 6, 1868: 10 – 11.

Armstrong, Nancy. *Fiction In The Age Of Photography: The Legacy Of British Realism*. Cambridge, Massachusetts and London, England: Harvard University Press, 2002.

Armstrong, Nancy. *How Novels Think: The Limits of Individualism from 1719–1900*. Colombia: Columbia University Press, 2006.

de Balzac, Honoré. La Comédie Humaine, I:1175, quoted in Yeazell, Ruth Bernard. *Art of the Everyday: Dutch Painting and the Realist Novel*, 61. Princeton, Princeton University Press, 2008.

di Bello, Patrizia. Women's Albums and Photography in. *Victorian England: Ladies, Mothers and. Flirts. Aldershot*, Hampshire and Burlington, VT: Ashgate, 2007.

Benjamin, Walter. "The Work of Art in the Age of Mechanical Reproduction." In *Illuminations*, edited by Hannah Arendt, 214–218. London: Fontana, 1968.

Bentham, Jeremy. *Panopticon; or, The Inspection-House*. London: T. Payne, 1791.

Bocard, Helene. "Great Exhibition of The Works of Industry of All Nations, Crystal Palace, Hyde Park (1851)." In *The Encyclopedia of Nineteenth-Century Photography*, edited by John Hannavy, 614–616. New York: Routledge, 2013.

Boehme-Neßler, Volker. *Pictorial Law: Modern Law and the Power of Pictures*. London: Springer, 2011.

Bogardus, Ralph F. *Pictures and Texts: Henry James, A. L. Coburn, and New Ways of Seeing in Literary Culture*. Ann Arbor, Michigan: UMI Research Press, 1984.

Brantlinger, Patrick. *The Reading Lesson: The Threat of Mass Literacy in Nineteenth-Century British Fiction*. Bloomington and Indianapolis: Indiana University Press, 1998.

Brontë, Charlotte. *The Letters of Charlotte Brontë*, vol. 2: 1848–1851, edited by Margaret Smith. Oxford: Clarendon Press, 2000.

Browning, Elizabeth Barrett. "On the Daguerreotype." In *Illuminations: Women Writing on Photography from the 1850s to the Present*, edited by Liz Heron and Val Williams, 2. Durham, NC: Duke University Press, 1996.

Burrows, Stuart. *A Familiar Strangeness: American Fiction and the Language of Photography, 1839–1945*. Athens: University of Georgia Press, 2010.

Clayton, Owen. "Flirting with Photography: Henry James and Photographic Exchange," *History of Photography*, 41:4 (2017), 329–342.

Clayton, Owen. *Literature and Photography in Transition, 1850–1915*. London: Palgrave Macmillan, 2015.

Collins, Wilkie. *Armadale*. New York: Harper & Brothers, [1866] 1874.

Collins, Wilkie. *Blind Love*. Piccadilly: Chatto & Windus, [1888] 1890).

Collins, Wilkie. *The Law and the Lady*. London: Chatto & Windus, Piccadilly, [1875] 1876.

Collins, Wilkie. *The Woman in White*. London: Chatto & Windus, [1859] 1896.

Conway, M. D. "My Lost Art." *The Atlantic Monthly*, 10 (1862): 228–235.

Crary, Jonathan. *Techniques of the Observer: On Vision and Modernity in the Nineteenth Century*. Cambridge, Massachusetts: MIT Press, 1992.

Culver, Stuart. "Law." In *Henry James in Context*, edited by David McWhirter, 180–191. Cambridge: Cambridge University Press, 2010.

Lord Darling. Speech to the House of Lords, 26 February 1924. *House of Lords Debates*, Vol. 56, columns 313–314. https://api.parliament.uk/historic-hansard/lords/1924/feb/26/criminal-justice-bill-hl#column_313

Daugherty, Sarah B. "James and the Representation of Women: Some Lessons of the Master(')s." In *Questioning the Master: Gender and Sexuality in Henry James's Writings*, edited by Peggy McCormack, 176–195. London: Associated University Presses, 2000.

Daum, Patrick. "Unity and Diversity in European Pictorialism." In *Impressionist Camera: Pictorial Photography in Europe, 1888–1918*, edited by Francis Ribemont and Patrick Daum, 15–30. London: Merrell, 2006.

Davies, Penelope. "Introduction." In *Janson's History of Art: The Western Tradition*, edited by Penelope Davies, xxi-xxxi. New Jersey: Prentice Hall, 2011.

Derrida, Jacques. *Memoirs of the Blind: The Self-Portrait and Other Ruins*. Translated by Pascale-Anne Brault and Michael Naas. Chicago and London: The University of Chicago Press, 1993.

Dickens, Charles. *Our Mutual Friend*. London: Chapman and Hall, 1865.

Dingley, Robert. "The Unreliable Camera: Photography as Evidence in Mid-Victorian Fiction." *Victorian Review*, Vol. 27, No. 2 (2001): 42–55.

Dominici, Sara. "*The democratisation of photography and the promotion of tourism: the Polytechnic Touring Association (1888–1939)*." PhD diss., University of Westminster, 2014. https://westminsterresearch.westminster.ac.uk/download/a45da892b67af59ca717b6c-1e11760cd99265b03d09db370873dd79caad654db/5855387/Sara_DOMINICI_2014.pdf accessed 09.01.19.

Douzinas, Costas. "The Legality of the Image." *The Modern Law Review*, Vol. 63, No. 6 (Nov., 2000), 813–830.

Doyle, Arthur Conan. "The Adventure of the Illustrious Client." In *The Complete Sherlock Holmes*. London: Magpie Books Ltd, 1993a. 984 – 999.

Doyle, Arthur Conan. "The Hound of the Baskervilles." In *The Complete Sherlock Holmes*. London: Magpie Books, 1993b. 669–766.

Doyle, Arthur Conan. "The Red-Headed League." in *The Complete Sherlock Holmes* (New York: Doubleday & Co Inc, 1927. 194–211.

Dwarris, Fortunatus. *A General Treatise on Statutes: Their Rules of Construction, and the Proper Boundaries of Legislation and of Judicial Interpretation*. Albany: William Gould & Son, 1875.

Eliot, George. "The Natural History of German Life." In *Selected Essays, Poems and Other Writings*, edited by A. S. Byatt, 107–139. London: Penguin Classics, [1859] 2005.

Ellenbogen, Josh. *Reasoned and Unreasoned Images: The Photography of Bertillon, Galton, and Marey*. University Park: Pennsylvania State University Press, 2012.

Fenster, Mark and Ohi, Kevin, eds. *Henry James and the Queerness of Style*. Minneapolis: University of Minnesota Press, 2008.

Finn, Jonathan Mathew. *Capturing the Criminal Image: From Mug Shot to Surveillance Society*. Minnesota: University of Minnesota Press, 2009.

Flint, Kate. "*Photographic Memory*", Romanticism and Victorianism on the Net 53 (2009) https://www.erudit.org/en/journals/ravon/2009-n53-ravon2916/029898ar/

Foucault, Michel. "Where Is the Law, And What Does It Do?" In *Maurice Blanchot: The Thought from Outside*, translated by Brian Massumi, 33–40. New York: Zone Books, 1987.

Foucault, Michel. *Discipline and Punish: The Birth of the Prison*. Translated by Alan Sheridan. New York: Vintage Books, 1995.

Frazier, Melissa. "The Science of Sensation: Dostoevsky, Wilkie Collins and the Detective Novel." *Dostoevsky Studies*, New Series, Vol. *XIX* (2015): 7–28.

Friedman, Stanley. "The Motif of Reading in Our Mutual Friend." *Nineteenth-Century Fiction*, Vol. 28, No. 1 (Jun., 1973): 38–61.

Gadamer, Hans-Georg. *Truth and Method*. Translated by J. Weinsheimer & D. Marshall. New York: Crossroad, 1990.

Goetz, William R. "The Allegory of Representation in "The Tragic Muse"." *The Journal of Narrative Technique* Vol. 8, No. 3 (Fall 1978): 151–164.

Goodrich, Peter. *Oedipus Lex: Psychoanalysis, History, Law*. Berkeley: University of California Press Berkeley, 1995.

Green-Lewis, Jennifer. "Victorian Photography and the Novel." In *The Oxford Handbook of the Victorian Novel*, edited by Lisa Rodensky, 313–336. Oxford: Oxford University Press, 2013.

Grossman, Julie. "'It's the Real Thing': Henry James, Photography, and The Golden Bowl." *The Henry James Review*, Volume 15, Number 3, Fall 1994: 309–328.

Haggard, H. Rider. "About Fiction." *Contemporary Review* 51 (February 1887): 172–180.

Haggard, H. Rider. *Mr Meeson's Will*. London: Spencer Blackett, 1888.

Hardy, Thomas. *Desperate Remedies*. London: Tinsley Brothers, 1871.

Harvey, Michael. "Ruskin and Photography." *Oxford Art Journal*, Vol. 7, No. 2, Photography (1984): 25–33.

H.C. "The Photograph Album." *The Gentleman's magazine* 11 (Aug 1873): 193–194.

Holmes, Oliver Wendell. "The Doings of the Sunbeam." In *Soundings from the Atlantic*, 228–281. Boston: Ticknor and Fields, 1864.

Howse, Geoffrey. *Murder and Mayhem in North London*. South Yorkshire: Wharncliffe Books: 2010.

Hutton, Christopher. "'I Crave the Law': Salomon v Salomon, Uncanny Personhood and the Jews." In *Reading The Legal Case: Cross-Currents Between Law and The Humanities*, edited by Marco Wan, 29–46. New York: Routledge, 2012.

James, Henry. *Autobiography*, edited by Frederick W. Dupee. New Jersey: Princeton University Publishing, 1956.

James, Henry. *The Bostonians*. London: Heron Books, 1976.

James, Henry. *The Letters of Henry James, edited by Percy Lubbock*. New York: Scribner's, 1920.

James, Henry. Nation (New York), 13 July 1865, i. 51–52, reprinted in Donald Smalley, ed., *Anthony Trollope: The Critical Heritage*, edited by Donald Smalley, 233–237. London: Routledge, 2013.

James, Henry. "The Picture Season in London." *The Galaxy*, Volume 24, Number 2 (August 1877): 149–161.

James, Henry. *The Princess Cassamassima*. London; New York: Macmillan and Co., 1889.

James, Henry. *The Princess Cassamassima, The Novels and Tales of Henry James, New York Edition*, Volume 5. New York: Charles Scribner's Sons, 1908a.

James, Henry. *Roderick Hudson. The New York Edition*, Vol. 1. London: Macmillan and Co, 1908b.

James, Henry. *Roderick Hudson*. The Atlantic Monthly, Vol. 35 (1875a).

James, Henry. *Roderick Hudson*. The Atlantic Monthly, Vol. 36 (1875b).

James, Henry. *Roderick Hudson*. Boston: James R. Osgood and Company, 1876.

James, Henry. *Roderick Hudson, edited by Geoffrey Moore*. New York: Penguin, 1986.

James, Henry. *The Tragic Muse. The Novels and Tales of Henry James, New York Edition, Volumes VII and VIII*. New York: Charles Scribner's Sons, 1908c.

James, Henry. *The Wings of the Dove. The Novels and Tales of Henry James, New York Edition, Volumes XIX and XX*. New York: Charles Scribner's Sons, 1909.

Kant, Immanuel. *Critique of Judgment, translated by Werner Pluhar*. Indianapolis: Hackett, 1987.

Kelvin, Norman. "The Painting as Physical Object in a Verbal Portrait: Pater's "A Prince of Court Painters" and Wilde's "The Portrait of Mr W. H"." In *Victorian Aesthetic Conditions: Pater Across the Arts*, edited by Elicia Clements and Lesley Higgins, 117–134. Basingstoke: Palgrave Macmillan, 2010.

Kernodle, George R. *The Theatre in History*. Fayetteville, AR: University of Arkansas Press, 1989.

Krueger, Christine L. "Henry Rider Haggard." In *Encyclopedia of British Writers, 19th and 20th Centuries*, edited by George Stade, Karen Karbiener and Christine L. Krueger, 151–152. New York: Facts On File, 2003.

Law Journal Reports 64 Law J. Rep. (n.s.) (1895), 693.

Lee, Vernon. "Ghosts in a Roman Photograph Album," *The English Review* (May 1920): 431–438.

Lee, Vernon. "On Modern Travelling." In *Limbo and Other Essays*, 85–106. London: Grant Richards, 1897.

Leighton, John. "On Photography as a Means or an End." *The Photographic Journal* (21 June 1853): 74–75.

Losano, Antonia. *The Woman Painter in Victorian Literature*. Columbus: Ohio State University Publishing, 2008.

Maseychik, William J. "Points of Departure from The American." In *Henry James: A Selection of Critical Essays*, edited by Tony Tanner, 116–127. London: Macmillan International Higher Education, 1968.

Maudsley, Henry. *The Physiology of Mind: Being the First Part of a Third Edition, Revised Enlarged and in Great Part Rewritten, of "The Physiology and Pathology of Mind"*. New York: D. Appleton, 1876 [1878].

MacCallum, Scott. Speech to the House of Commons, 18 March 1912. *House of Commons Debates*, Vol. 35, column 1529. https://hansard.parliament.uk/commons/1912-03-18/debates/83ef70ec-6d0a-46aa-ab54-735eb65aa675/CommonsChamber

McLeod, Ian. "Literal and Purposive Techniques of Legislative Interpretation: Some European Community and English Common Law Perspective". 29 *Brooklyn Journal of International Law* (2004), 1109–1134.

Mulcahy, Linda. "Revolting consumers: a revisionist account of the 1925 ban on photography in English and Welsh courts and its implications for debate about who is able to produce, manage and consume images of the trial," *International Journal of Law in Context* (2018), 14, 559–580.

Murphy, Sara. "Inadmissible Evidence: The Trial Of Madeleine Smith And Collins's The Law And The Lady." *Victorian Literature and Culture* (2016), 44: 163–188.

Nead, Linda. *The Female Nude: Art, Obscenity and Sexuality*. London and New York: Routledge, 2001.

Novak, Daniel A. *Realism, Photography and Nineteenth-Century Fiction*. Cambridge: Cambridge University Press, 2008.

O'Neal, Philip. *Wilkie Collins: Women, Property, and Propriety*. Totowa, New Jersey: Barnes & Noble Books, 1988, 198.

Palgrave, Francis Turner. *Essays on Art*. New York: Hurd & Houghton, 1867.

Poole, Adrian. *"Introduction". In Charles Dickens, Our Mutual Friend*. London: Penguin Books, 1997.

Posner, Richard A. "Legislation and Its Interpretation: A Primer". 68 *Nebraska Law Review* (1989), 431–453.

Prodger, Phillip. "Darwin, Charles Robert." In *Encyclopedia of Nineteenth Century Photography*, edited by John Hannavy, 384–385. New York and London: Routledge, 2008.

Pykett, Lyn. *Wilkie Collins (Authors in Context)*. Oxford: Oxford University Press, 2009.

Rabb, Jane M. *Literature and Photography Interactions 1840 – 1990: A Critical Anthology*. Albuquerque: University of New Mexico Press, 1995.

Rose, Phyllis. *Parallel Lives: Five Victorian Marriages*. New York: Knopf, 1983.

Royal Commissioners. Reports by the Juries on the Subjects in the Thirty Classes into which the Exhibition was Divided. London: Spicer Brothers and W. Clowes and Sons, 1852.

Ruskin, John. *The Complete Works of John Ruskin*, volume 3, edited by E. T. Cook and Alexander Wedderburn. London: George Allen, 1903a.

Ruskin, John. *The Complete Works of John Ruskin*, volume 5, edited by E. T. Cook and Alexander Wedderburn. London: George Allen, 1903b.

Ruskin, John. *The Complete Works of John Ruskin*, volume 6, edited by E. T. Cook and Alexander Wedderburn. London: George Allen, 1903c.

Ruskin, John. *The Complete Works of John Ruskin*, volume 11, edited by E. T. Cook and Alexander Wedderburn. London: George Allen, 1903d.

Ruskin, John. *The Complete Works of John Ruskin*, volume 12, edited by E. T. Cook and Alexander Wedderburn. London: George Allen, 1903e.

Ruskin, John. *The Complete Works of John Ruskin*, volume 14, edited by E. T. Cook and Alexander Wedderburn. London: George Allen, 1903f.

Ruskin, John. *The Complete Works of John Ruskin*, volume 18, edited by E. T. Cook and Alexander Wedderburn. London: George Allen, 1903g.

Ruskin, John. *The Complete Works of John Ruskin,* volume 19, *edited by E. T. Cook and Alexander Wedderburn*. London: George Allen, 1903h.

Ruskin, John. *The Complete Works of John Ruskin*, volume 20, edited by E. T. Cook and Alexander Wedderburn. London: George Allen, 1903i.

Ruskin, John. *The Complete Works of John Ruskin*, volume 22, edited by E. T. Cook and Alexander Wedderburn. London: George Allen, 1903j.

Ruskin, John. *The Complete Works of John Ruskin*, volume 28, edited by E. T. Cook and Alexander Wedderburn. London: George Allen, 1903k.

Ruskin, John. *The Complete Works of John Ruskin*, volume 33, edited by E. T. Cook and Alexander Wedderburn. London: George Allen, 1903l.

Saltz, Laura. "Henry James's Overexposures." *The Henry James Review*, Volume 25, Number 3, (Fall 2004): 254–266.

Sampson, Edward C. "Thomas Hardy-Justice of the Peace." *Colby Library Quarterly*, Volume 13, no.4, (December 1977): 263–274.

Schor, Naomi. *Reading in Detail: Aesthetics and the Feminine*. New York and London: Routledge, 2007.

Schwanebeck, Wieland. "'It's Never Twins?'—It's Always Twins: The Notting Hill Mystery (1865) and the Specter of Twinship in Early Detective Fiction." *CLUES: A Journal Of Detection*, Volume 36, Number 1 (Spring 2018): 58–68.

Schwarzschild, Edward L. "Revising Vulnerability: Henry James's Confrontation with Photography." *Texas Studies in Literature and Language*, Vol. 38, No. 1, Representative Paradoxes (SPRING 1996): 51–78

Sekula, Alan. "The Body and the Archive," October 39 (1986): 4 – 64.

Simpson, Alfred William Brian. "Innovation in Nineteenth Century Contract Law." In *Legal Theory and Legal History: Essays on the Common Law*. London: The Hambledon Press, 1987.

Simpson, Roddy. *The Photography of Victorian Scotland*. Edinburgh: Edinburgh University Press, 2012.

Smith, Jonathan. *Charles Darwin and Victorian Visual Culture*. Cambridge: Cambridge University Press, 2006.

Smith, Peter and Lefley, Carolyn. *Rethinking Photography: Histories, Theories and Education*. London: Routledge, 2015.

Sobieszek, Robert A. "Sculpture as the Sum of Its Profiles: François Willème and Photosculpture in France, 1859–1868." *The Art Bulletin*, Vol. 62, No. 4 (Dec., 1980): 617–630.

Sonstegard, Adam. "*Painting, Photography and Fidelity in The Tragic Muse*." English Faculty Publications. 27 (2003). http://engagedscholarship.csuohio.edu/cleng_facpub/27 accessed 18.09.2018.

Speake, Jennifer. "Biography" (Robert Louis Stevenson). In *Literature of Travel and Exploration: R to Z, index*, edited by Jennifer Speake, 1152. New York; London: Taylor & Francis, 2003.

Stepniak, Daniel. "British Justice: not Suitable for Public Viewing?" In *Criminal Visions: Media Representations of Crime and Justice*, edited by Paul Mason, 254–277. Cullompton, Devon, UK: Willan Publishing, 2003.

Stevenson, Robert Louis and Osbourne, Lloyd. *The Wrecker*. New York: Charles Scribner's Sons, 1895.

Strassler, Karen. "Ethnography and the National Identity Photograph." In *Photography, History, Difference*, edited by Tanya Sheehan, 151–171. Dartmouth College Press, 2014.

Sumara, Dennis J. "Fictionalizing Acts: Reading and the Making of Identity." *Theory Into Practice*, Vol. 37, No. 3, Literary Theory in the High School English Classroom (Summer, 1998): 203–210.

Tagg, John (1988) *The Burden of Representation: Essays on Photographies and Histories* The Macmillan Press Ltd: London.

Taylor, David. *Foundation Course Black And White Photography*. East Sussex: AE Publications, 2015.

Thomas, Julia. *Victorian Narrative Painting*. London: Tate Publishing, 2000.

Thomas, Ronald R. "Making Darkness Visible: Capturing the Criminal and Observing the Law in Victorian Photography and Detective Fiction." In *Victorian Literature and the Victorian Visual Imagination,* edited by Carol T. Christ and John O. Jordan, 134–168. California: California University Press, 1995.

Thomas, Ronald R. "The Moonstone, Detective Fiction and Forensic Science." In *The Cambridge Companion to Wilkie Collins,* edited by Jenny Bourne Taylor. Cambridge: Cambridge University Press, 2006.

Tick, Stanley. ""Positives and Negatives: Henry James vs. Photography"." In *Essays on Charles Dickens, Henry James, and George Eliot,* 195–229. Philadelphia, PA: Xlibris Corporation, 2005.

Tintner, A. R. Henry *James and the Lust of the Eyes: Thirteen Artists in His Work*. Baton Rouge, LA: Louisiana State University Press, 1993.

Tomaiuolo, Saverio. *Victorian Unfinished Novels: The Imperfect Page*. London: Palgrave Macmillan, 2012.

Tucker, Irene. "Paranoid Imagining: Wilkie Collins, the Rugeley Poisoner, and the Invisibility of Novelistic Exphrasis." In *The Moment of Racial Sight: A History*, 75–118. Chicago and London: The University of Chicago Press, 2012.

Tucker, Jennifer. *Nature Exposed: Photography as Eyewitness in Victorian Science*. Baltimore: The John Hopkins University Press, 2005.

Turner, J. M. W. Light and *Colour (Goethe's Theory) – the Morning after the Deluge - Moses Writing the Book of Genesis*, 1843. Oil paint on canvas, 787 x 787 mm. Tate Gallery.

Weltman, Sharon Aronofsky. "Sexuality and Gender." In *The Cambridge Companion to John Ruskin,* edited by Francis O'Gorman, 157–170. Cambridge: Cambridge University Press, 2015.

Werner, Jean-François. "Photography and Industrialization in Contemporary Africa: An Ivoirian Case-Study." *Visual Anthropology* 14 (2001): 251–268.

Wichelns, Kathryn. *Henry James's Feminist Afterlives: Annie Fields, Emily Dickinson, Marguerite Duras*. Cham, Switzerland: Palgrave Macmillan, 2018.

Wilde, Oscar. "The Decay of Lying." In *Intentions*, 1–57. New York: Brentano's, 1905.

Wootton, Sarah. "Henry James's Venice and the Visual Arts." In *Venice and the Cultural Imagination: 'This Strange Dream upon the Water'*, edited by Michael O'Neill, Mark Sandy and Sarah Wootton, 127–140. New York: Routledge, 2015.

Index

Page numbers followed by n indicate notes

For Product Safety Concerns and Information please contact our EU representative GPSR@taylorandfrancis.com
Taylor & Francis Verlag GmbH, Kaufingerstraße 24, 80331 München, Germany

www.ingramcontent.com/pod-product-compliance
Ingram Content Group UK Ltd.
Pitfield, Milton Keynes, MK11 3LW, UK
UKHW022123190926
475702UK00013B/1619

* 9 7 8 1 0 3 2 0 0 3 7 2 6 *